SCHOLA

2010 ALMANAC for KIDS

FACTS, FIGURES, & STATS

SCHOLASTIC INC.
New York · Toronto · London · Auckland
Sydney · Mexico City · New Delhi · Hong Kong

Scholastic 2010 Almanac for Kids is produced by becker&mayer! LLC, 11120 NE 33rd Place, Suite 101, Bellevue, WA 98004.
www.beckermayer.com

Art Director: Shane Hartley
Editor: Delia Greve
Project Director: Jacqueline A. Ball, J.A. Ball Associates, Inc.
Head Writer: Lynn Brunelle
Writers: Jim Brunelle, Delia Greve, Sandra Will
Designer: Mathew McInelly

ISBN-13: 978-0-545-16063-6
ISBN-10: 0-545-16063-4

10 9 8 7 6 5 4 3 2 1 09 10 11 12 13

Printed in the U.S.A. 23
First printing, September 2009
Cover design by Kay Petronio

08155 8/1/09

Due to the publication date, statistics are current as of June 2009.

CONTENTS

Animals

You Animal

From aphids to zebras, animals come in a great variety of shapes and sizes. The amazing variety of animal life on Earth is called biodiversity. Scientists have counted and named 1.5 million species, and most estimate there are from 5 to 20 million more. In fact, at the present rate of describing new species, it could take hundreds of years to finish identifying them.

Bug Bites

More than half of these species are insects. The world is so full of bugs that scientists are suggesting they be eaten in places where food is scarce. Why not? They're plentiful and full of protein. Researchers say that grubs, ants, wasps, and other insects are already eaten in 113 countries.

Polar Bears in Danger

Animals that eat only bugs are called insectivores. Herbivores eat plants. Carnivores eat other animals, and omnivores eat pretty much everything. All animals have to eat, and they all need something else: a healthy habitat. Sometimes human activity or development destroys animal habitats. On May 14, 2008, polar bears were added to the endangered species list because their habitat is being threatened by global climate change. There are 936 other animals on that list.

Pet Projects

Until about 12,000 years ago, all dogs were wolves. After years of breeding for specific characteristics, there are now over 400 breeds, from chihuahuas to German shepherds. Domestic cats go back about 5,000 years. Experts say they've changed very little since ancient times. See page 17 for the top dogs—and cats—in the United States. Did your pet make the list?

TAKE a LOOK

Do you know your hogs from your hounds? What's a group of each of them called? And if you've got a "murder" or a "charm" of animals on your front lawn, should you run or stick around? Find out on page 12.

CHECK IT OUT!

The next time you're around a cat, notice the way it walks. How is it different from the way a dog walks? Hint: Only camels and giraffes move like a cat. (The answer is on page 271.)

THE ANIMAL KINGDOM

Porifera SPONGES

Cnidaria COELENTERATES

Platyhelminthes FLATWORMS

Nematoda ROUNDWORMS

Mollusca MOLLUSKS

Annelida TRUE WORMS

Hydrozoa HYDRAS, HYDROIDS

Scyphozoa JELLYFISH

Anthozoa SEA ANEMONES, CORAL

Turbellaria FREE-LIVING FLATWORMS

Monogenea PARASITIC FLUKES

Trematoda PARASITIC FLUKES

Cestoda TAPEWORMS

Polyplacophora CHITONS

Gastropoda SNAILS, SLUGS

Bivalvia CLAMS, SCALLOPS, MUSSELS

Cephalopoda OCTOPUSES, SQUID

Polychaeta MARINE WORMS

Oligochaeta EARTHWORMS, FRESHWATER WORMS

Hirudinea LEECHES

Insecta INSECTS

Chilopoda CENTIPEDES

Diplopoda MILLIPEDES

Symphyla SYMPHYLANS, PAUROPODS

Collembola, SPRINGTAILS
Thysanura, SILVERFISH, BRISTLETAILS
Ephemeroptera, MAYFLIES
Odonata, DRAGONFLIES
Isoptera, TERMITES
Orthoptera, LOCUSTS, CRICKETS, GRASSHOPPERS
Dictyptera, COCKROACHES, MANTIDS
Dermaptera, EARWIGS
Phasmida, STOCK INSECTS, LEAF INSECTS
Psocoptera, BOOK LICE, BARK LICE
Diplura, SIMPLE INSECTS
Protura, TELSONTAILS
Plecoptera, STONEFLIES
Grylloblattodea, TINY MOUNTAIN INSECTS
Strepsiptera, TWISTED-WINGED STYLOPIDS
Trichoptera, CADDISFLIES
Embioptera, WEBSPINNERS
Thysanoptera, THRIPS
Mecoptera, SCORPIONFLIES
Zoraptera, RARE TROPICAL INSECTS
Hemiptera, TRUE BUGS
Anoplura, SUCKING LICE
Mallophaga, BITING LICE, BIRD LICE
Homoptera, WHITEFLIES, APHIDS, SCALE INSECTS, CICADAS
Coleoptera, BEETLES, WEEVILS
Neuroptera, ALDERFLIES, LACEWINGS, ANT LIONS, SNAKEFLIES, DOBSONFLIES
Hymenoptera, ANTS, BEES, WASPS
Siphonaptera, FLEAS
Diptera, TRUE FLIES, MOSQUITOES, GNATS
Lepidoptera, BUTTERFLIES, MOTHS

Insectivora, INSECTIVORES (e.g., shrews, moles, hedgehogs)
Chiroptera, BATS
Dermoptera, FLYING LEMURS
Edentata, ANTEATERS, SLOTHS, ARMADILLOS
Pholidota, PANGOLINS
Primates, PROSIMIANS (e.g., lemurs, tarsiers, monkeys, apes, humans)
Rodentia, RODENTS (e.g., squirrels, rats, beavers, mice, porcupines)
Lagomorpha, RABBITS, HARES, PIKAS
Cetacea, WHALES, DOLPHINS, PORPOISES
Carnivora, CARNIVORES (e.g., cats, dogs, weasels, bears, hyenas)
Pinnipedia, SEALS, SEA LIONS, WALRUSES
Tubulidentata, AARDVARKS
Hyracoidea, HYDRAXES
Proboscidea, ELEPHANTS
Sirenia, SEA COWS (e.g., manatees, dugongs)
Perissodactyla, ODD-TOED HOOFED ANIMALS (e.g., horses, rhinoceroses, tapirs)
Artiodactyla, EVEN-TOED HOOFED ANIMALS (e.g., hogs, cattle, camels, hippopotamuses)

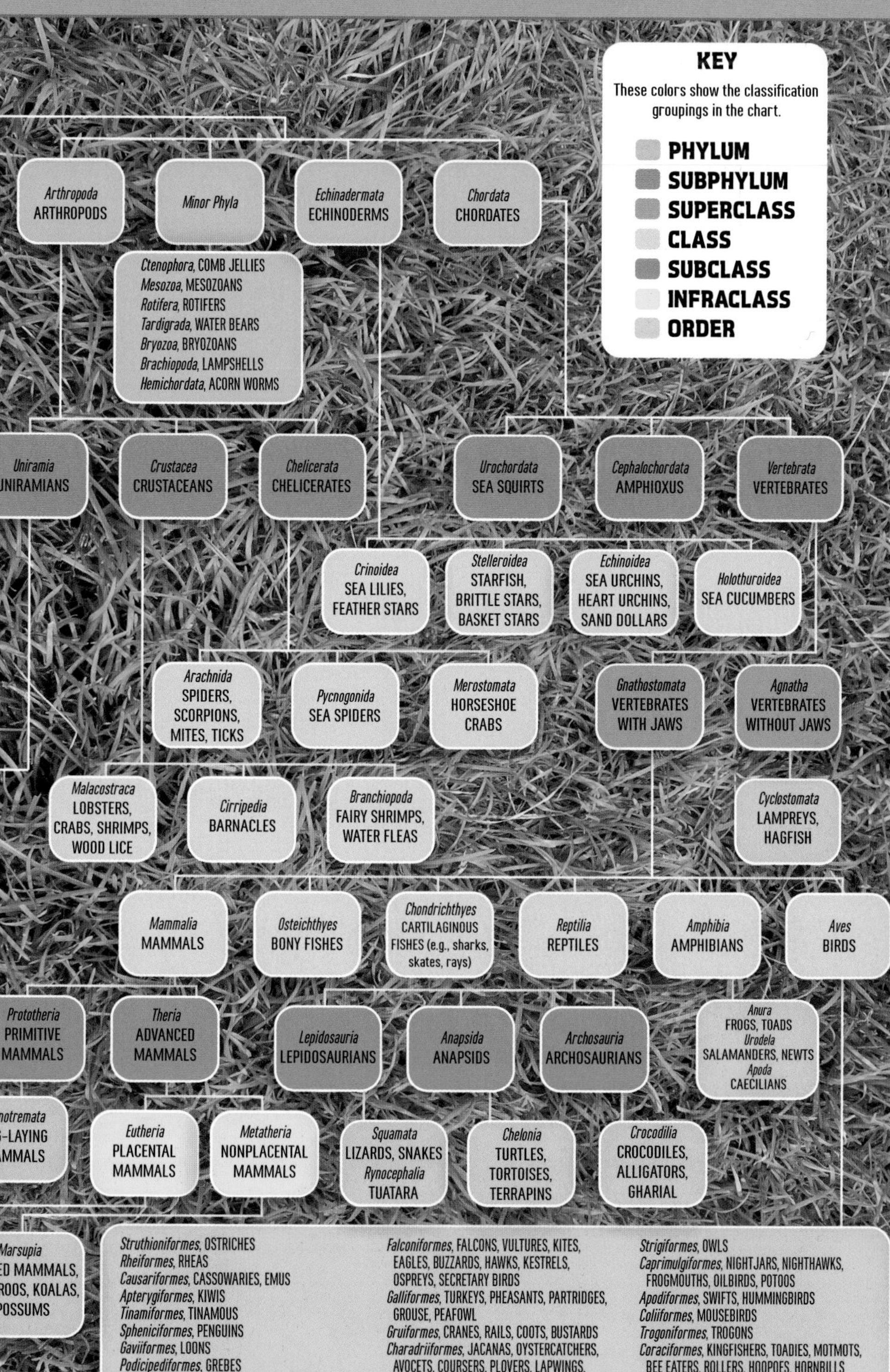
KEY
These colors show the classification groupings in the chart.
PHYLUM
SUBPHYLUM
SUPERCLASS
CLASS
SUBCLASS
INFRACLASS
ORDER
Arthropoda ARTHROPODS
Minor Phyla
Echinadermata ECHINODERMS
Chordata CHORDATES
Ctenophora, COMB JELLIES
Mesozoa, MESOZOANS
Rotifera, ROTIFERS
Tardigrada, WATER BEARS
Bryozoa, BRYOZOANS
Brachiopoda, LAMPSHELLS
Hemichordata, ACORN WORMS
Uniramia UNIRAMIANS
Crustacea CRUSTACEANS
Chelicerata CHELICERATES
Urochordata SEA SQUIRTS
Cephalochordata AMPHIOXUS
Vertebrata VERTEBRATES
Crinoidea SEA LILIES, FEATHER STARS
Stelleroidea STARFISH, BRITTLE STARS, BASKET STARS
Echinoidea SEA URCHINS, HEART URCHINS, SAND DOLLARS
Holothuroidea SEA CUCUMBERS
Arachnida SPIDERS, SCORPIONS, MITES, TICKS
Pycnogonida SEA SPIDERS
Merostomata HORSESHOE CRABS
Gnathostomata VERTEBRATES WITH JAWS
Agnatha VERTEBRATES WITHOUT JAWS
Malacostraca LOBSTERS, CRABS, SHRIMPS, WOOD LICE
Cirripedia BARNACLES
Branchiopoda FAIRY SHRIMPS, WATER FLEAS
Cyclostomata LAMPREYS, HAGFISH
Mammalia MAMMALS
Osteichthyes BONY FISHES
Chondrichthyes CARTILAGINOUS FISHES (e.g., sharks, skates, rays)
Reptilia REPTILES
Amphibia AMPHIBIANS
Aves BIRDS
Prototheria PRIMITIVE MAMMALS
Theria ADVANCED MAMMALS
Lepidosauria LEPIDOSAURIANS
Anapsida ANAPSIDS
Archosauria ARCHOSAURIANS
Anura FROGS, TOADS *Urodela* SALAMANDERS, NEWTS *Apoda* CAECILIANS
onotremata G-LAYING AMMALS
Eutheria PLACENTAL MAMMALS
Metatheria NONPLACENTAL MAMMALS
Squamata LIZARDS, SNAKES *Rynocephalia* TUATARA
Chelonia TURTLES, TORTOISES, TERRAPINS
Crocodilia CROCODILES, ALLIGATORS, GHARIAL
Marsupia HED MAMMALS, AROOS, KOALAS, POSSUMS
Struthioniformes, OSTRICHES
Rheiformes, RHEAS
Causariformes, CASSOWARIES, EMUS
Apterygiformes, KIWIS
Tinamiformes, TINAMOUS
Spheniciformes, PENGUINS
Gaviiformes, LOONS
Podicipediformes, GREBES
Procellariiformes, PETRELS, ALBATROSSES, SHEARWATERS, FULMARS
Pelecaniformes, PELICANS, GANNETS, BOOBIES, CORMORANTS, SHAGS, DARTERS, FRIGATE BIRDS
Ciconiiformes, HERONS, BITTERNS
Anseriformes, DUCKS, GEESE, SWANS, SCREAMERS
Falconiformes, FALCONS, VULTURES, KITES, EAGLES, BUZZARDS, HAWKS, KESTRELS, OSPREYS, SECRETARY BIRDS
Galliformes, TURKEYS, PHEASANTS, PARTRIDGES, GROUSE, PEAFOWL
Gruiformes, CRANES, RAILS, COOTS, BUSTARDS
Charadriiformes, JACANAS, OYSTERCATCHERS, AVOCETS, COURSERS, PLOVERS, LAPWINGS, SNIPE, SKUAS, GULLS, TERNS, SKIMMERS, AUKS
Pteroclidformes, SAND GROUSE
Columbiformes, DOVES, PIGEONS
Psittaciformes, PARROTS, PARAKEETS, LORIES, LORIKEETS, COCKATOOS, MACAWS
Cuculiformes, CUCKOOS, TURACOS, HOATZIN
Strigiformes, OWLS
Caprimulgiformes, NIGHTJARS, NIGHTHAWKS, FROGMOUTHS, OILBIRDS, POTOOS
Apodiformes, SWIFTS, HUMMINGBIRDS
Coliiformes, MOUSEBIRDS
Trogoniformes, TROGONS
Coraciformes, KINGFISHERS, TOADIES, MOTMOTS, BEE EATERS, ROLLERS, HOOPOES, HORNBILLS
Piciformes, WOODPECKERS, BARBETS
Passeriformes, PERCHING BIRDS (e.g., larks, swallows, shrikes, wrens, thrushes, warblers, sunbirds, honey eaters, buntings, blackbirds, finches, weavers, sparrows, starlings, birds of paradise, crows)

Animals with Most Known Species

Animal	Known species
Insects and Other Arthropods	1,000,000
Mollusks	100,000
Fish	24,000
Worms	20,000
Birds	9,600
Reptiles	8,700
Mammals	5,000

10 Longest Animal Life Spans

Animal	Maximum age (years)
Quahog (marine clam)	400
Giant tortoise	150
Human	122
Sturgeon	100
Killer whale	90
Blue Whale	80
Golden Eagle	80
Elephant	75
Sea anemone	70
Crocodile	60

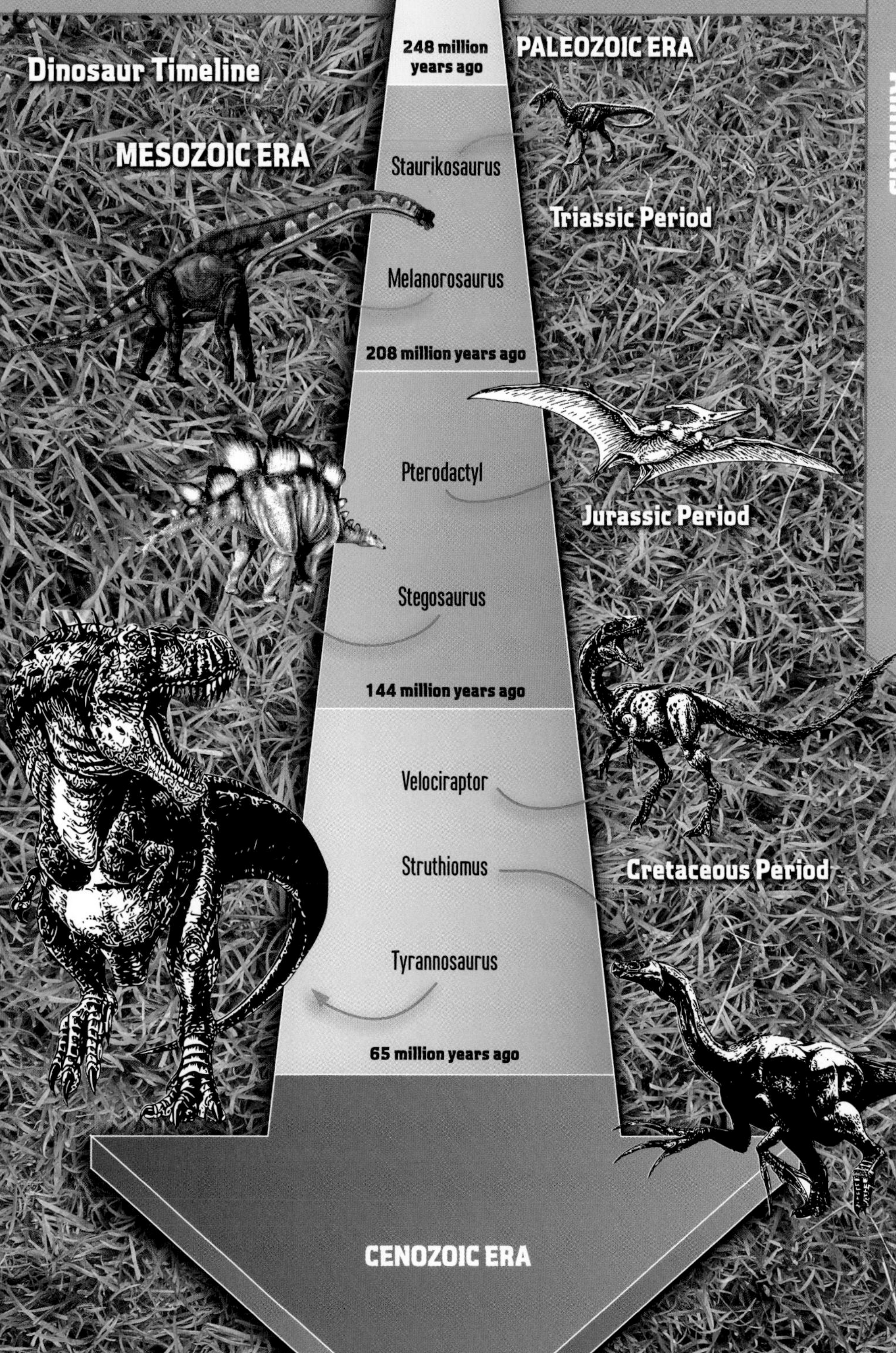
Dinosaur Timeline
248 million years ago
PALEOZOIC ERA
MESOZOIC ERA
Staurikosaurus
Triassic Period
Melanorosaurus
208 million years ago
Pterodactyl
Jurassic Period
Stegosaurus
144 million years ago
Velociraptor
Struthiomus
Cretaceous Period
Tyrannosaurus
65 million years ago
CENOZOIC ERA

Animal Multiples

ants: colony
bears: sleuth, sloth
bees: grist, hive, swarm
birds: flight, volery
cats: clutter, clowder
cattle: drove
chicks: brood, clutch
clams: bed
cranes: sedge, seige
crows: murder
doves: dule
ducks: brace, team
elephants: herd
elks: gang
finches: charm
fish: school, shoal, drought
foxes: leash, skulk
geese: flock, gaggle, skein
gnats: cloud, horde
goats: trip
gorillas: band
hares: down, husk
hawks: cast
hens: brood
hogs: drift
horses: pair, team
hounds: cry, mute, pack
kangaroos: troop
kittens: kindle, litter

larks: exaltation
lions: pride
locusts: plague
magpies: tidings
mules: span
nightingales: watch
oxen: yoke
oysters: bed
parrots: company
partridges: covey
peacocks: muster, ostentation
pheasants: nest, bouquet
pigs: litter
ponies: string
quail: bevy, covey
rabbits: nest
seals: pod
sheep: drove, flock
sparrows: host
storks: mustering
swans: bevy, wedge
swine: sounder
toads: knot
turkeys: rafter
turtles: bale
vipers: nest
whales: gam, pod
wolves: pack, route
woodcocks: fall

Top 10 Most Common Insects

Insect	Approximate number of known species
Beetles	350,000
Butterflies and moths	150,000
True flies	120,000
Ants, bees, and wasps	50,000
True bugs	40,000
Grasshoppers, crickets, and locusts	20,000
Caddisflies	7,000
Lacewings	4,000
Lice	2,900
Dragonflies and damselflies	2,500

Most Popular Official State Insects

Insect	Number of states	
Honeybee	AR, GA, KS, LA, ME, MO, MS, NC, NE, NJ, SD, UT, VT, WI	14
Ladybird beetle/ladybug	DE, MA, NH, NY, OH, TN*	6
Monarch butterfly	AL, ID, IL	3
Swallowtail butterfly	OR, VA	2
Firefly	PA, TN*	2

*Tennessee has two official insects.

Heaviest Land Mammals

Mammal	Weight
African elephant	15,000 lb. (6,804 kg)
Hippopotamus	9,920 lb. (4,500 kg)
White rhinoceros	5,000 lb. (2,268 kg)
Giraffe	3,000 lb. (1,361 kg)
Asian water buffalo	2,600 lb. (1,179 kg)
Arabian camel (dromedary)	1,520 lb. (689 kg)
Grizzly bear	1,500 lb. (680 kg)
Gorilla	500 lb. (227 kg)
Siberian tiger	400 lb. (181 kg)

Heaviest Marine Mammals

Mammal	Weight
Blue whale	150 tons
Fin whale	80 tons
Right whale	70 tons
Sperm whale	60 tons
Humpback whale	40 tons
Sei whale	40 tons
Gray whale	15 tons
Baird's beaked whale	14 tons
Killer whale	10 tons

Smallest Mammals

Mammal	Length
Kitti's hog-nosed bat	1.2 in. (3.2 cm)
Pipistrelle bat	1.4 in. (3.6 cm)
Masked shrew	1.8 in. (4.6 cm)
Common (Eurasian) shrew	2.0 in. (5.1 cm)
Harvest mouse	2.0 in. (5.1 cm)
Southern blossom bat	2.0 in. (5.1 cm)
House mouse	2.5 in. (6.4 cm)
Pygmy glider	2.8 in. (7.1 cm)
Little brown bat	3.0 in. (7.6 cm)
Pygmy shrew	3.0 in. (7.6 cm)

Fastest Mammals

Mammal	Maximum speed
Cheetah	70 mph (113 kph)
Pronghorn antelope	61 mph (98 kph)
Springbok	55 mph (89 kph)
Blue wildebeest	50 mph (80 kph)
Lion	50 mph (80 kph)
Brown hare	48 mph (77 kph)
Red fox	30 mph (48 kph)

Names of Male, Female, and Young Animals

Animal	Male	Female	Young
Bear	Boar	Sow	Cub
Cat	Tom	Queen	Kitten
Cattle	Bull	Cow	Calf
Chicken	Rooster	Hen	Chick
Deer	Buck	Doe	Fawn
Dog	Dog	Bitch	Pup
Donkey	Jack	Jenny	Foal
Duck	Drake	Duck	Duckling
Elephant	Bull	Cow	Calf
Fox	Dog	Vixen	Kit
Goose	Gander	Goose	Gosling
Horse	Stallion	Mare	Foal
Lion	Lion	Lioness	Cub
Rabbit	Buck	Doe	Bunny
Sheep	Ram	Ewe	Lamb
Swan	Cob	Pen	Cygnet
Swine	Boar	Sow	Piglet
Tiger	Tiger	Tigress	Cub
Whale	Bull	Cow	Calf
Wolf	Dog	Bitch	Pup

Types of Pets in the United States

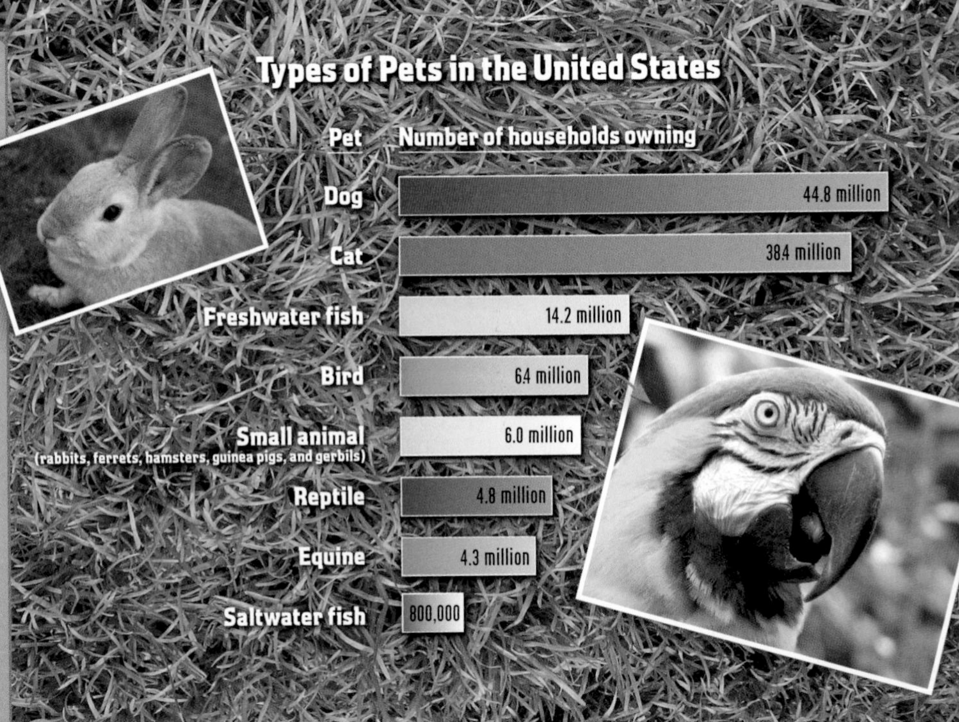

Top 10 Registered U.S. Dog Breeds

Top 10 Registered U.S. Cat Breeds

Breed	Number registered
Persian	16,657
Maine coon	3,932
Exotic shorthair	3,006
Siamese	1,445
Abyssinian	1,344
Ragdoll	1,215
Birman	991
American shorthair	802
Oriental shorthair	764
Tonkinese	704

Buildings & Landmarks

The Face of a Place

Humans have been building remarkable structures out of a variety of materials since ancient times. In fact, buildings are probably the clearest symbols of civilization. Different cities have unique buildings and landmarks that set them apart from one another. The skyline of Manhattan cannot be confused with that of any other city on Earth. The Golden Gate Bridge says San Francisco the same way the Space Needle says Seattle. And the Great Pyramids and Sphinx can only mean Egypt.

A Big Buildup

Why do we build the things we do? Bridges, roads, and tunnels are practical pathways for people to travel over, on, and through. Dams hold water back to create new space, harness power, and control waterways. Buildings provide shelter, spaces to work, and places to gather and worship.

In this section you'll see what kinds of buildings people have been making through time. How can a building reflect a culture's personality?

SUPER SKYSCRAPERS

Churches and castles were once the biggest, most impressive buildings around. Created out of stone, wood, and metal, these structures were a symbol of power and gave focus to a culture. Nowadays the biggest buildings in many cities are skyscrapers. These towering buildings—crafted from modern materials like steel, wire, concrete, and glass—can contain residences, shops, banks, offices, schools, hospitals, museums, and more.

TAKE a LOOK

The Pyramids at Giza were built around 2600 to 2500 BC as elaborate royal tombs. Created without the use of modern machinery or iron tools, they are the only "Wonder of the Ancient World" still standing. How do modern "wonders" differ from the ancient ones? (See pages 22 and 23.)

CHECK IT OUT!

At one time, a landmark was something in the natural landscape, like a mountain or river, that could be used to guide explorers. Now a landmark can be any recognizable human-built or natural structure. What kinds of landmarks are in your town? Have you ever used one to find your way?

Milestones in Modern Architecture Timeline

1884

First modern metal-frame skyscraper, Chicago's ten-story Home Insurance Company Building, is designed by U.S. architect William Jenney (1832—1907). It features a metal skeleton of cast-iron columns and nonsupporting curtain walls, which become characteristic of modern design.

1900

U.S. architect Frank Lloyd Wright (1867—1959) becomes famous for designing houses in the Prairie style, characterized by low, horizontal lines and use of natural earth colors. Wright believes buildings should complement settings.

1919

Walter Gropius (1883—1969) founds Bauhaus, a German school of design, to combine art and architecture with modern industrial technology. Bauhaus styles are notable for geometric lines and use of steel, glass, and concrete.

1928

Noted American architect (Richard) Buckminster Fuller (1895—1983) designs a self-contained "4-D" prefabricated house. Fuller becomes known for his "Dymaxion" principle of trying to get the most from the least amount of material and energy.

1937

Ludwig Mies van der Rohe (1886—1969) emigrates to the United States and becomes a leader in glass-and-steel architecture. He pioneers rectangular lines in design, including cubelike brick structures, uncovered steel columns, and large areas of tinted glass.

1948

Finnish-born American architect Eero Saarinen (1910—1961) becomes known for innovative designs for various buildings in the United States. His sweeping style features soaring rooflines, extensive use of glass, and curved lines.

1996

Petronas Twin Towers in Kuala Lumpur, Malaysia, are built and become the world's tallest buildings at a height of 1,483 feet (452 m). In 2003, the towers lose their title to the Taipei 101 Tower in Taiwan. Taipei 101 measures 1,674 feet (508 m) tall.

Construction of Important Earthworks, Dams, and Canals Timeline

1718 Elaborate system of earthen levees is built along the Mississippi River at New Orleans, LA, to control floodwaters.

1825 United States opens New York's Erie Canal, linking the Great Lakes with New York City by way of the Hudson River. The canal leads to increased development of western New York State.

1869 Suez Canal, 101 miles (163 km) long, is completed, built by French engineer Ferdinand de Lesseps (1805—1894) to connect the Mediterranean and Red seas. It is enlarged in 1980 to enable passage of supertankers.

1902 Aswan Dam is built on the Nile River in Egypt. Considered one of the finest dams of all time, it has a record-setting length of 6,400 feet (1,951 m).

1904–1914 Panama Canal, dug across Isthmus of Panama, connects the Atlantic and Pacific oceans. It is built by U.S. military engineers on land leased from the Republic of Panama. The Canal Zone is returned to Panama in 1979.

1942 Grand Coulee Dam, built for electric generation and irrigation, is completed on the Columbia River in Washington State. At 550 feet (168 m) high and 5,223 feet (1,592 m) long, it is the world's largest concrete structure.

1944 World's longest tunnel, Delaware Aqueduct, is complete. It is 105 miles (169 km) long and supplies water to New York City.

1959 United States and Canada complete construction of the St. Lawrence Seaway. It provides access to Lake Ontario for oceangoing traffic by way of the St. Lawrence River.

1970 Aswan High Dam, on the Nile River in Egypt, is completed. The dam is 364 feet (111 m) high and 12,562 feet (3,829 m) long.

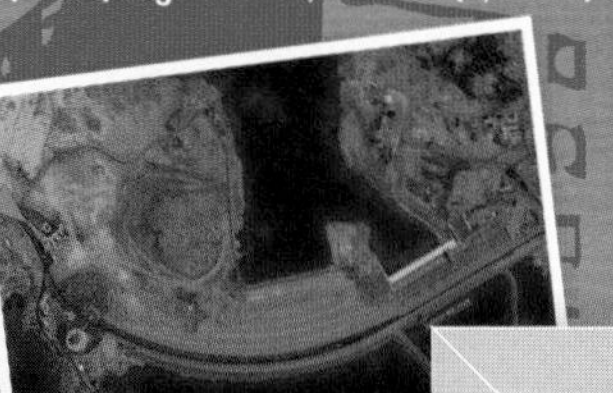

1988 Construction on the world's longest railroad tunnel is completed in Japan. Almost 33.4 miles (54 km) long, the Seikan Tunnel connects the islands of Hokkaido and Honshu.

2000 Laerdal-Aurland Tunnel, the world's longest road tunnel, opens in Norway. This 15.2-mile (24.5 km) tunnel connects Oslo to the port of Bergen.

The Seven Wonders of the Modern World

Wonder/Location		Description
Channel Tunnel England and France		The 31-mile (50 km) Channel Tunnel (Chunnel) is actually three concrete tubes, each 5 feet (2 m) thick, which burrow through the English Channel. They enter the earth at Coquelles, France, and reemerge at Folkstone, England, behind the white cliffs of Dover.
CN Tower Toronto		The world's tallest freestanding structure soars 1,815 feet (553 m) above Toronto, Canada. The CN Tower was designed to withstand 260-mph (418 kph) gusts.
Empire State Building New York City		At 1,250 feet (381 m), the Empire State Building is the best-known skyscraper in the world. For more than 40 years it was the tallest building in the world. Construction took only one year and 45 days.
Netherlands North Sea Protection Works Netherlands		This is not just one structure but a complex system of dams, floodgates, storm surge barriers, and other engineered works that protect the country against destructive floods.
Golden Gate Bridge San Francisco		Once the world's tallest suspension bridge, the Golden Gate Bridge hangs from two 746-foot (227 m) towers and is supported by enough cable to circle the earth three times.
Itaipu Dam Brazil/Paraguay		Five miles (8 km) wide and as high as a 65-story building, the main dam is made of concrete while the flanking wings are earth and rock fill. The dam generates enough energy to power most of California.
Panama Canal Panama		To build the Panama Canal, 42,000 workers dredged, blasted, and excavated from Colón to Balboa. They moved enough earth and rubble to bury the island of Manhattan to a depth of 12 feet (4 m)—or enough to open a 16-foot (5 m) tunnel to the center of the earth.

The Seven Wonders of the Ancient World

Wonder/Location	Description
Colossus of Rhodes Harbor of Rhodes, in Aegean Sea, off coast of Turkey	This huge bronze statue of the sun god, Helios, took 12 years to build and stood about 105 feet (32 m) tall. It was destroyed by an earthquake in 225 BC.
Hanging Gardens of Babylon Ancient city of Babylon (now near Baghdad, Iraq)	The hanging gardens were a series of landscaped terraces along the banks of the Euphrates River, planted with trees, flowers, and shrubs. The gardens were probably built by King Nebuchadnezzar II for his wife.
Pharos (lighthouse) Pharos Island, off coast of Alexandria, Egypt	Built around 270 BC, this was the world's first important lighthouse. It stood in the harbor for 1,000 years until it was destroyed by an earthquake. It served as a prototype for all other lighthouses built by the Roman Empire.
Mausoleum of Halicarnassus Ancient city of Halicarnassus, now Turkish town of Bodrum	This monumental marble tomb was built by the widow of Mausolus, king of Anatolia, in 353 BC.
Statue of Zeus Olympia, Greece	This huge, ornate statue of the god on his throne was almost 60 feet (18 m) tall.
Pyramids of Egypt Giza, Egypt	The oldest pyramid was built with more than two million limestone blocks and stands more than 480 feet (146 m) high. This is the only one of the ancient wonders still in existence.
Temple of Artemis Ancient Greek city of Ephesus, now in Turkey near Selçuk	Built in the sixth century BC to honor the goddess Artemis, this was one of the largest Greek temples ever built. It was famous for the artistic decoration and use of marble.

World's Tallest Dams

Name/Location	Completed	Height above lowest formation
Rogun Vakhsh River, Tajikistan	*	1,099 ft. (335 m)
Nurek Vakhsh River, Tajikistan	1980	984 ft. (300 m)
Xiaowan Lancang River, China	*	958 ft. (292 m)
Grande Dixence Dixence River, Switzerland	1961	935 ft. (285 m)
Inguri Inguri River, Georgia	1980	892 ft. (272 m)
Vaiont Vaiont River, Italy	1961	859 ft. (262 m)
Manuel M. Torres Grijalva River, Mexico	1980	856 ft. (261 m)
Tehri Bhagirathi, India	*	856 ft. (261 m)
Alvaro Obregon Mextiquic, Mexico	1946	853 ft. (260 m)
Mauvoisin Drance de Bagnes, Switzerland	1957	820 ft. (250 m)

*Planned or under construction

Top 10 Longest Suspension Bridges in North America

Name/Location	Completed	Length of main span
Verrazano-Narrows Lower New York Bay, NY	1964	4,260 ft. (1,298 m)
Golden Gate San Francisco Bay, CA	1937	4,200 ft. (1,280 m)
Mackinac Lakes Michigan and Huron, MI	1957	3,800 ft. (1,158 m)
George Washington Hudson River at New York City, NY	1931	3,500 ft. (1,067 m)
Tacoma Narrows II Puget Sound at Tacoma, WA	1950	2,800 ft. (853 m)
Carquinez Carquinez Strait, CA	2003	2,388 ft. (728 m)
San Francisco–Oakland Bay San Francisco Bay, CA	1936	2,310 ft. (704 m)
Bronx-Whitestone East River, New York City, NY	1939	2,300 ft. (701 m)
Pierre Laporte Quebec City, QC	1970	2,190 ft. (668 m)
Delaware Memorial (twin) Delaware River near Wilmington, DE	1951, 1968	2,150 ft. (655 m)

Top 10 Longest Road Tunnels in the World

Name/Location	Completed	Tunnel length
Laerdal-Aurland Norway	2000	15.2 mi. (24.5 km)
Zhongnanshan China	2007	11.2 mi. (18 km)
St. Gotthard Switzerland	1980	10.5 mi. (16.9 km)
Arlberg Austria	1978	8.7 mi. (14.0 km)
Fréjus France/Italy	1980	8.0 mi. (12.9 km)
Hsuehshan Taiwan	2007	8.0 mi. (12.9 km)
Mont Blanc France/Italy	1965	7.3 mi. (11.7 km)
Gudvanga Norway	1991	7.1 mi. (11.4 km)
Folgefonn Norway	2001	7.0 mi. (11.2 km)
Kanetsu Japan	1991	6.9 mi. (11.1 km)

Top 10 "Tallest" Cities in the World

City	Towers 700–999 ft. (213–304.5 m)	Towers 1000+ ft. (304.8 m)
New York, New York, U.S.	31	4
Hong Kong, China	25	5
Dubai, United Arab Emirates	17	8
Shanghai, China	18	3
Chicago, Illinois, U.S.	12	5
Shenzen, China	12	1
Tokyo, Japan	11	0
Houston, Texas, U.S.	9	1
Singapore	10	0
Los Angeles, California, U.S.	7	1

Top 10 Tallest Buildings in the World

Name/Location	Height
Burj Dubai* Dubai, United Arab Emirates	2,600+ ft. (800 m)
Taipei 101 Taipei, Taiwan	1,670 ft. (508 m)
Shanghai World Financial Center Shanghai, China	1,614 ft. (492 m)
International Commerce Centre* Hong Kong, China	1,585 ft. (483 m)
Petronas Tower 1 Kuala Lumpur, Malaysia	1,483 ft. (452 m)
Petronas Tower 2 Kuala Lumpur, Malaysia	1,483 ft. (452 m)
Nanjing Greenland Financial Center* Nanjing, China	1,476 ft. (450 m)
Willis (formerly Sears) Tower Chicago, Illinois	1,451 ft. (442 m)
Jin Mao Building Shanghai, China	1,381 ft. (421 m)
Trump International Hotel & Tower* Chicago, United States	1,362 ft. (415 m)

*Buildings not completed but under construction and "topped out" as of December 31, 2008

Calendars & Holidays

Mark Your Calendar!

We use calendars to keep track of all the things we need to do in our busy days, weeks, months, and years. But in one way or another, human beings have always been creating calendars. Ever since people first noticed the passing of time, they have figured out interesting ways to measure and record it. They used sticks in the ground to show how shadows changed throughout a day. They made marks on a wall to show how many nights passed until the Moon became full again.

Luna-tics!

The Moon was an essential tool in creating early calendars. Ancient Egyptians noticed that the Nile flooded every 12 moons, leaving rich soils for growing crops. This was an important event to plan for. They figured out that it took about 365 days for these 12 moons to pass and for the floods to begin again.

The Spin Is In

Ancient peoples understood that time never stands still. Earth is constantly in motion, rotating on its axis while it makes its slow orbit around the Sun. A day is 24 hours—the time it takes for Earth to make one rotation. A year is the time it takes for Earth to revolve around the Sun—365 ¼ days. Every four years we have to add a day to make the math right, resulting in what we call a leap year.

When in Rome

There are several kinds of calendars in use around the world today. The months in the calendar used most often, called the Gregorian calendar, were originally named by the Romans after rulers and gods. July is named for Roman ruler Julius Caesar. March is named for Mars, the god of war. Some days of the week were also named after gods. The French word for Tuesday is *mardi*, after the same god of war.

TAKE a LOOK

In this chapter, read about holidays and special occasions celebrated around the world. If you were in charge, what event or events would you want celebrated with a special day? (Besides your birthday, of course!)

Every day of the year, there's something to celebrate or honor:

JAN 21 — National Hugging Day

MAY 1 — Save the Rhino Day

JUNE 6 — National Yo-Yo Day

SEPT 19 — National Butterscotch Pudding Day

OCT 9 — Moldy Cheese Day

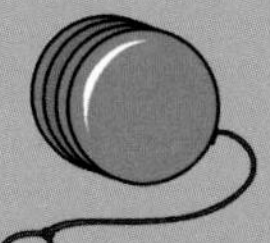

Periods of Time

annual	yearly
biannual	twice a year
bicentennial	marking a period of 200 years
biennial	marking a period of 2 years
bimonthly	every 2 months; twice a month
biweekly	every 2 weeks; twice a week
centennial	marking a period of 100 years
decennial	marking a period of 10 years
diurnal	daily; of a day
duodecennial	marking a period of 12 years
millennial	marking a period of 1,000 years
novennial	marking a period of 9 years
octennial	marking a period of 8 years
perennial	occurring year after year
quadrennial	marking a period of 4 years
quadricentennial	marking a period of 400 years
quincentennial	marking a period of 500 years
quindecennial	marking a period of 15 years
quinquennial	marking a period of 5 years
semiannual	twice a year
semicentennial	marking a period of 50 years
semidiurnal	twice a day
semiweekly	twice a week
septennial	marking a period of 7 years
sesquicentennial	marking a period of 150 years
sexennial	marking a period of 6 years
thrice weekly	3 times a week
tricennial	marking a period of 30 years
triennial	marking a period of 3 years
trimonthly	every 3 months
triweekly	every 3 weeks; 3 times a week
undecennial	marking a period of 11 years
vicennial	marking a period of 20 years

Months of the Year in Different Calendars

Gregorian	Jewish	Hindu	Muslim
January	Shevat	Magha	Muharram
February	Adar	Phalgun	Safar
March	Nisan	Cait	Rabi I
April	Iyar	Baisakh	Rabi II
May	Sivan	Jyeshtha	Jumada I
June	Tammuz	Asarh	Jumada II
July	Av	Sravan	Rajab
August	Elul	Bhadon	Sha'ban
September	Tishrei	Asvin	Ramadan
October	Cheshvan	Kartik	Shawwal
November	Kislev	Margasira	Dhu'l-Qa'dah
December	Tevet	Pus	Dhu'l-Hijja

Birthstones by Month

garnet

FEB: amethyst

MARCH: aquamarine

diamond

emerald

pearl

JULY: ruby

AUG: peridot

SEPT: sapphire

OCT: opal

NOV: topaz

DEC: turquoise

Wedding Anniversary Gift Chart

Anniversary	Traditional	Modern
1st	paper	clocks
2nd	cotton	china
3rd	leather	crystal
4th	fruit/flowers	linen/silk
5th	wood	silverware
6th	iron	wood
7th	wool	desk sets
8th	bronze	linen
9th	pottery	leather
10th	tin	diamond jewelry
11th	steel	fashion jewelry
12th	silk/linen	pearls
13th	lace	textiles
14th	ivory	gold jewelry
15th	crystal	watches
20th	china	platinum
25th	silver	silver
30th	pearls	diamonds
35th	coral	jade
40th	rubies	rubies
45th	sapphires	sapphires
50th	gold	gold
55th	emeralds	emeralds
60th	diamonds	diamonds

Chinese Years, 1900–2019

Rat	Ox	Tiger	Hare (Rabbit)	Dragon	Snake
1900	1901	1902	1903	1904	1905
1912	1913	1914	1915	1916	1917
1924	1925	1926	1927	1928	1929
1936	1937	1938	1939	1940	1941
1948	1949	1950	1951	1952	1953
1960	1961	1962	1963	1964	1965
1972	1973	1974	1975	1976	1977
1984	1985	1986	1987	1988	1989
1996	1997	1998	1999	2000	2001
2008	2009	2010	2011	2012	2013

Horse	Sheep (Goat)	Monkey	Rooster	Dog	Pig
1906	1907	1908	1909	1910	1911
1918	1919	1920	1921	1922	1923
1930	1931	1932	1933	1934	1935
1942	1943	1944	1945	1946	1947
1954	1955	1956	1957	1958	1959
1966	1967	1968	1969	1970	1971
1978	1979	1980	1981	1982	1983
1990	1991	1992	1993	1994	1995
2002	2003	2004	2005	2006	2007
2014	2015	2016	2017	2018	2019

Perpetual Calendar, 1775–2050

A perpetual calendar lets you find the day of the week for any date in any year. The number next to each year below corresponds to one of the 14 calendars that follow.

Year	Cal.	Year	Cal.	Year	Cal.	Year	Cal.	Year	Cal.	Year	Cal.
1775	1	1821	2	1867	3	1913	4	1959	5	2005	7
1776	9	1822	3	1868	11	1914	5	1960	13	2006	1
1777	4	1823	4	1869	6	1915	6	1961	1	2007	2
1778	5	1824	12	1870	7	1916	14	1962	2	2008	10
1779	6	1825	7	1871	1	1917	2	1963	3	2009	5
1780	14	1826	1	1872	9	1918	3	1964	11	2010	6
1781	2	1827	2	1873	4	1919	4	1965	6	2011	7
1782	3	1828	10	1874	5	1920	12	1966	7	2012	8
1783	4	1829	5	1875	6	1921	7	1967	1	2013	3
1784	12	1830	6	1876	14	1922	1	1968	9	2014	4
1785	7	1831	7	1877	2	1923	2	1969	4	2015	5
1786	1	1832	8	1878	3	1924	10	1970	5	2016	13
1787	2	1833	3	1879	4	1925	5	1971	6	2017	1
1788	10	1834	4	1880	12	1926	6	1972	14	2018	2
1789	5	1835	5	1881	7	1927	7	1973	2	2019	3
1790	6	1836	13	1882	1	1928	8	1974	3	2020	11
1791	7	1837	1	1883	2	1929	3	1975	4	2021	6
1792	8	1838	2	1884	10	1930	4	1976	12	2022	7
1793	3	1839	3	1885	5	1931	5	1977	7	2023	1
1794	4	1840	11	1886	6	1932	13	1978	1	2024	9
1795	5	1841	6	1887	7	1933	1	1979	2	2025	4
1796	13	1842	7	1888	8	1934	2	1980	10	2026	5
1797	1	1843	1	1889	3	1935	3	1981	5	2027	6
1798	2	1844	9	1890	4	1936	11	1982	6	2028	14
1799	3	1845	4	1891	5	1937	6	1983	7	2029	2
1800	4	1846	5	1892	13	1938	7	1984	8	2030	3
1801	5	1847	6	1893	1	1939	1	1985	3	2031	4
1802	6	1848	14	1894	2	1940	9	1986	4	2032	12
1803	7	1849	2	1895	3	1941	4	1987	5	2033	7
1804	8	1850	3	1896	11	1942	5	1988	13	2034	1
1805	3	1851	4	1897	6	1943	6	1989	1	2035	2
1806	4	1852	12	1898	7	1944	14	1990	2	2036	10
1807	5	1853	7	1899	1	1945	2	1991	3	2037	5
1808	13	1854	1	1900	2	1946	3	1992	11	2038	6
1809	1	1855	2	1901	3	1947	4	1993	6	2039	7
1810	2	1856	10	1902	4	1948	12	1994	7	2040	8
1811	3	1857	5	1903	5	1949	7	1995	1	2041	3
1812	11	1858	6	1904	13	1950	1	1996	9	2042	4
1813	6	1859	7	1905	1	1951	2	1997	4	2043	5
1814	7	1860	8	1906	2	1952	10	1998	5	2044	13
1815	1	1861	3	1907	3	1953	5	1999	6	2045	1
1816	9	1862	4	1908	11	1954	6	2000	14	2046	2
1817	4	1863	5	1909	6	1955	7	2001	2	2047	3
1818	5	1864	13	1910	7	1956	8	2002	3	2048	11
1819	6	1865	1	1911	1	1957	3	2003	4	2049	6
1820	14	1866	2	1912	9	1958	4	2004	12	2050	7

1

JANUARY

S	M	T	W	T	F	S
1	2	3	4	5	6	7
8	9	10	11	12	13	14
15	16	17	18	19	20	21
22	23	24	25	26	27	28
29	30	31				

FEBRUARY

S	M	T	W	T	F	S
			1	2	3	4
5	6	7	8	9	10	11
12	13	14	15	16	17	18
19	20	21	22	23	24	25
26	27	28				

MARCH

S	M	T	W	T	F	S
			1	2	3	4
5	6	7	8	9	10	11
12	13	14	15	16	17	18
19	20	21	22	23	24	25
26	27	28	29	30	31	

APRIL

S	M	T	W	T	F	S
						1
2	3	4	5	6	7	8
9	10	11	12	13	14	15
16	17	18	19	20	21	22
23	24	25	26	27	28	29
30						

MAY

S	M	T	W	T	F	S
	1	2	3	4	5	6
7	8	9	10	11	12	13
14	15	16	17	18	19	20
21	22	23	24	25	26	27
28	29	30	31			

JUNE

S	M	T	W	T	F	S
				1	2	3
4	5	6	7	8	9	10
11	12	13	14	15	16	17
18	19	20	21	22	23	24
25	26	27	28	29	30	

JULY

S	M	T	W	T	F	S
						1
2	3	4	5	6	7	8
9	10	11	12	13	14	15
16	17	18	19	20	21	22
23	24	25	26	27	28	29
30	31					

AUGUST

S	M	T	W	T	F	S
		1	2	3	4	5
6	7	8	9	10	11	12
13	14	15	16	17	18	19
20	21	22	23	24	25	26
27	28	29	30	31		

SEPTEMBER

S	M	T	W	T	F	S
					1	2
3	4	5	6	7	8	9
10	11	12	13	14	15	16
17	18	19	20	21	22	23
24	25	26	27	28	29	30

OCTOBER

S	M	T	W	T	F	S
1	2	3	4	5	6	7
8	9	10	11	12	13	14
15	16	17	18	19	20	21
22	23	24	25	26	27	28
29	30	31				

NOVEMBER

S	M	T	W	T	F	S
			1	2	3	4
5	6	7	8	9	10	11
12	13	14	15	16	17	18
19	20	21	22	23	24	25
26	27	28	29	30		

DECEMBER

S	M	T	W	T	F	S
					1	2
3	4	5	6	7	8	9
10	11	12	13	14	15	16
17	18	19	20	21	22	23
24	25	26	27	28	29	30
31						

2

JANUARY

S	M	T	W	T	F	S
	1	2	3	4	5	6
7	8	9	10	11	12	13
14	15	16	17	18	19	20
21	22	23	24	25	26	27
28	29	30	31			

FEBRUARY

S	M	T	W	T	F	S
				1	2	3
4	5	6	7	8	9	10
11	12	13	14	15	16	17
18	19	20	21	22	23	24
25	26	27	28			

MARCH

S	M	T	W	T	F	S
				1	2	3
4	5	6	7	8	9	10
11	12	13	14	15	16	17
18	19	20	21	22	23	24
25	26	27	28	29	30	31

APRIL

S	M	T	W	T	F	S
1	2	3	4	5	6	7
8	9	10	11	12	13	14
15	16	17	18	19	20	21
22	23	24	25	26	27	28
29	30					

MAY

S	M	T	W	T	F	S
		1	2	3	4	5
6	7	8	9	10	11	12
13	14	15	16	17	18	19
20	21	22	23	24	25	26
27	28	29	30	31		

JUNE

S	M	T	W	T	F	S
					1	2
3	4	5	6	7	8	9
10	11	12	13	14	15	16
17	18	19	20	21	22	23
24	25	26	27	28	29	30

JULY

S	M	T	W	T	F	S
1	2	3	4	5	6	7
8	9	10	11	12	13	14
15	16	17	18	19	20	21
22	23	24	25	26	27	28
29	30	31				

AUGUST

S	M	T	W	T	F	S
			1	2	3	4
5	6	7	8	9	10	11
12	13	14	15	16	17	18
19	20	21	22	23	24	25
26	27	28	29	30	31	

SEPTEMBER

S	M	T	W	T	F	S
						1
2	3	4	5	6	7	8
9	10	11	12	13	14	15
16	17	18	19	20	21	22
23	24	25	26	27	28	29
30						

OCTOBER

S	M	T	W	T	F	S
	1	2	3	4	5	6
7	8	9	10	11	12	13
14	15	16	17	18	19	20
21	22	23	24	25	26	27
28	29	30	31			

NOVEMBER

S	M	T	W	T	F	S
				1	2	3
4	5	6	7	8	9	10
11	12	13	14	15	16	17
18	19	20	21	22	23	24
25	26	27	28	29	30	

DECEMBER

S	M	T	W	T	F	S
						1
2	3	4	5	6	7	8
9	10	11	12	13	14	15
16	17	18	19	20	21	22
23	24	25	26	27	28	29
30	31					

3

JANUARY

S	M	T	W	T	F	S
		1	2	3	4	5
6	7	8	9	10	11	12
13	14	15	16	17	18	19
20	21	22	23	24	25	26
27	28	29	30	31		

FEBRUARY

S	M	T	W	T	F	S
					1	2
3	4	5	6	7	8	9
10	11	12	13	14	15	16
17	18	19	20	21	22	23
24	25	26	27	28		

MARCH

S	M	T	W	T	F	S
					1	2
3	4	5	6	7	8	9
10	11	12	13	14	15	16
17	18	19	20	21	22	23
24	25	26	27	28	29	30
31						

APRIL

S	M	T	W	T	F	S
	1	2	3	4	5	6
7	8	9	10	11	12	13
14	15	16	17	18	19	20
21	22	23	24	25	26	27
28	29	30				

MAY

S	M	T	W	T	F	S
			1	2	3	4
5	6	7	8	9	10	11
12	13	14	15	16	17	18
19	20	21	22	23	24	25
26	27	28	29	30	31	

JUNE

S	M	T	W	T	F	S
						1
2	3	4	5	6	7	8
9	10	11	12	13	14	15
16	17	18	19	20	21	22
23	24	25	26	27	28	29
30						

JULY

S	M	T	W	T	F	S
	1	2	3	4	5	6
7	8	9	10	11	12	13
14	15	16	17	18	19	20
21	22	23	24	25	26	27
28	29	30	31			

AUGUST

S	M	T	W	T	F	S
				1	2	3
4	5	6	7	8	9	10
11	12	13	14	15	16	17
18	19	20	21	22	23	24
25	26	27	28	29	30	31

SEPTEMBER

S	M	T	W	T	F	S
1	2	3	4	5	6	7
8	9	10	11	12	13	14
15	16	17	18	19	20	21
22	23	24	25	26	27	28
29	30					

OCTOBER

S	M	T	W	T	F	S
		1	2	3	4	5
6	7	8	9	10	11	12
13	14	15	16	17	18	19
20	21	22	23	24	25	26
27	28	29	30	31		

NOVEMBER

S	M	T	W	T	F	S
					1	2
3	4	5	6	7	8	9
10	11	12	13	14	15	16
17	18	19	20	21	22	23
24	25	26	27	28	29	30

DECEMBER

S	M	T	W	T	F	S
1	2	3	4	5	6	7
8	9	10	11	12	13	14
15	16	17	18	19	20	21
22	23	24	25	26	27	28
29	30	31				

4

JANUARY

S	M	T	W	T	F	S
			1	2	3	4
5	6	7	8	9	10	11
12	13	14	15	16	17	18
19	20	21	22	23	24	25
26	27	28	29	30	31	

FEBRUARY

S	M	T	W	T	F	S
						1
2	3	4	5	6	7	8
9	10	11	12	13	14	15
16	17	18	19	20	21	22
23	24	25	26	27	28	

MARCH

S	M	T	W	T	F	S
						1
2	3	4	5	6	7	8
9	10	11	12	13	14	15
16	17	18	19	20	21	22
23	24	25	26	27	28	29
30	31					

APRIL

S	M	T	W	T	F	S
		1	2	3	4	5
6	7	8	9	10	11	12
13	14	15	16	17	18	19
20	21	22	23	24	25	26
27	28	29	30			

MAY

S	M	T	W	T	F	S
				1	2	3
4	5	6	7	8	9	10
11	12	13	14	15	16	17
18	19	20	21	22	23	24
25	26	27	28	29	30	31

JUNE

S	M	T	W	T	F	S
1	2	3	4	5	6	7
8	9	10	11	12	13	14
15	16	17	18	19	20	21
22	23	24	25	26	27	28
29	30					

JULY

S	M	T	W	T	F	S
		1	2	3	4	5
6	7	8	9	10	11	12
13	14	15	16	17	18	19
20	21	22	23	24	25	26
27	28	29	30	31		

AUGUST

S	M	T	W	T	F	S
					1	2
3	4	5	6	7	8	9
10	11	12	13	14	15	16
17	18	19	20	21	22	23
24	25	26	27	28	29	30
31						

SEPTEMBER

S	M	T	W	T	F	S
	1	2	3	4	5	6
7	8	9	10	11	12	13
14	15	16	17	18	19	20
21	22	23	24	25	26	27
28	29	30				

OCTOBER

S	M	T	W	T	F	S
			1	2	3	4
5	6	7	8	9	10	11
12	13	14	15	16	17	18
19	20	21	22	23	24	25
26	27	28	29	30	31	

NOVEMBER

S	M	T	W	T	F	S
						1
2	3	4	5	6	7	8
9	10	11	12	13	14	15
16	17	18	19	20	21	22
23	24	25	26	27	28	29
30						

DECEMBER

S	M	T	W	T	F	S
	1	2	3	4	5	6
7	8	9	10	11	12	13
14	15	16	17	18	19	20
21	22	23	24	25	26	27
28	29	30	31			

5

JANUARY

S	M	T	W	T	F	S
				1	2	3
4	5	6	7	8	9	10
11	12	13	14	15	16	17
18	19	20	21	22	23	24
25	26	27	28	29	30	31

FEBRUARY

S	M	T	W	T	F	S
1	2	3	4	5	6	7
8	9	10	11	12	13	14
15	16	17	18	19	20	21
22	23	24	25	26	27	28

MARCH

S	M	T	W	T	F	S
1	2	3	4	5	6	7
8	9	10	11	12	13	14
15	16	17	18	19	20	21
22	23	24	25	26	27	28
29	30	31				

APRIL

S	M	T	W	T	F	S
			1	2	3	4
5	6	7	8	9	10	11
12	13	14	15	16	17	18
19	20	21	22	23	24	25
26	27	28	29	30		

MAY

S	M	T	W	T	F	S
					1	2
3	4	5	6	7	8	9
10	11	12	13	14	15	16
17	18	19	20	21	22	23
24	25	26	27	28	29	30
31						

JUNE

S	M	T	W	T	F	S
	1	2	3	4	5	6
7	8	9	10	11	12	13
14	15	16	17	18	19	20
21	22	23	24	25	26	27
28	29	30				

JULY

S	M	T	W	T	F	S
			1	2	3	4
5	6	7	8	9	10	11
12	13	14	15	16	17	18
19	20	21	22	23	24	25
26	27	28	29	30	31	

AUGUST

S	M	T	W	T	F	S
						1
2	3	4	5	6	7	8
9	10	11	12	13	14	15
16	17	18	19	20	21	22
23	24	25	26	27	28	29
30	31					

SEPTEMBER

S	M	T	W	T	F	S
		1	2	3	4	5
6	7	8	9	10	11	12
13	14	15	16	17	18	19
20	21	22	23	24	25	26
27	28	29	30			

OCTOBER

S	M	T	W	T	F	S
				1	2	3
4	5	6	7	8	9	10
11	12	13	14	15	16	17
18	19	20	21	22	23	24
25	26	27	28	29	30	31

NOVEMBER

S	M	T	W	T	F	S
1	2	3	4	5	6	7
8	9	10	11	12	13	14
15	16	17	18	19	20	21
22	23	24	25	26	27	28
29	30					

DECEMBER

S	M	T	W	T	F	S
		1	2	3	4	5
6	7	8	9	10	11	12
13	14	15	16	17	18	19
20	21	22	23	24	25	26
27	28	29	30	31		

6

JANUARY

S	M	T	W	T	F	S
					1	2
3	4	5	6	7	8	9
10	11	12	13	14	15	16
17	18	19	20	21	22	23
24	25	26	27	28	29	30
31						

FEBRUARY

S	M	T	W	T	F	S
	1	2	3	4	5	6
7	8	9	10	11	12	13
14	15	16	17	18	19	20
21	22	23	24	25	26	27
28						

MARCH

S	M	T	W	T	F	S
	1	2	3	4	5	6
7	8	9	10	11	12	13
14	15	16	17	18	19	20
21	22	23	24	25	26	27
28	29	30	31			

APRIL

S	M	T	W	T	F	S
				1	2	3
4	5	6	7	8	9	10
11	12	13	14	15	16	17
18	19	20	21	22	23	24
25	26	27	28	29	30	

MAY

S	M	T	W	T	F	S
						1
2	3	4	5	6	7	8
9	10	11	12	13	14	15
16	17	18	19	20	21	22
23	24	25	26	27	28	29
30	31					

JUNE

S	M	T	W	T	F	S
		1	2	3	4	5
6	7	8	9	10	11	12
13	14	15	16	17	18	19
20	21	22	23	24	25	26
27	28	29	30			

JULY

S	M	T	W	T	F	S
				1	2	3
4	5	6	7	8	9	10
11	12	13	14	15	16	17
18	19	20	21	22	23	24
25	26	27	28	29	30	31

AUGUST

S	M	T	W	T	F	S
1	2	3	4	5	6	7
8	9	10	11	12	13	14
15	16	17	18	19	20	21
22	23	24	25	26	27	28
29	30	31				

SEPTEMBER

S	M	T	W	T	F	S
			1	2	3	4
5	6	7	8	9	10	11
12	13	14	15	16	17	18
19	20	21	22	23	24	25
26	27	28	29	30		

OCTOBER

S	M	T	W	T	F	S
					1	2
3	4	5	6	7	8	9
10	11	12	13	14	15	16
17	18	19	20	21	22	23
24	25	26	27	28	29	30
31						

NOVEMBER

S	M	T	W	T	F	S
	1	2	3	4	5	6
7	8	9	10	11	12	13
14	15	16	17	18	19	20
21	22	23	24	25	26	27
28	29	30				

DECEMBER

S	M	T	W	T	F	S
			1	2	3	4
5	6	7	8	9	10	11
12	13	14	15	16	17	18
19	20	21	22	23	24	25
26	27	28	29	30	31	

7

JANUARY

S	M	T	W	T	F	S
						1
2	3	4	5	6	7	8
9	10	11	12	13	14	15
16	17	18	19	20	21	22
23	24	25	26	27	28	29
30	31					

FEBRUARY

S	M	T	W	T	F	S
		1	2	3	4	5
6	7	8	9	10	11	12
13	14	15	16	17	18	19
20	21	22	23	24	25	26
27	28					

MARCH

S	M	T	W	T	F	S
		1	2	3	4	5
6	7	8	9	10	11	12
13	14	15	16	17	18	19
20	21	22	23	24	25	26
27	28	29	30	31		

APRIL

S	M	T	W	T	F	S
					1	2
3	4	5	6	7	8	9
10	11	12	13	14	15	16
17	18	19	20	21	22	23
24	25	26	27	28	29	30

MAY

S	M	T	W	T	F	S
1	2	3	4	5	6	7
8	9	10	11	12	13	14
15	16	17	18	19	20	21
22	23	24	25	26	27	28
29	30	31				

JUNE

S	M	T	W	T	F	S
			1	2	3	4
5	6	7	8	9	10	11
12	13	14	15	16	17	18
19	20	21	22	23	24	25
26	27	28	29	30		

JULY

S	M	T	W	T	F	S
					1	2
3	4	5	6	7	8	9
10	11	12	13	14	15	16
17	18	19	20	21	22	23
24	25	26	27	28	29	30
31						

AUGUST

S	M	T	W	T	F	S
	1	2	3	4	5	6
7	8	9	10	11	12	13
14	15	16	17	18	19	20
21	22	23	24	25	26	27
28	29	30	31			

SEPTEMBER

S	M	T	W	T	F	S
				1	2	3
4	5	6	7	8	9	10
11	12	13	14	15	16	17
18	19	20	21	22	23	24
25	26	27	28	29	30	

OCTOBER

S	M	T	W	T	F	S
						1
2	3	4	5	6	7	8
9	10	11	12	13	14	15
16	17	18	19	20	21	22
23	24	25	26	27	28	29
30	31					

NOVEMBER

S	M	T	W	T	F	S
		1	2	3	4	5
6	7	8	9	10	11	12
13	14	15	16	17	18	19
20	21	22	23	24	25	26
27	28	29	30			

DECEMBER

S	M	T	W	T	F	S
				1	2	3
4	5	6	7	8	9	10
11	12	13	14	15	16	17
18	19	20	21	22	23	24
25	26	27	28	29	30	31

8

JANUARY

S	M	T	W	T	F	S
1	2	3	4	5	6	7
8	9	10	11	12	13	14
15	16	17	18	19	20	21
22	23	24	25	26	27	28
29	30	31				

FEBRUARY

S	M	T	W	T	F	S
			1	2	3	4
5	6	7	8	9	10	11
12	13	14	15	16	17	18
19	20	21	22	23	24	25
26	27	28	29			

MARCH

S	M	T	W	T	F	S
				1	2	3
4	5	6	7	8	9	10
11	12	13	14	15	16	17
18	19	20	21	22	23	24
25	26	27	28	29	30	31

APRIL

S	M	T	W	T	F	S
1	2	3	4	5	6	7
8	9	10	11	12	13	14
15	16	17	18	19	20	21
22	23	24	25	26	27	28
29	30					

MAY

S	M	T	W	T	F	S
		1	2	3	4	5
6	7	8	9	10	11	12
13	14	15	16	17	18	19
20	21	22	23	24	25	26
27	28	29	30	31		

JUNE

S	M	T	W	T	F	S
					1	2
3	4	5	6	7	8	9
10	11	12	13	14	15	16
17	18	19	20	21	22	23
24	25	26	27	28	29	30

JULY

S	M	T	W	T	F	S
1	2	3	4	5	6	7
8	9	10	11	12	13	14
15	16	17	18	19	20	21
22	23	24	25	26	27	28
29	30	31				

AUGUST

S	M	T	W	T	F	S
			1	2	3	4
5	6	7	8	9	10	11
12	13	14	15	16	17	18
19	20	21	22	23	24	25
26	27	28	29	30	31	

SEPTEMBER

S	M	T	W	T	F	S
						1
2	3	4	5	6	7	8
9	10	11	12	13	14	15
16	17	18	19	20	21	22
23	24	25	26	27	28	29
30						

OCTOBER

S	M	T	W	T	F	S
	1	2	3	4	5	6
7	8	9	10	11	12	13
14	15	16	17	18	19	20
21	22	23	24	25	26	27
28	29	30	31			

NOVEMBER

S	M	T	W	T	F	S
				1	2	3
4	5	6	7	8	9	10
11	12	13	14	15	16	17
18	19	20	21	22	23	24
25	26	27	28	29	30	

DECEMBER

S	M	T	W	T	F	S
						1
2	3	4	5	6	7	8
9	10	11	12	13	14	15
16	17	18	19	20	21	22
23	24	25	26	27	28	29
30	31					

9

JANUARY
S	M	T	W	T	F	S
	1	2	3	4	5	6
7	8	9	10	11	12	13
14	15	16	17	18	19	20
21	22	23	24	25	26	27
28	29	30	31			

FEBRUARY
S	M	T	W	T	F	S
				1	2	3
4	5	6	7	8	9	10
11	12	13	14	15	16	17
18	19	20	21	22	23	24
25	26	27	28	29		

MARCH
S	M	T	W	T	F	S
					1	2
3	4	5	6	7	8	9
10	11	12	13	14	15	16
17	18	19	20	21	22	23
24	25	26	27	28	29	30
31						

APRIL
S	M	T	W	T	F	S
	1	2	3	4	5	6
7	8	9	10	11	12	13
14	15	16	17	18	19	20
21	22	23	24	25	26	27
28	29	30				

MAY
S	M	T	W	T	F	S
			1	2	3	4
5	6	7	8	9	10	11
12	13	14	15	16	17	18
19	20	21	22	23	24	25
26	27	28	29	30	31	

JUNE
S	M	T	W	T	F	S
						1
2	3	4	5	6	7	8
9	10	11	12	13	14	15
16	17	18	19	20	21	22
23	24	25	26	27	28	29
30						

JULY
S	M	T	W	T	F	S
	1	2	3	4	5	6
7	8	9	10	11	12	13
14	15	16	17	18	19	20
21	22	23	24	25	26	27
28	29	30	31			

AUGUST
S	M	T	W	T	F	S
				1	2	3
4	5	6	7	8	9	10
11	12	13	14	15	16	17
18	19	20	21	22	23	24
25	26	27	28	29	30	31

SEPTEMBER
S	M	T	W	T	F	S
1	2	3	4	5	6	7
8	9	10	11	12	13	14
15	16	17	18	19	20	21
22	23	24	25	26	27	28
29	30					

OCTOBER
S	M	T	W	T	F	S
		1	2	3	4	5
6	7	8	9	10	11	12
13	14	15	16	17	18	19
20	21	22	23	24	25	26
27	28	29	30	31		

NOVEMBER
S	M	T	W	T	F	S
					1	2
3	4	5	6	7	8	9
10	11	12	13	14	15	16
17	18	19	20	21	22	23
24	25	26	27	28	29	30

DECEMBER
S	M	T	W	T	F	S
1	2	3	4	5	6	7
8	9	10	11	12	13	14
15	16	17	18	19	20	21
22	23	24	25	26	27	28
29	30	31				

10

JANUARY
S	M	T	W	T	F	S
		1	2	3	4	5
6	7	8	9	10	11	12
13	14	15	16	17	18	19
20	21	22	23	24	25	26
27	28	29	30	31		

FEBRUARY
S	M	T	W	T	F	S
					1	2
3	4	5	6	7	8	9
10	11	12	13	14	15	16
17	18	19	20	21	22	23
24	25	26	27	28	29	

MARCH
S	M	T	W	T	F	S
						1
2	3	4	5	6	7	8
9	10	11	12	13	14	15
16	17	18	19	20	21	22
23	24	25	26	27	28	29
30	31					

APRIL
S	M	T	W	T	F	S
		1	2	3	4	5
6	7	8	9	10	11	12
13	14	15	16	17	18	19
20	21	22	23	24	25	26
27	28	29	30			

MAY
S	M	T	W	T	F	S
				1	2	3
4	5	6	7	8	9	10
11	12	13	14	15	16	17
18	19	20	21	22	23	24
25	26	27	28	29	30	31

JUNE
S	M	T	W	T	F	S
1	2	3	4	5	6	7
8	9	10	11	12	13	14
15	16	17	18	19	20	21
22	23	24	25	26	27	28
29	30					

JULY
S	M	T	W	T	F	S
		1	2	3	4	5
6	7	8	9	10	11	12
13	14	15	16	17	18	19
20	21	22	23	24	25	26
27	28	29	30	31		

AUGUST
S	M	T	W	T	F	S
					1	2
3	4	5	6	7	8	9
10	11	12	13	14	15	16
17	18	19	20	21	22	23
24	25	26	27	28	29	30
31						

SEPTEMBER
S	M	T	W	T	F	S
	1	2	3	4	5	6
7	8	9	10	11	12	13
14	15	16	17	18	19	20
21	22	23	24	25	26	27
28	29	30				

OCTOBER
S	M	T	W	T	F	S
			1	2	3	4
5	6	7	8	9	10	11
12	13	14	15	16	17	18
19	20	21	22	23	24	25
26	27	28	29	30	31	

NOVEMBER
S	M	T	W	T	F	S
						1
2	3	4	5	6	7	8
9	10	11	12	13	14	15
16	17	18	19	20	21	22
23	24	25	26	27	28	29
30						

DECEMBER
S	M	T	W	T	F	S
	1	2	3	4	5	6
7	8	9	10	11	12	13
14	15	16	17	18	19	20
21	22	23	24	25	26	27
28	29	30	31			

11

JANUARY
S	M	T	W	T	F	S
			1	2	3	4
5	6	7	8	9	10	11
12	13	14	15	16	17	18
19	20	21	22	23	24	25
26	27	28	29	30	31	

FEBRUARY
S	M	T	W	T	F	S
						1
2	3	4	5	6	7	8
9	10	11	12	13	14	15
16	17	18	19	20	21	22
23	24	25	26	27	28	29

MARCH
S	M	T	W	T	F	S
1	2	3	4	5	6	7
8	9	10	11	12	13	14
15	16	17	18	19	20	21
22	23	24	25	26	27	28
29	30	31				

APRIL
S	M	T	W	T	F	S
			1	2	3	4
5	6	7	8	9	10	11
12	13	14	15	16	17	18
19	20	21	22	23	24	25
26	27	28	29	30		

MAY
S	M	T	W	T	F	S
					1	2
3	4	5	6	7	8	9
10	11	12	13	14	15	16
17	18	19	20	21	22	23
24	25	26	27	28	29	30
31						

JUNE
S	M	T	W	T	F	S
	1	2	3	4	5	6
7	8	9	10	11	12	13
14	15	16	17	18	19	20
21	22	23	24	25	26	27
28	29	30				

JULY
S	M	T	W	T	F	S
			1	2	3	4
5	6	7	8	9	10	11
12	13	14	15	16	17	18
19	20	21	22	23	24	25
26	27	28	29	30	31	

AUGUST
S	M	T	W	T	F	S
						1
2	3	4	5	6	7	8
9	10	11	12	13	14	15
16	17	18	19	20	21	22
23	24	25	26	27	28	29
30	31					

SEPTEMBER
S	M	T	W	T	F	S
		1	2	3	4	5
6	7	8	9	10	11	12
13	14	15	16	17	18	19
20	21	22	23	24	25	26
27	28	29	30			

OCTOBER
S	M	T	W	T	F	S
				1	2	3
4	5	6	7	8	9	10
11	12	13	14	15	16	17
18	19	20	21	22	23	24
25	26	27	28	29	30	31

NOVEMBER
S	M	T	W	T	F	S
1	2	3	4	5	6	7
8	9	10	11	12	13	14
15	16	17	18	19	20	21
22	23	24	25	26	27	28
29	30					

DECEMBER
S	M	T	W	T	F	S
		1	2	3	4	5
6	7	8	9	10	11	12
13	14	15	16	17	18	19
20	21	22	23	24	25	26
27	28	29	30	31		

12

JANUARY
S	M	T	W	T	F	S
				1	2	3
4	5	6	7	8	9	10
11	12	13	14	15	16	17
18	19	20	21	22	23	24
25	26	27	28	29	30	31

FEBRUARY
S	M	T	W	T	F	S
1	2	3	4	5	6	7
8	9	10	11	12	13	14
15	16	17	18	19	20	21
22	23	24	25	26	27	28
29						

MARCH
S	M	T	W	T	F	S
	1	2	3	4	5	6
7	8	9	10	11	12	13
14	15	16	17	18	19	20
21	22	23	24	25	26	27
28	29	30	31			

APRIL
S	M	T	W	T	F	S
				1	2	3
4	5	6	7	8	9	10
11	12	13	14	15	16	17
18	19	20	21	22	23	24
25	26	27	28	29	30	

MAY
S	M	T	W	T	F	S
						1
2	3	4	5	6	7	8
9	10	11	12	13	14	15
16	17	18	19	20	21	22
23	24	25	26	27	28	29
30	31					

JUNE
S	M	T	W	T	F	S
		1	2	3	4	5
6	7	8	9	10	11	12
13	14	15	16	17	18	19
20	21	22	23	24	25	26
27	28	29	30			

JULY
S	M	T	W	T	F	S
				1	2	3
4	5	6	7	8	9	10
11	12	13	14	15	16	17
18	19	20	21	22	23	24
25	26	27	28	29	30	31

AUGUST
S	M	T	W	T	F	S
1	2	3	4	5	6	7
8	9	10	11	12	13	14
15	16	17	18	19	20	21
22	23	24	25	26	27	28
29	30	31				

SEPTEMBER
S	M	T	W	T	F	S
			1	2	3	4
5	6	7	8	9	10	11
12	13	14	15	16	17	18
19	20	21	22	23	24	25
26	27	28	29	30		

OCTOBER
S	M	T	W	T	F	S
					1	2
3	4	5	6	7	8	9
10	11	12	13	14	15	16
17	18	19	20	21	22	23
24	25	26	27	28	29	30
31						

NOVEMBER
S	M	T	W	T	F	S
	1	2	3	4	5	6
7	8	9	10	11	12	13
14	15	16	17	18	19	20
21	22	23	24	25	26	27
28	29	30				

DECEMBER
S	M	T	W	T	F	S
			1	2	3	4
5	6	7	8	9	10	11
12	13	14	15	16	17	18
19	20	21	22	23	24	25
26	27	28	29	30	31	

13

JANUARY
S	M	T	W	T	F	S
					1	2
3	4	5	6	7	8	9
10	11	12	13	14	15	16
17	18	19	20	21	22	23
24	25	26	27	28	29	30
31						

FEBRUARY
S	M	T	W	T	F	S
	1	2	3	4	5	6
7	8	9	10	11	12	13
14	15	16	17	18	19	20
21	22	23	24	25	26	27
28	29					

MARCH
S	M	T	W	T	F	S
		1	2	3	4	5
6	7	8	9	10	11	12
13	14	15	16	17	18	19
20	21	22	23	24	25	26
27	28	29	30	31		

APRIL
S	M	T	W	T	F	S
					1	2
3	4	5	6	7	8	9
10	11	12	13	14	15	16
17	18	19	20	21	22	23
24	25	26	27	28	29	30

MAY
S	M	T	W	T	F	S
1	2	3	4	5	6	7
8	9	10	11	12	13	14
15	16	17	18	19	20	21
22	23	24	25	26	27	28
29	30	31				

JUNE
S	M	T	W	T	F	S
			1	2	3	4
5	6	7	8	9	10	11
12	13	14	15	16	17	18
19	20	21	22	23	24	25
26	27	28	29	30		

JULY
S	M	T	W	T	F	S
					1	2
3	4	5	6	7	8	9
10	11	12	13	14	15	16
17	18	19	20	21	22	23
24	25	26	27	28	29	30
31						

AUGUST
S	M	T	W	T	F	S
	1	2	3	4	5	6
7	8	9	10	11	12	13
14	15	16	17	18	19	20
21	22	23	24	25	26	27
28	29	30	31			

SEPTEMBER
S	M	T	W	T	F	S
				1	2	3
4	5	6	7	8	9	10
11	12	13	14	15	16	17
18	19	20	21	22	23	24
25	26	27	28	29	30	

OCTOBER
S	M	T	W	T	F	S
						1
2	3	4	5	6	7	8
9	10	11	12	13	14	15
16	17	18	19	20	21	22
23	24	25	26	27	28	29
30	31					

NOVEMBER
S	M	T	W	T	F	S
		1	2	3	4	5
6	7	8	9	10	11	12
13	14	15	16	17	18	19
20	21	22	23	24	25	26
27	28	29	30			

DECEMBER
S	M	T	W	T	F	S
				1	2	3
4	5	6	7	8	9	10
11	12	13	14	15	16	17
18	19	20	21	22	23	24
25	26	27	28	29	30	31

14

JANUARY
S	M	T	W	T	F	S
						1
2	3	4	5	6	7	8
9	10	11	12	13	14	15
16	17	18	19	20	21	22
23	24	25	26	27	28	29
30	31					

FEBRUARY
S	M	T	W	T	F	S
		1	2	3	4	5
6	7	8	9	10	11	12
13	14	15	16	17	18	19
20	21	22	23	24	25	26
27	28	29				

MARCH
S	M	T	W	T	F	S
			1	2	3	4
5	6	7	8	9	10	11
12	13	14	15	16	17	18
19	20	21	22	23	24	25
26	27	28	29	30	31	

APRIL
S	M	T	W	T	F	S
						1
2	3	4	5	6	7	8
9	10	11	12	13	14	15
16	17	18	19	20	21	22
23	24	25	26	27	28	29
30						

MAY
S	M	T	W	T	F	S
	1	2	3	4	5	6
7	8	9	10	11	12	13
14	15	16	17	18	19	20
21	22	23	24	25	26	27
28	29	30	31			

JUNE
S	M	T	W	T	F	S
				1	2	3
4	5	6	7	8	9	10
11	12	13	14	15	16	17
18	19	20	21	22	23	24
25	26	27	28	29	30	

JULY
S	M	T	W	T	F	S
						1
2	3	4	5	6	7	8
9	10	11	12	13	14	15
16	17	18	19	20	21	22
23	24	25	26	27	28	29
30	31					

AUGUST
S	M	T	W	T	F	S
		1	2	3	4	5
6	7	8	9	10	11	12
13	14	15	16	17	18	19
20	21	22	23	24	25	26
27	28	29	30	31		

SEPTEMBER
S	M	T	W	T	F	S
					1	2
3	4	5	6	7	8	9
10	11	12	13	14	15	16
17	18	19	20	21	22	23
24	25	26	27	28	29	30

OCTOBER
S	M	T	W	T	F	S
1	2	3	4	5	6	7
8	9	10	11	12	13	14
15	16	17	18	19	20	21
22	23	24	25	26	27	28
29	30	31				

NOVEMBER
S	M	T	W	T	F	S
			1	2	3	4
5	6	7	8	9	10	11
12	13	14	15	16	17	18
19	20	21	22	23	24	25
26	27	28	29	30		

DECEMBER
S	M	T	W	T	F	S
					1	2
3	4	5	6	7	8	9
10	11	12	13	14	15	16
17	18	19	20	21	22	23
24	25	26	27	28	29	30
31						

Important Dates in the United States and Canada

Fixed Dates

These events are celebrated on the same date every year, regardless of where the date falls in the week.

Event	Date
New Year's Day[1]	January 1
Groundhog Day	February 2
Abraham Lincoln's Birthday	February 12
Valentine's Day	February 14
Susan B. Anthony Day	February 15
George Washington's Birthday	February 22
St. Patrick's Day	March 17
April Fool's Day	April 1
Earth Day	April 22
National Maritime Day	May 22
Flag Day	June 14
Canada Day[2]	July 1
Independence Day[1]	July 4
Citizenship Day	September 17
United Nations Day	October 24
Halloween	October 31
Veterans Day[1,3]	November 11
Remembrance Day[2]	November 11
Christmas	December 25
Boxing Day[2]	December 26
New Year's Eve	December 31

Changing Dates

These events are celebrated on different dates every year, but are always on a certain day of a certain week of a certain month.

Event	Day
Martin Luther King Jr. Day[1]	third Monday in January
Presidents' Day[1]	third Monday in February
Daylight saving time begins	second Sunday in March
Arbor Day	last Friday in April
National Teacher Day	Tuesday of the first full week in May
Mother's Day	second Sunday in May
Armed Forces Day	third Saturday in May
Victoria Day[2]	Monday on or before May 24
Memorial Day[1]	last Monday in May
Father's Day	third Sunday in June
Labor Day[1,2]	first Monday in September
Columbus Day[1]	second Monday in October
Thanksgiving Day (Canada)[2]	second Monday in October
Daylight saving time ends	first Sunday in November
Thanksgiving Day (U.S.)[1]	fourth Thursday in November

Why do we celebrate . . .

New Year's Day
The first record of a new year festival is from about 2,000 BC in Mesopotamia. The festival took place not in January but in mid-March, with the new moon after the spring equinox.

Martin Luther King Jr. Day
This holiday honors the birthday of the slain civil rights leader who preached nonviolence and led the March on Washington in 1963. Dr. King's most famous speech is entitled "I Have a Dream."

Groundhog Day
According to legend, if a groundhog in Punxsutawney, Pennsylvania, peeks his head out of his burrow and sees his shadow, he'll return to his hole and there will be six more weeks of winter.

Lincoln's Birthday
This holiday honors the 16th president of the United States, who led the nation through the Civil War (1861–1865) and was then assassinated. It was first formally observed in Washington, DC, in 1866, when both houses of congress gathered to pay tribute to the slain president.

Valentine's Day
This holiday of love originated as a festival for several martyrs from the third century, all named St. Valentine. The holiday's association with romance may have come from an ancient belief that birds mate on this day.

Presidents' Day
This official government holiday was created in observance of both Washington's and Lincoln's birthdays.

Washington's Birthday
This holiday honors the first president of the United States, known as the Father of Our Country. It was first officially observed in America in 1879.

St. Patrick's Day
This holiday honors the patron saint of Ireland. Most often celebrated in the United States with parties and special dinners, the most famous event is the annual St. Patrick's Day parade on Fifth Avenue in New York City.

Mother's Day
First proposed by Anna Jarvis of Philadelphia in 1907, this holiday has become a national time for family gatherings and showing appreciation for mothers.

Memorial Day
Also known as Decoration Day, this legal holiday was created in 1868 by order of General John A. Logan as a day on which the graves of Civil War soldiers would be decorated. Since that time, the day has been set aside to honor all American soldiers who have given their lives for their country.

Flag Day
This holiday was set aside to commemorate the adoption of the Stars and Stripes by the Continental Congress on June 14, 1777. It is a legal holiday only in Pennsylvania but is generally acknowledged and observed in many states each year.

Father's Day
This holiday honors the role of the father in the American family, as Mother's Day honors the role of the mother.

Independence Day
This holiday celebrates the signing of the Declaration of Independence, July 4, 1776. It has been celebrated nationwide since 1777, the first anniversary of the signing.

Labor Day
First proposed by Peter J. McGuire in New York in 1882, this holiday was created to honor the labor unions and workers who built the nation.

Columbus Day
This holiday commemorates the discovery of the New World by Italian explorer Christopher Columbus in 1492. Even though the land was already populated by Native Americans when Columbus arrived, this discovery marks the beginning of European influence in America.

United Nations Day
This holiday marks the founding of the United Nations, which began in its present capacity in 1945 but had already been in operation as the League of Nations.

Halloween
Also known as All Hallows' Eve, this holiday has its origins in ancient Celtic rituals that marked the beginning of winter with bonfires, masquerades, and dressing in costume to frighten away spirits.

Election Day
Since it was declared an official holiday by Congress in 1845, presidential elections have been taking place on this day every four years. Most statewide elections are also held on this day, but election years vary according to state.

Veterans Day
Originally called Armistice Day, this holiday was created to celebrate the end of World War I in 1918. In June 1954, Congress changed the name of the holiday to Veterans Day and declared that the day would honor all men and women who have served in America's armed forces.

Thanksgiving
President Lincoln was the first president to proclaim Thanksgiving a national holiday, in 1863. Most people believe the tradition of reserving a day of thanks began with an order given by Governor Bradford of Plymouth Colony in New England in 1621.

Major World Holidays

January 1 New Year's Day throughout the Western world and in India, Indonesia, Japan, Korea, the Philippines, Singapore, Taiwan, and Thailand; founding of Republic of China (Taiwan)

January 2 Berchtoldstag in Switzerland

January 3 Genshi-Sai (First Beginning) in Japan

January 5 Twelfth Night (Wassail Eve or Eve of Epiphany) in England

January 6 Epiphany, observed by Catholics throughout Europe and Latin America

Mid-January Martin Luther King Jr.'s Birthday on the third Monday in the Virgin Islands

January 15 Adults' Day in Japan

January 20 St. Agnes Eve in Great Britain

JAN 20

January 24 Australia Day in Australia

January 26 Republic Day in India

January–February Chinese New Year and Vietnamese New Year (Tet)

February 3 Setsubun (Bean-throwing Festival) in Japan

February 5 Promulgation of the Constitution Day in Mexico

February 11 National Foundation Day in Japan

February 27 Independence Day in the Dominican Republic

March 1 Independence Movement Day in Korea

March 8 International Women's Day in China, Russia, Great Britain, and the United States

March 17 St. Patrick's Day in Ireland and Northern Ireland

March 19 St. Joseph's Day in Colombia, Costa Rica, Italy, and Spain

March 21 Benito Juarez's Birthday in Mexico

March 22 Arab League Day in Arab League countries

March 23 Pakistan Day in Pakistan

March 25 Independence Day in Greece; Lady Day (Quarter Day) in Great Britain

March 26 Fiesta del Arbol (Arbor Day) in Spain

March 29 Youth and Martyr's Day in Taiwan

March 30 Muslim New Year in Indonesia

March-April Carnival/Lent/Easter: The pre-Lenten celebration of Carnival (Mardi Gras) and the post-Lenten celebration of Easter are movable feasts widely observed in Christian countries

April 1 April Fools' Day (All Fools' Day) in Great Britain and the United States

April 5 Arbor Day in Korea

April 7 World Health Day in UN member nations

April 8 Buddha's Birthday in Korea and Japan; Hana Matsuri (Flower Festival) in Japan

April 14 Pan American Day in the Americas

April 19 Declaration of Independence Day in Venezuela

April 22 Queen Isabella Day in Spain

April 23 St. George's Day in England

April 25 Liberation Day in Italy; ANZAC Day in Australia and New Zealand

April 30 Queen's Birthday in the Netherlands; Walpurgis Night in Germany and Scandinavia

May 3 Constitution Day in Japan

May 1 May Day (Labor Day) in Russia and most of Europe and Latin America

May 5 Children's Day in Japan and Korea; Cinco de Mayo in Mexico; Liberation Day in the Netherlands

May 8 V-E Day in Europe

May 9 Victory over Fascism Day in Russia

MAY 9

Late May Victoria Day on Monday before May 25 in Canada

June 2 Founding of the Republic Day in Italy

June 5 Constitution Day in Denmark

June 6 Memorial Day in Korea; Flag Day in Sweden

June 10 Portugal Day in Portugal

June 12 Independence Day in the Philippines

Mid-June Queen's Official Birthday on second Saturday in Great Britain

June 16 Soweto Day in UN member nations

JUNE 20

June 20 Flag Day in Argentina

June 24 Midsummer's Day in Great Britain

June 29 Feasts of Saints Peter and Paul in Chile, Colombia, Italy, Peru, Spain, and Venezuela

July 1 Canada Day in Canada; Half-year Holiday in Hong Kong; Bank Holiday in Taiwan

July 5 Independence Day in Venezuela

July 9 Independence Day in Argentina

July 12 Orangemen's Day in Northern Ireland

July 14 Bastille Day in France

Mid-July Feria de San Fermin during second week in Spain

July 17 Constitution Day in Korea

July 20 Independence Day in Colombia

July 21 National Holiday in Belgium

July 22 National Liberation Day in Poland

July 24 Simon Bolivar's Birthday in Ecuador and Venezuela

July 25 St. James Day in Spain

July 28 Independence Day in Peru

August Holiday on first Monday in Grenada, Guyana, and Ireland

August 1 Lammas Day in England; National Day in Switzerland

August 6 Independence Day in Jamaica

August 9 National Day in Singapore

August 10 Independence Day in Ecuador

August 12 Queen's Birthday in Thailand

August 14 Independence Day in Pakistan

August 15 Independence Day in India and Korea; Assumption Day in Catholic countries

August 16 National Restoration Day in the Dominican Republic

August 17 Independence Day in Indonesia

August 31 Independence Day in Trinidad and Tobago

September Respect for the Aged Day in Japan on third Monday

September 7 Independence Day in Brazil

September 9 Choxo-no-Sekku (Chrysanthemum Day) in Japan

September 14 Battle of San Jacinto Day in Nicaragua

Mid-September Sherry Wine Harvest in Spain

September 15 Independence Day in Costa Rica, Guatemala, and Nicaragua

September 16 Independence Day in Mexico and Papua New Guinea

September 18–19 Independence Day in Chile; St. Gennaro Day in Italy

September 28 Confucius's Birthday in Taiwan

October 1 National Day in People's Republic of China; Armed Forces Day in Korea; National Holiday in Nigeria

October 2 Mahatma Gandhi's Birthday in India

October 3 National Foundation Day in Korea; Day of German Unity in Germany

October 5 Proclamation of the Portuguese Republic Day in Portugal

October 9 Korean Alphabet Day in Korea

October 10 Kruger Day in South Africa; Founding Day of the Republic of China in Taiwan

October 12 Columbus Day in Spain and widely throughout Mexico, and Central and South America

October 20 Revolution Day in Guatemala; Kenyatta Day in Kenya

October 24 United Nations Day in UN member nations

October 26 National Holiday in Austria

October 28 Greek National Day in Greece

November 1 All Saints' Day, observed by Catholics in most countries

November 2 All Souls' Day in Ecuador, El Salvador, Luxembourg, Macao, Mexico (Day of the Dead), San Marino, Uruguay, and Vatican City

NOV 5

November 4 National Unity Day in Italy

November 5 Guy Fawkes Day in Great Britain

November 7–8 October Revolution Day in Russia

November 11 Armistice Day in Belgium, France, French Guiana, and Tahiti; Remembrance Day in Canada

November 12 Sun Yat-sen's Birthday in Taiwan

November 15 Proclamation of the Republic Day in Brazil

November 17 Day of Penance in Federal Republic of Germany

November 19 National Holiday in Monaco

November 20 Anniversary of the Revolution in Mexico

November 23 Kinro-Kansha-no-Hi (Labor Thanksgiving Day) in Japan

DEC 5

November 30 Bonifacio Day in the Philippines

December 5 Discovery by Columbus Day in Haiti; Constitution Day in Russia

December 6 Independence Day in Finland

December 8 Feast of the Immaculate Conception, widely observed in Catholic countries

December 10 Constitution Day in Thailand; Human Rights Day in UN member nations

December 12 Jamhuri Day in Kenya; Guadalupe Day in Mexico

Mid-December Nine Days of Posada during third week in Mexico

December 25 Christmas Day, widely observed in all Christian countries

December 26 St. Stephen's Day in Christian countries; Boxing Day in Canada, Australia, and Great Britain

December 26–January 1 Kwanzaa in the United States

December 31 New Year's Eve throughout the world; Omisoka (Grand Last Day) in Japan; Hogmanay Day in Scotland

WHAT'S YOUR SIGN?

The original zodiac signs are thought to have originated in Mesopotamia as far back as 2000 B.C. The Greeks later picked up some of the symbols from the Babylonians and then passed them on to other ancient cultures. Some other societies that developed their own zodiac charts based on these early ideas include the Egyptians, the Chinese, and the Aztecs.

The positions of the Sun, Moon, and planets in the zodiac on the day you are born determine your astrological sign. **What's yours?**

March 21–April 19

Planet: Mars
Element: Fire
Personality Traits: Independent, enthusiastic, bold, impulsive, confident

April 20–May 20

Planet: Venus
Element: Earth
Personality Traits: Decisive, determined, stubborn, stable

May 21–June 21

Planet: Mercury
Element: Air
Personality Traits: Curious, sociable, ambitious, alert, intelligent, temperamental

June 22–July 22

Planet (Celestial Object): Moon
Element: Water
Personality Traits: Organized, busy, moody, sensitive, supportive

Leo, the Lion

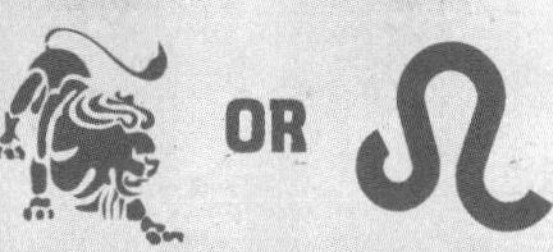

July 23–August 22

Planet (Celestial Object): Sun
Element: Water
Personality Traits: Born leader, bold, noble, generous, enthusiastic, sympathetic

Virgo, the Virgin

August 23–September 22

Planet: Mercury
Element: Earth
Personality Traits: Analytical, critical, intellectual, clever

Libra, the Scales

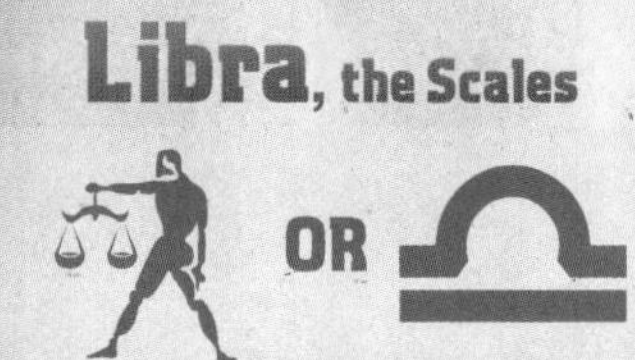

September 23–October 23

Planet: Venus
Element: Water
Personality Traits: Affectionate, thoughtful, sympathetic, orderly, persuasive

Scorpio, the Scorpion

October 24–November 21

Planet: Mars
Element: Water
Personality Traits: Intense, fearless, loyal, willful

Sagittarius, the Archer

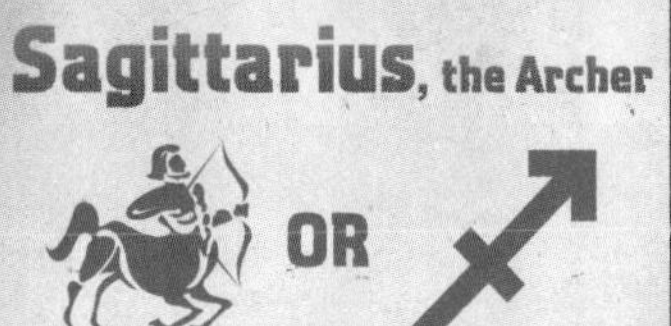

November 22–December 21

Planet: Jupiter
Element: Fire
Personality Traits: Energetic, good-natured, practical, clever

Capricorn, the Goat

OR

December 22–January 19

Planet: Saturn
Element: Earth
Personality Traits: Serious, domineering, ambitious, blunt, loyal, persistent

Aquarius, the Water Bearer

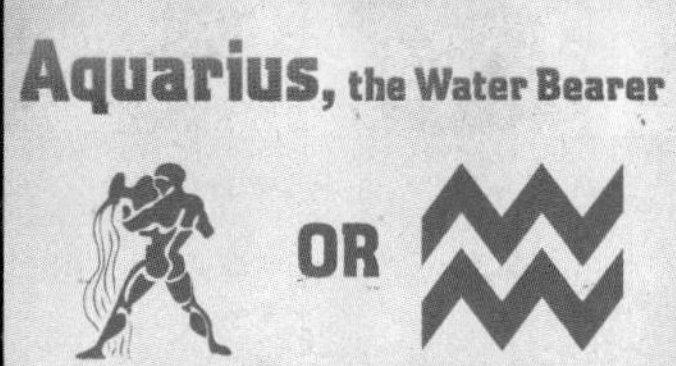

January 20–February 18

Planet: Uranus
Element: Air
Personality Traits: Independent, unselfish, generous, idealistic

Pisces, the Fishes

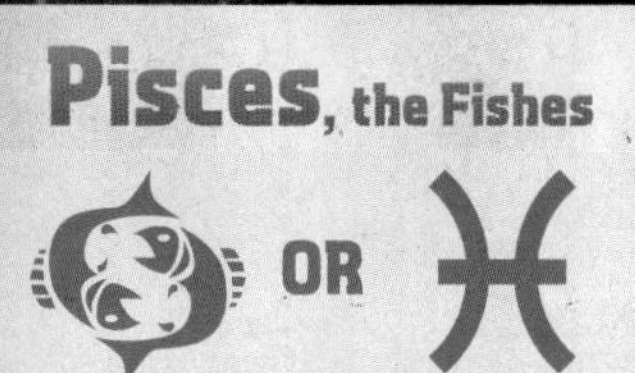

February 19–March 20

Planet: Neptune
Element: Water
Personality Traits: Compassionate, sympathetic, sensitive, timid, methodical

Environment

A Place to Call Home

From deserts to oceans, our planet offers a wide variety of environments. Environments are made up of living and nonliving things. Water, sunlight, soil, and climate are the nonliving elements of an environment. Plants and animals (including humans) are the living part.

Power Trip

All living things need energy to survive, but energy is not all the same. The energy that comes from the Sun, wind, and ocean tides is renewable. There is an unlimited supply in nature. However, some energy sources, such as petroleum, coal, and other fossil fuels, are nonrenewable. In time we could use every last one of them up.

Don't Be a (Carbon) Bigfoot

Using fossil fuels such as gasoline to power our cars, and burning oil and coal to heat our homes, releases harmful gases into the atmosphere. These gases, known as greenhouse gases, include methane and carbon dioxide, and can increase the temperature and change the weather on Earth. The amount of carbon dioxide humans create through activities and energy choices is called their carbon footprint.

The Three Rs

Three key things we can do to protect our planet are: reduce, reuse, and recycle. Reduce trash production by buying only what you need. Be creative and see how many new uses you can find for things you ordinarily toss out after one use. Recycle plastic, glass, and paper.

TAKE a LOOK

Trash Talk

Reducing the amount of trash we produce every day can have a significant impact in protecting our environment. The average person creates about 3 pounds (1.4 kg) of trash every day. That adds up to over 1,130 pounds (512.6 kg) every year. Recycling makes a huge difference. Each ton of recycled paper can save 17 trees, 380 gallons (1,440 L) of oil, 3 cubic yards (2.3 cu m) of landfill space, 4,000 kilowatts of energy, and 7,000 gallons (26,500 L) of water! (See page 42 for examples of what's in the average landfill.)

EARTH DAY

In the 1970s, Americans were fighting against pollution—oil spills, raw sewage, and pesticides. On April 22, 1970, about 20 million Americans celebrated the first Earth Day to raise environmental awareness. That same year, the Environmental Protection Agency was created to enforce environmental standards. Every year millions of people in the United States still celebrate environmental awareness on Earth Day.

What's Filling Up U.S. Landfills?

(in millions of tons)

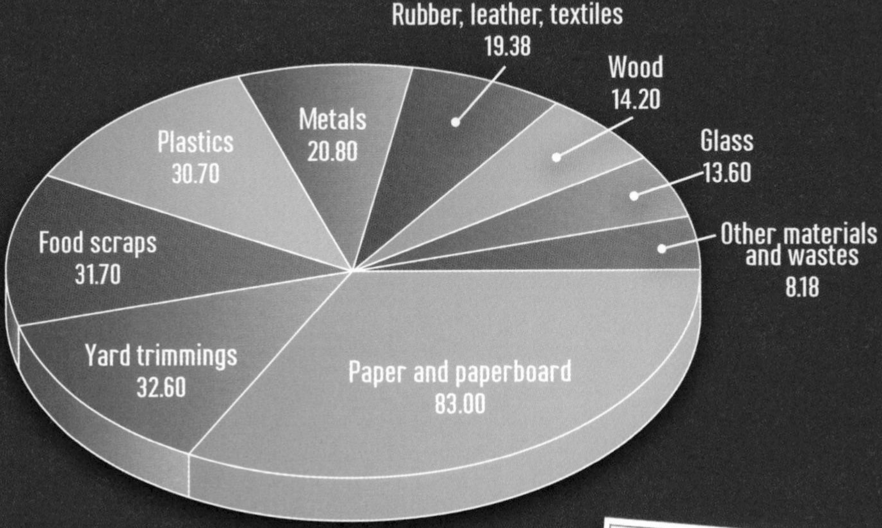

Material	Millions of tons
Rubber, leather, textiles	19.38
Wood	14.20
Glass	13.60
Other materials and wastes	8.18
Paper and paperboard	83.00
Yard trimmings	32.60
Food scraps	31.70
Plastics	30.70
Metals	20.80

Total amount of trash = 254.1 million tons

How Much Is Recycled?

Material	Percent recycled yearly
Yard trimmings	64.1
Paper and paperboard	54.5
Metals	34.8
Rubber, leather, textiles	30.6
Glass	23.7
Wood	9.3
Plastics	6.8
Food scraps	2.6
Other	26.2

Top 5 Paper Recycling Countries

For every 1,000 people in the United States, about 160 tons of paper are recycled every year. That's a lot, but other countries recycle even more.

Country	Amount recycled (per 1,000 people)
Sweden	186 tons
Austria	182 tons
Switzerland	179 tons
Germany	176 tons
The Netherlands	162 tons

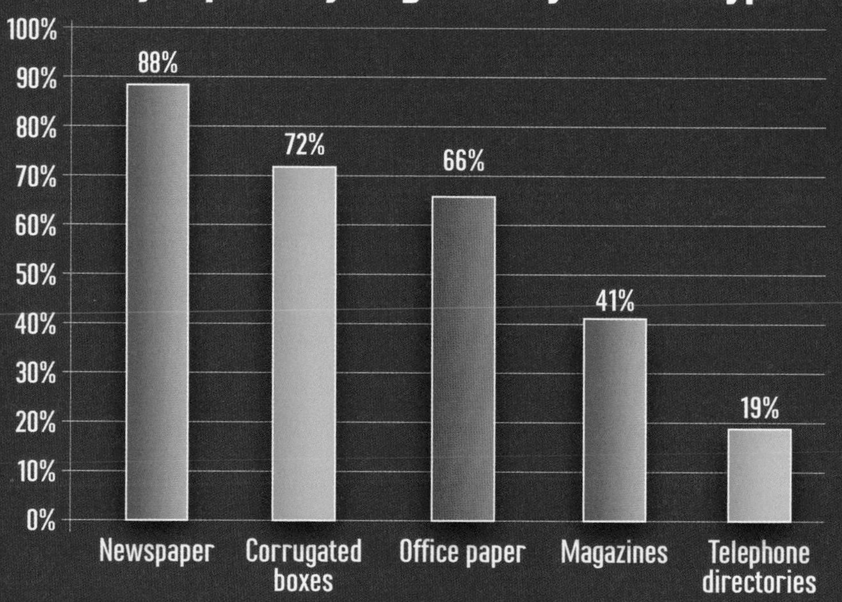

CHECK IT OUT!

More than 5,000 different products can be made from recycled paper, including lampshades, money, and bandages.

Rising Carbon Dioxide Levels

The amount of the main greenhouse gas, carbon dioxide (CO_2), in the atmosphere has been steadily rising for more than a century. Experts say the increase comes mostly from the burning of fossil fuels for energy.

Carbon Dioxide in the Atmosphere, 1903–2007

Year	CO_2 (parts per million)
1903	295
1915	301
1927	306
1943	308
1960	317
1970	326
1980	339
1990	354
2000	367
2004	375
2005	377
2006	379
2007	381

Average Global Temperatures, 1900–2007

The earth has been heating up for more than a century. Most experts have concluded that the CO_2 increase has been at least partly responsible for the increase in global surface temperature.

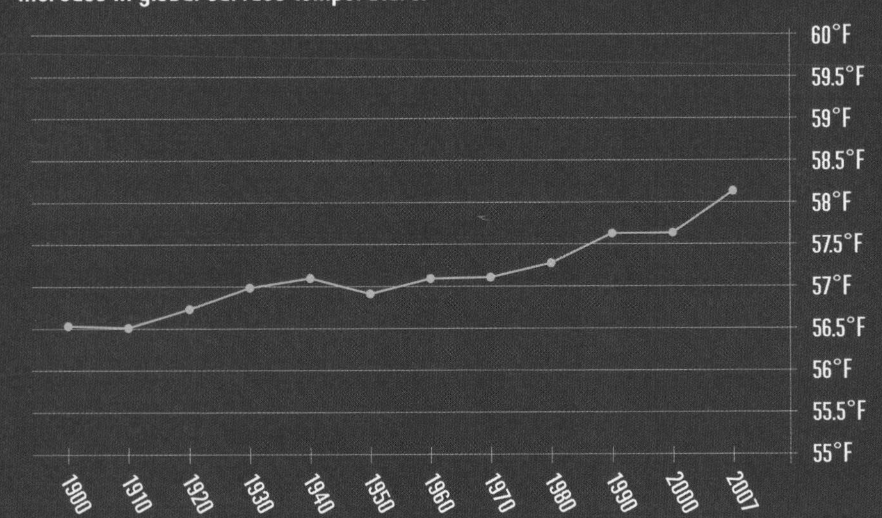

Environment

10 Worst Carbon Dioxide–Producing Countries

Country	Millions of metric tons produced annually
China	6,017.69
United States	5,902.75
Russia	1,704.35
India	1,293.17
Japan	1,246.76
Germany	857.60
Canada	614.33
United Kingdom	585.71
South Korea	514.53
Iran	471.48

10 U.S. Urban Areas with the Worst Ozone Levels

There are six common air pollutants: ground-level ozone, carbon monoxide, sulfur and nitrogen oxides, lead, and particulate matter such as soot and smoke. Find out more at www.epa.gov. These ten urban areas have the highest ozone levels in the United States.

Rank	City
1	Los Angeles—Long Beach—Riverside, CA
2	Bakersfield, CA
3	Visalia—Porterville, CA
4	Houston—Baytown—Huntsville, TX
5	Fresno—Madera, CA
6	Sacramento—Arden-Arcade—Yuba City, CA
7	Dallas—Fort Worth, TX
8	New York—Newark—Bridgeport, NY—NJ—CT
9	Washington—Baltimore—Northern Virginia, DC—MD—VA
10	Baton Rouge—Pierre Part, LA

What's the quality of the air where you live? Find out at

www.airnow.gov

Countries of the World

There are 195 independent countries in the world. Each one has its own traditions, history, culture, foods, and more. Each country has different challenges, too, like weather and natural disasters. But in two ways every country is the same as every other one. Its citizens are all part of the same human race. And every country has its own, unique national flag.

Some flags show a country's religious beliefs with symbols:

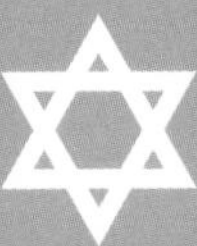

An ancient symbol of the Jewish people called the Star of David appears on the flag of Israel.

Flying Colors

Strictly speaking, a country's flag is a piece of cloth. But it's so much more than that. Every color, pattern, shape, and image on a flag stands for something about the country—its land, history, geography, people, government, or beliefs. The flag is a country's most important source of pride, and countries demand that their flags be respected. Most countries have strict rules about how to treat their flag, such as never allowing it to touch the ground or be made into clothing.

Most national flags use these colors: red, white, blue, green, yellow, black, and orange. The South African flag uses six colors, the most of any nation. The Libyan flag uses the fewest. Its flag is solid green, the traditional color of Islam.

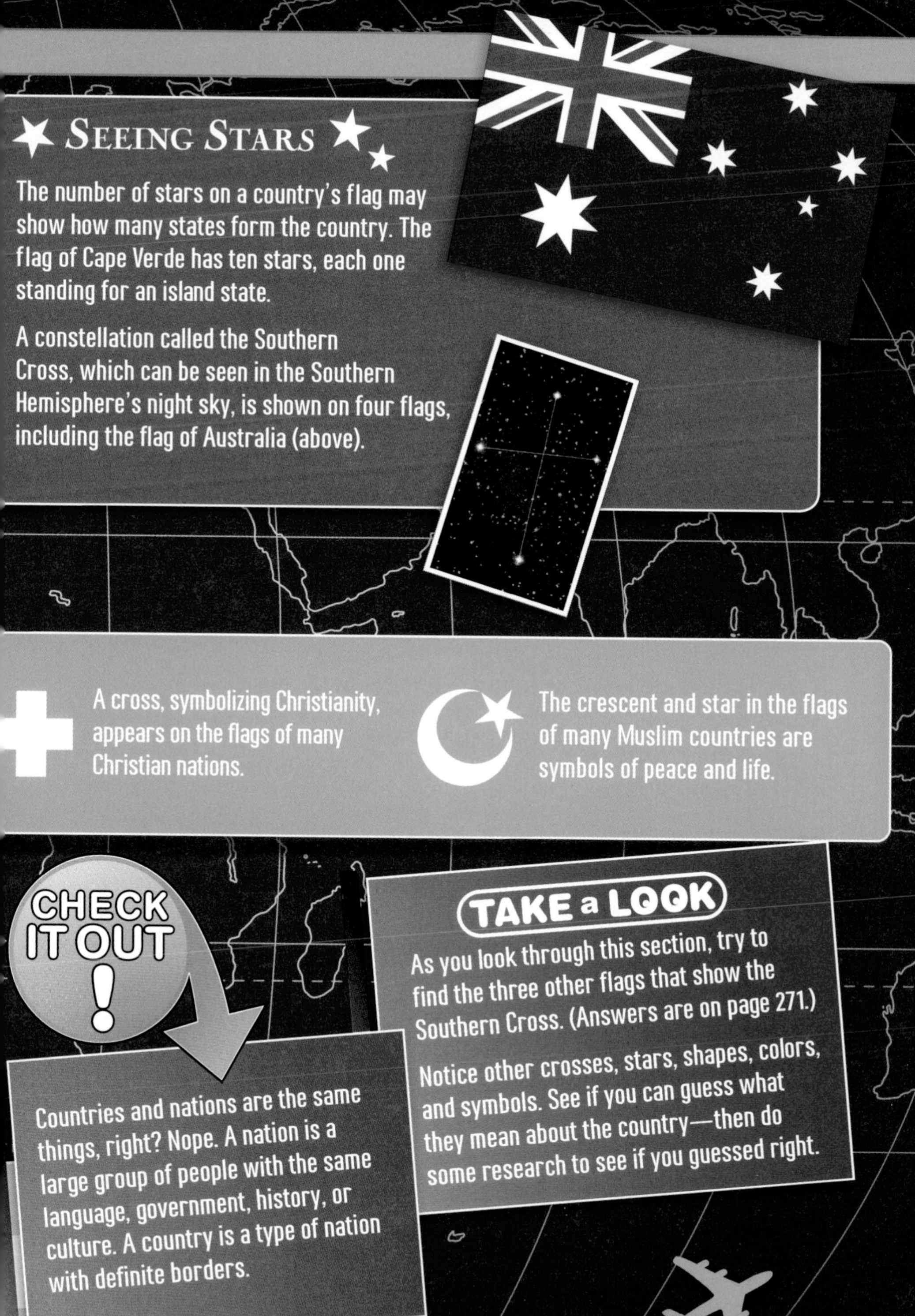

★ Seeing Stars ★

The number of stars on a country's flag may show how many states form the country. The flag of Cape Verde has ten stars, each one standing for an island state.

A constellation called the Southern Cross, which can be seen in the Southern Hemisphere's night sky, is shown on four flags, including the flag of Australia (above).

A cross, symbolizing Christianity, appears on the flags of many Christian nations.

The crescent and star in the flags of many Muslim countries are symbols of peace and life.

CHECK IT OUT!

Countries and nations are the same things, right? Nope. A nation is a large group of people with the same language, government, history, or culture. A country is a type of nation with definite borders.

TAKE a LOOK

As you look through this section, try to find the three other flags that show the Southern Cross. (Answers are on page 271.)

Notice other crosses, stars, shapes, colors, and symbols. See if you can guess what they mean about the country—then do some research to see if you guessed right.

Countries of the World

ARCTIC OCEAN
ARCTIC OCEAN
RUSSIA
FINLAND
ESTONIA
LATVIA
LITHUANIA
BELARUS
UKRAINE
MOLDOVA
ROMANIA
BULGARIA
GREECE
TURKEY
GEORGIA
ARMENIA
AZERBAIJAN
KAZAKHSTAN
UZBEKISTAN
TURKMENISTAN
KYRGYZSTAN
TAJIKISTAN
MONGOLIA
CHINA
NORTH KOREA
SOUTH KOREA
JAPAN
PACIFIC OCEAN
CYPRUS
SYRIA
LEBANON
ISRAEL
JORDAN
IRAQ
IRAN
AFGHANISTAN
PAKISTAN
KUWAIT
BAHRAIN
QATAR
U.A.E.
OMAN
SAUDI ARABIA
EGYPT
NEPAL
BHUTAN
INDIA
BANGLADESH
MYANMAR
LAOS
THAILAND
VIETNAM
CAMBODIA
Tropic of Cancer
NORTHERN MARIANA ISLANDS (U.S.)
PHILIPPINES
SUDAN
ERITREA
YEMEN
DJIBOUTI
SOMALIA
ETHIOPIA
SRI LANKA
MALDIVES
BRUNEI
MALAYSIA
PALAU
FEDERATED STATES OF MICRONESIA
MARSHALL ISLANDS
DEMOCRATIC REPUBLIC OF THE CONGO
UGANDA
KENYA
RWANDA
BURUNDI
TANZANIA
Equator
INDONESIA
PAPUA NEW GUINEA
TIMOR-LESTE
SOLOMON ISLANDS
KIRIBATI
TUVALU
COMOROS
MALAWI
ZAMBIA
ZIMBABWE
MOZAMBIQUE
MADAGASCAR
BOTSWANA
INDIAN OCEAN
Tropic of Capricorn
SAMOA
VANUATU
FIJI
NEW CALEDONIA (France)
TONGA
AUSTRALIA
SWAZILAND
SOUTH AFRICA
LESOTHO
NEW ZEALAND
N
W
E
S
30°E
45°E
60°E
75°E
90°E
105°E
120°E
135°E
150°E
165°E
180°
ANTARCTICA

AFGHANISTAN

Capital: Kabul
Population: 32,738,376
Area: 250,001 sq. mi. (647,500 sq km)
Language: Dari (Afghan Persian), Pashto
Money: Afghani
Government: Islamic republic

CHECK IT OUT

Kite running is a popular sport in Afghanistan. Kids fly kites, cut them loose, and then race to recover them.

ALBANIA

Capital: Tirana
Population: 3,619,778
Area: 11,100 sq. mi. (28,748 sq km)
Language: Albanian, Greek
Money: Lek
Government: Republic

CHECK IT OUT

The Adriatic and Ionian Seas border the western coast of Albania.

ALGERIA

Capital: Algiers
Population: 33,769,669
Area: 919,595 sq. mi. (2,381,740 sq km)
Language: Arabic, Berber, French
Money: Dinar
Government: Republic

CHECK IT OUT

Algeria is the second-largest country in Africa.

ANDORRA

Capital: Andorra la Vella
Population: 82,627
Area: 180 sq. mi. (468 sq km)
Language: Catalan, French, Castillan, Portuguese
Money: Euro
Government: Parliamentary democracy

CHECK IT OUT

Andorra is about half the size of New York City. For 700 years, until 1993, this little country had two rulers: France and Spain.

ANGOLA

Capital: Luanda
Population: 12,531,357
Area: 481,400 sq. mi. (1,246,700 sq km)
Language: Portuguese, Bantu, others
Money: Kwanza
Government: Republic

CHECK IT OUT

Eighty-five percent of the country's revenue (GDP) comes from oil production.

ANTIGUA AND BARBUDA

Capital: St. John's
Population: 84,522
Area: 171 sq. mi. (443 sq km)
Language: English
Money: Dollar
Government: Parliamentary democracy; independent sovereign state within the Commonwealth

CHECK IT OUT

Thousands of frigate birds live in a sanctuary on Barbuda. A frigate bird's wingspan can reach nearly eight feet (2.4 m).

ARGENTINA

Capital: Buenos Aires
Population: 40,481,998
Area: 1,068,302 sq. mi. (2,766,890 sq km)
Language: Spanish, Italian, English, German, French
Money: Peso
Government: Republic

CHECK IT OUT

The Andes mountains run along the western edge of Argentina, on the border with Chile.

ARMENIA

Capital: Yerevan
Population: 2,968,586
Area: 11,484 sq. mi. (29,743 sq km)
Language: Armenian, Yezidi, Russian
Money: Dram
Government: Republic

CHECK IT OUT

Armenia was the first nation to formally adopt Christianity (in the early fourth century).

AUSTRALIA

Capital: Canberra
Population: 21,007,310
Area: 2,967,909 sq. mi. (7,686,850 sq km)
Language: English, Chinese, Italian, aboriginal languages
Money: Dollar
Government: Constitutional monarchy; democratic, federal-state system recognizing British monarchy as sovereign

CHECK IT OUT

The Great Barrier Reef, off the coast of Australia, is larger than the Great Wall of China.

AUSTRIA

Capital: Vienna
Population: 8,205,533
Area: 32,382 sq. mi. (83,870 sq km)
Language: German
Money: Euro
Government: Federal parliamentary democracy

CHECK IT OUT

The Habsburg family ruled Austria for nearly 750 years, until the Treaty of St. Germain in 1919 established the Republic of Austria.

AZERBAIJAN

Capital: Baku
Population: 8,177,717
Area: 33,436 sq. mi. (83,600 sq km)
Language: Azerbaijani, Russian, Armenian, others
Money: Manat
Government: Republic

CHECK IT OUT

The country's name is thought to come from the ancient Persian phrase that means "Land of Fire."

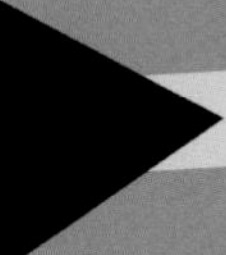

THE BAHAMAS

Capital: Nassau
Population: 307,451
Area: 5,382 sq. mi. (13,940 sq km)
Language: English, Creole
Money: Dollar
Government: Constitutional parliamentary democracy

CHECK IT OUT

More than eight out of ten Bahamians are of African heritage.

BAHRAIN

Capital: Manama
Population: 718,308
Area: 257 sq. mi. (665 sq km)
Language: Arabic, English, Farsi, Urdu
Money: Dinar
Government: Constitutional monarchy

CHECK IT OUT

The land area of Bahrain is only three and a half times the size of Washington, DC.

BANGLADESH

Capital: Dhaka
Population: 153,546,901
Area: 55,599 sq. mi. (144,000 sq km)
Language: Bengali, Chakma, Bagh
Money: Taka
Government: Parliamentary democracy

CHECK IT OUT

The Bengal tiger is the national animal of Bangladesh.

BARBADOS

Capital: Bridgetown
Population: 281,968
Area: 166 sq. mi. (431 sq km)
Language: English
Money: Dollar
Government: Parliamentary democracy

CHECK IT OUT

The British settled Barbados in 1627. When they arrived, there was no one living there.

BELARUS

Capital: Minsk
Population: 9,685,768
Area: 80,155 sq. mi. (207,600 sq km)
Language: Belarusian, Russian
Money: Ruble
Government: Republic

CHECK IT OUT

The name of this Eastern European country means "White Russia."

BELGIUM

Capital: Brussels
Population: 10,403,951
Area: 11,787 sq. mi. (30,528 sq km)
Language: Dutch, French, German
Money: Euro
Government: Parliamentary democracy under a constitutional monarchy

CHECK IT OUT

Many people call Belgium the chocolate capital of the world. Hundreds of thousands of tons of the sweet stuff are produced here yearly.

BELIZE

Capital: Belmopan
Population: 301,270
Area: 8,867 sq. mi. (22,966 sq km)
Language: English, Creole, Spanish, Mayan dialects
Money: Dollar
Government: Parliamentary democracy

CHECK IT OUT

The mahogany industry was central to Belize's economy hundreds of years ago. That's why a mahogany tree is pictured on the country's flag.

BENIN

Capital: Porto-Novo
Population: 8,532,547
Area: 43,483 sq. mi. (116,622 sq km)
Language: French, Fon, Yoruba in the south; Nagot, Bariba, Dendi in the north
Money: CFA franc
Government: Republic under multiparty democratic rule

CHECK IT OUT

Benin is only 215 miles across (about 325 km) at its widest point. It's eight times smaller than Nigeria, its neighbor.

BHUTAN

Capital: Thimphu
Population: 682,321
Area: 18,147 sq. mi. (47,000 sq km)
Language: Dzongkha, Nepali, Tibetan
Money: Ngultrum
Government: Constitutional monarchy

CHECK IT OUT

The Great Himalaya Range, the highest mountain system in the world, runs through northern Bhutan.

BOLIVIA

Capital: La Paz
Population: 9,247,816
Area: 424,164 sq. mi. (1,098,580 sq km)
Language: Spanish, Quecha, Aymara, Guarani
Money: Boliviano
Government: Republic

CHECK IT OUT

Bolivia is named after independence fighter Simón Bolívar.

BOSNIA AND HERZEGOVINA

Capital: Sarajevo
Population: 4,590,310
Area: 19,772 sq. mi. (51,209 sq km)
Language: Bosnian, Serbian, Croatian
Money: Convertible marka
Government: Federal democratic republic

CHECK IT OUT

Sarajevo, the country's capital, hosted the 1984 Winter Olympics.

BOTSWANA

Capital: Gaborone
Population: 1,842,323
Area: 3,286,488 sq. mi. (8,511,965 sq km)
Language: English, Setswana, Kalanga
Money: Pula
Government: Parliamentary republic

CHECK IT OUT

Botswana has one of the healthiest economies in Africa. About 70—80 percent of its export revenues come from diamond mining.

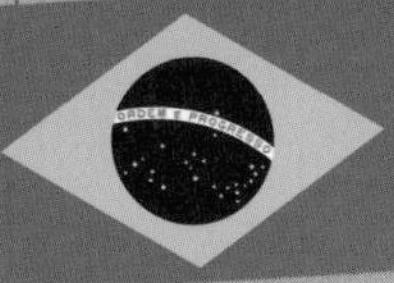

BRAZIL

Capital: Brasilia
Population: 196,342,587
Area: 3,286,488 sq. mi. (8,511,965 sq km)
Language: Portuguese
Money: Real
Government: Federative republic

CHECK IT OUT

Brazil has the largest population in Latin America and the fifth-largest in the world.

BRUNEI

Capital: Bandar Seri Begawan
Population: 381,371
Area: 2,228 sq. mi. (5,770 sq km)
Language: Malay, English, Chinese
Money: Dollar
Government: Constitutional sultanate

For more than six centuries, the same royal family has ruled Brunei.

BULGARIA

Capital: Sofia
Population: 7,262,675
Area: 42,823 sq. mi. (110,910 sq km)
Language: Bulgarian, Turkish, Roma
Money: Lev
Government: Parliamentary democracy

CHECK IT OUT

One of Bulgaria's sweetest exports is rose oil, which is used throughout the world to make perfume.

BURKINA FASO

Capital: Ouagadougou
Population: 15,264,735
Area: 105,869 sq. mi. (274,200 sq km)
Language: French
Money: CFA franc
Government: Republic

CHECK IT OUT

Burkina Faso has western Africa's largest elephant population.

BURMA

Capital: Yangon (Rangoon)
Population: 47,758,181
Area: 261,970 sq. mi. (678,500 sq km)
Language: Burmese, many ethnic languages
Money: Kyat
Government: Military junta

CHECK IT OUT

The military junta ruling the nation changed Burma's name to Myanmar in 1989, but several countries, including the United States, refused to acknowledge the change. Others recognize Myanmar as the official name.

BURUNDI

Capital: Bujumbura
Population: 8,691,005
Area: 10,745 sq. mi. (27,830 sq km)
Language: Kirundi, French, Swahili
Money: Franc
Government: Republic

CHECK IT OUT

Burundi is on the shoreline of Lake Tanganyika, the second-deepest lake in the world.

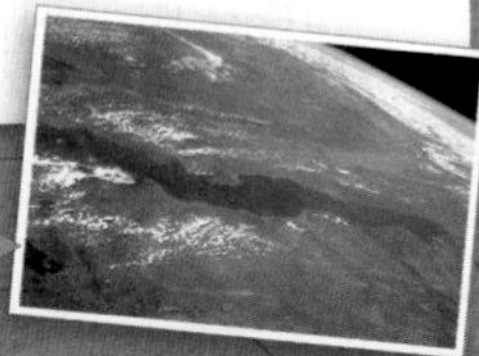

CAMBODIA

Capital: Phnom Penh
Population: 14,241,640
Area: 69,900 sq. mi. (181,040 sq km)
Language: Khmer, French, English
Money: Riel
Government: Multiparty democracy under a constitutional monarchy

CHECK IT OUT

The Mekong River system, which runs through Cambodia, is the home of the giant catfish. These fish can reach 10 feet (3 m) in length and weigh up to 650 pounds (295 kg).

CAMEROON

Capital: Yaoundé
Population: 18,467,692
Area: 183,568 sq. mi. (475,440 sq km)
Language: French, English, 24 major African language groups
Money: CFA franc
Government: Republic

CHECK IT OUT

Mount Cameroon, the highest mountain in Sub-Saharan West Africa, is an active volcano that last erupted in 2000.

CANADA

Capital: Ottawa
Population: 33,212,696
Area: 3,855,103 sq. mi. (9,093,507 sq km)
Language: English, French
Money: Dollar
Government: Confederation with parliamentary democracy and constitutional monarchy

CHECK IT OUT

In land area, Canada is the second-largest country in the world. In population, it ranks only 39.

CAPE VERDE

Capital: Praia
Population: 426,998
Area: 1,557 sq. mi. (4,033 sq km)
Language: Portuguese, Crioulo
Money: Escudo
Government: Republic

CHECK IT OUT

The group of islands that make up Cape Verde was uninhabited until the Portuguese discovered them in 1460.

CENTRAL AFRICAN REPUBLIC

Capital: Bangui
Population: 4,444,330
Area: 240,535 sq. mi. (622,984 sq km)
Language: Sangho, French, tribal languages
Money: CFA franc
Government: Republic

CHECK IT OUT

There are more than 80 ethnic groups in the Central African Republic. Each group speaks its own language.

CHAD

Capital: N'Djaména
Population: 10,111,337
Area: 495,755 sq. mi. (1,284,000 sq km)
Language: French, Arabic, more than 120 others
Money: CFA franc
Government: Republic

CHECK IT OUT

Chad is about three times the size of California.

CHILE

Capital: Santiago
Population: 16,454,143
Area: 292,260 sq. mi. (756,950 sq km)
Language: Spanish
Money: Peso
Government: Republic

CHECK IT OUT

The blue in Chile's flag stands for the sky and the white for the snow of the Andes mountains, on its eastern border.

CHINA

Capital: Beijing
Population: 1,330,044,605
Area: 3,705,407 million sq. mi. (9,596,960 sq km)
Language: Mandarin, Yue, Wu, Minhel, Minnan, Xiang, Gan, Hakka dialects, others
Money: Yuan
Government: Communist Party–led state

CHECK IT OUT

The name *China* comes from the Qin (or Ch'in) Dynasty, under which China was unified in 221 BC.

COLOMBIA

Capital: Bogotá
Population: 45,013,674
Area: 439,736 sq. mi. (1,138,910 sq km)
Language: Spanish
Money: Peso
Government: Republic

CHECK IT OUT

Historically Colombia has been the world's top producer of emeralds.

COMOROS

Capital: Moroni
Population: 731,775
Area: 838 sq. mi. (2,170 sq km)
Language: Arabic, French, Shikomoro
Money: Franc
Government: Republic

CHECK IT OUT

The three islands that make up Comoros are sometimes called the Perfume Islands. The country is the world's leading producer of essence of ylang-ylang, a flower oil used to make perfumes and soaps.

CONGO, Democratic Republic of the

Capital: Kinshasa
Population: 66,514,506
Area: 905,588 sq. mi. (2,345,410 sq km)
Language: French, Lingala, Swahili, Kikongo, Tshiluba
Money: CFA franc
Government: Republic

CHECK IT OUT

This country's enormous land area is equal to the United States east of the Mississippi River, or all of western Europe.

CONGO, Republic of the

Capital: Brazzaville
Population: 3,903,318
Area: 132,047 sq. mi. (342,000 sq km)
Language: French, Lingala, Monokutuba, Kikongo
Money: CFA franc
Government: Republic

CHECK IT OUT

Oil is the country's largest revenue-generating industry.

COSTA RICA

Capital: San José
Population: 4,195,914
Area: 19,730 sq. mi. (51,100 sq km)
Language: Spanish, English
Money: Colón
Government: Democratic republic

CHECK IT OUT

For a bird's-eye view of the rain forest, tourists in Costa Rica swing through the canopy on pulleys attached to treetops.

CÔTE d'IVOIRE (Ivory Coast)

Capital: Yamoussoukro
Population: 20,179,602
Area: 124,503 sq. mi. (322,460 sq km)
Language: French, Dioula, 59 other native dialects
Money: CFA franc
Government: Republic with multiparty presidential regime

Côte d'Ivoire is home to more than 60 ethnic groups.

CROATIA

Capital: Zagreb
Population: 4,491,543
Area: 21,831 sq. mi. (56,542 sq km)
Language: Croatian, Serbian
Money: Kuna
Government: Parliamentary democracy

CHECK IT OUT

Civil war ended in Croatia in 1998. Now tourists flock to its beautiful islands and national parks.

CUBA

Capital: Havana
Population: 11,423,952
Area: 42,803 sq. mi. (110,860 sq km)
Language: Spanish
Money: Peso
Government: Communist state

CHECK IT OUT

Cuba was controlled by the same leader, Fidel Castro, for nearly 50 years.

CYPRUS

Capital: Nicosia
Population: 792,604
Area: 3,571 sq. mi. (9,250 sq km)
Language: Greek, Turkish, English
Money: Euro
Government: Republic

CHECK IT OUT

Mythology says the goddess Aphrodite arose from the waves at a rock formation in Cyprus called *Petra tou Romiou*.

CZECH REPUBLIC

Capital: Prague
Population: 10,220,911
Area: 30,450 sq. mi. (78,866 sq km)
Language: Czech, Slovak
Money: Koruna
Government: Parliamentary democracy

CHECK IT OUT

Prague Castle in the country's capital is the largest medieval castle in the world. It was built about 1,200 years ago.

DENMARK

Capital: Copenhagen
Population: 5,484,723
Area: 16,639 sq. mi. (43,094 sq km)
Language: Danish, Faroese, Greenlandic, English
Money: Krone
Government: Constitutional monarchy

CHECK IT OUT

Lego™ blocks were invented in Denmark. The name comes from the Danish words *leg* and *godt*, which mean "play well."

DJIBOUTI

Capital: Djibouti
Population: 506,221
Area: 8,880 sq. mi. (23,000 sq km)
Language: French, Arabic, Afar, Somali
Money: Franc
Government: Republic

CHECK IT OUT

The Djibouti countryside features dramatic limestone chimneys created by deposits of calcium carbonate from hot springs.

DOMINICA

Capital: Roseau
Population: 72,514
Area: 291 sq. mi. (754 sq km)
Language: English, French patois
Money: Dollar
Government: Parliamentary democracy

CHECK IT OUT

Parts of Dominica can receive as much as 300 inches (762 cm) of rain every year.

DOMINICAN REPUBLIC

Capital: Santo Domingo
Population: 9,507,133
Area: 18,815 sq. mi. (48,730 sq km)
Language: Spanish
Money: Peso
Government: Democratic republic

CHECK IT OUT

The Dominican Republic is the second-largest country in the West Indies.

ECUADOR

Capital: Quito
Population: 13,927,650
Area: 109,483 sq. mi. (283,560 sq km)
Language: Spanish, Quechua, Jivaroan
Money: Dollar
Government: Republic

CHECK IT OUT

The Galápagos Islands, off Ecuador's coast, are home to the Galápagos tortoise. These ancient creatures can weigh up to 475 pounds (215 kg) and live more than 100 years.

EGYPT

Capital: Cairo
Population: 81,713,517
Area: 386,662 sq. mi. (1,001,450 sq km)
Language: Arabic, English, French
Money: Pound
Government: Republic

CHECK IT OUT

The Great Pyramid of Khufu (Cheops) is 480 feet (146 m) high—about the height of a 48-story building.

EL SALVADOR

Capital: San Salvador
Population: 7,066,403
Area: 8,124 sq. mi. (21,040 sq km)
Language: Spanish, Nahua
Money: Colón
Government: Republic

CHECK IT OUT

El Salvador is the smallest and most densely populated country in Central America.

EQUATORIAL GUINEA

Capital: Malabo
Population: 616,459
Area: 10,831 sq. mi. (28,051 sq km)
Language: Spanish, French, Fang, Bubi
Money: CFA franc
Government: Republic

CHECK IT OUT

Scientists come to Bioko Island, where this country's capital is located, to study unique species of plants and animals, including a rare monkey called a drill.

ERITREA

Capital: Asmara
Population: 5,502,026
Area: 46,842 sq. mi. (121,320 sq km)
Language: Afar, Arabic, Tigre, Kunama
Money: Nakfa
Government: In transition

CHECK IT OUT

Many Eritreans wear a traditional shawl known as a *gabbi*.

ESTONIA

Capital: Tallinn
Population: 1,307,605
Area: 17,462 sq. mi. (45,226 sq km)
Language: Estonian, Russian, Latvian
Money: Kroon
Government: Parliamentary republic

CHECK IT OUT

Estonia is home to Old Town Tallinn, one of Europe's best-preserved medieval communities. It has 26 watchtowers and cobblestone streets.

ETHIOPIA

Capital: Addis Ababa
Population: 82,544,838
Area: 435,186 sq. mi. (1,127,127 sq km)
Language: Amarigna, Oromigna, Tigrigna, Somaligna, English
Money: Birr
Government: Federal republic

CHECK IT OUT

The Blue Nile river runs for more than 500 miles (800 km) through Ethiopia and carries the runoff from the highlands to the desert.

FIJI

Capital: Suva
Population: 931,741
Area: 7,054 sq. mi. (18,270 sq km)
Language: English, Fijian, Hindustani
Money: Dollar
Government: Republic

CHECK IT OUT

Fiji is composed of 333 different islands in the South Pacific, but most people live on the largest one—Viti Levu.

FINLAND

Capital: Helsinki
Population: 5,244,749
Area: 130,559 sq. mi. (338,145 sq km)
Language: Finnish, Swedish
Money: Euro
Government: Constitutional republic

One-fourth of Finland is north of the Arctic Circle, making winters there long and very cold.

FRANCE

Capital: Paris
Population: 64,057,790
Area: 248,429 sq. mi. (643,427 sq km)
Language: French
Money: Euro
Government: Republic

CHECK IT OUT

The TGV train, France's high-speed rail service, runs at speeds of up to 200 miles per hour (322 kph).

GABON

Capital: Libreville
Population: 1,485,832
Area: 103,347 sq. mi. (267,667 sq km)
Language: French, Fang, others
Money: CFA franc
Government: Republic

CHECK IT OUT

The Kongou Falls, located in Gabon's Invindo National Park, is 2 miles (3.2 km) wide.

THE GAMBIA

Capital: Banjul
Population: 1,735,464
Area: 4,363 sq. mi. (11,300 sq km)
Language: English, Mandinka, Wolof, Fula, others
Money: Dalasi
Government: Republic

CHECK IT OUT

The Gambia is the smallest country on the African continent.

GEORGIA

Capital: Tbilisi
Population: 4,630,841
Area: 26,911 sq. mi. (69,700 sq km)
Language: Georgian, Russian, Abkhaz
Money: Lari
Government: Republic

CHECK IT OUT

Krubera Cave, in Georgia's Caucasus Mountains, is said to be deepest cave in the world. It has been explored to depths of 7,185 feet (2190 m).

GERMANY

Capital: Berlin
Population: 82,369,548
Area: 137,847 sq. mi. (357,021 sq km)
Language: German
Money: Euro
Government: Federal republic

CHECK IT OUT

The spires of the Cologne Cathedral are an amazing 515 feet (157 m) high—taller than a 50-story building.

GHANA

Capital: Accra
Population: 23,382,848
Area: 92,456 sq. mi. (239,460 sq km)
Language: English, Asante, Ewe, Fante
Money: Cedi
Government: Constitutional democracy

CHECK IT OUT

Until 1957 Ghana was known as the Gold Coast because of the vast amounts of gold Portuguese explorers found there.

GREECE

Capital: Athens
Population: 10,722,816
Area: 50,942 sq. mi. (131,940 sq km)
Language: Greek, Turkish, English
Money: Euro
Government: Parliamentary republic

CHECK IT OUT

The Parthenon in Athens is one of the oldest and most famous buildings in the world. The ancient temple was built to honor the Greek goddess Athena almost 2,500 years ago.

GRENADA

Capital: St. George's
Population: 90,343
Area: 133 sq. mi. (344 sq km)
Language: English, French patois
Money: Dollar
Government: Parliamentary democracy

CHECK IT OUT

Grenada is known as "The Spice of the Caribbean." The country produces one-third of the world's nutmeg.

GUATEMALA

Capital: Guatemala City
Population: 13,002,206
Area: 42,043 sq. mi. (108,890 sq km)
Language: Spanish, 23 Amerindian dialects
Money: Quetzal
Government: Constitutional democratic republic

CHECK IT OUT

More than one-half of Guatemalans are descended from the Mayas. The Mayan Indian civilization developed a calendar with a 365-day year, among many other achievements.

GUINEA

Capital: Conakry
Population: 9,806,509
Area: 94,926 sq. mi. (245,857 sq km)
Language: French, Peul, Malinke, Soussou
Money: Franc
Government: Republic

CHECK IT OUT

Despite its name, the guinea pig does not come from Guinea. It is native to South America. (And it's not a pig!)

GUINEA-BISSAU

Capital: Bissau
Population: 1,503,182
Area: 13,946 sq. mi. (36,120 sq km)
Language: Portuguese, Creole, French, others
Money: CFA franc
Government: Republic

CHECK IT OUT

Guinea-Bissau's main export crop is cashew nuts.

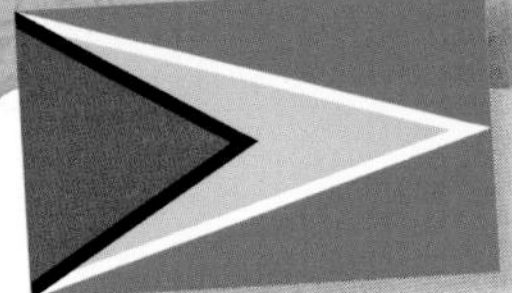

GUYANA

Capital: Georgetown
Population: 760,200
Area: 83,000 sq. mi. (214,970 sq km)
Language: English, Guyanese, Creole
Money: Dollar
Government: Republic

CHECK IT OUT

Guyana's Kaieteur Falls is five times as tall as Niagara Falls.

HAITI

Capital: Port-au-Prince
Population: 8,924,553
Area: 10,714 sq. mi. (27,750 sq km)
Language: French, Creole
Money: Gourde
Government: Republic

CHECK IT OUT

Haiti achieved independence in 1804. It was the first Caribbean state to become independent.

THE HOLY SEE (VATICAN CITY)

Capital: Vatican City
Population: 824
Area: 0.17 sq. mi. (0.44 sq km)
Language: Italian, Latin, French, various others
Money: Euro
Government: Ecclesiastical

CHECK IT OUT

Vatican City, the seat of the Roman Catholic Church, is the world's smallest independent nation.

HONDURAS

Capital: Tegucigalpa
Population: 7,639,327
Area: 43,278 sq. mi. (112,090 sq km)
Language: Spanish, Amerindian dialects
Money: Lempira
Government: Democratic constitutional republic

CHECK IT OUT

The word *honduras* means "depths" in Spanish. Christopher Columbus named the area when he landed here in 1502, after the deep water off its coast.

HUNGARY

Capital: Budapest
Population: 9,930,915
Area: 35,919 sq. mi. (93,030 sq km)
Language: Hungarian
Money: Forint
Government: Parliamentary democracy

CHECK IT OUT

The Danube River splits the capital city into two sides: Buda and Pest.

ICELAND

Capital: Reykjavik
Population: 304,367
Area: 39,769 sq. mi. (103,000 sq km)
Language: Icelandic
Money: Krona
Government: Constitutional republic

CHECK IT OUT

Iceland's glaciers, geysers, and warm, mineral-rich pools attract more than a quarter of a million tourists every year.

INDIA

Capital: New Delhi
Population: 1,147,995,898
Area: 1,269,346 sq. mi. (3,287,590 sq km)
Language: Hindi, English, 21 others
Money: Rupee
Government: Federal republic

CHECK IT OUT

India's Taj Mahal is one of the wonders of the world. It was built in the 1600s by Shah Jahan for his wife, Mumtaz Mahal.

INDONESIA

Capital: Jakarta
Population: 237,512,365
Area: 741,100 sq. mi. (1,919,440 sq km)
Language: Bahasa Indonesia, English, Dutch, Javanese
Money: Rupiah
Government: Republic

CHECK IT OUT

The largest volcanic eruption in history happened on the Indonesian island of Sumbawa in 1815. Scientists say that the eruption of Mount Tambora sent a massive cloud of ash 30 miles (43 km) into the atmosphere—much higher than a plane can fly—and killed 100,000 people.

IRAN

Capital: Tehran
Population: 65,875,223
Area: 636,296 sq. mi. (1,648,000 sq km)
Language: Persian, Turkic, Kurdish, Arabic, others
Money: Rial
Government: Islamic republic

CHECK IT OUT

For most of its history, Iran was called Persia.

IRAQ

Capital: Baghdad
Population: 28,221,181
Area: 168,754 sq. mi. (437,072 sq km)
Language: Arabic, Kurdish, Turkoman, Assyrian, Armenian
Money: Dinar
Government: Parliamentary democracy

CHECK IT OUT

Iraq contains more oil than any country in the world, except for Saudi Arabia and Canada.

IRELAND

Capital: Dublin
Population: 4,156,119
Area: 27,135 sq. mi. (70,280 sq km)
Language: English, Gaelic
Money: Euro
Government: Parliamentary republic

CHECK IT OUT

Ireland is known as the Emerald Isle because of its beautiful green fields and hillsides.

ISRAEL

Capital: Jerusalem
Population: 7,112,359
Area: 8,019 sq. mi. (20,770 sq km)
Language: Hebrew, Arabic, English
Money: New Shekel
Government: Republic

CHECK IT OUT

The Western Wall in Jerusalem is also called the Wailing Wall. It is one of Judaism's holiest places and most sacred symbols.

ITALY

Capital: Rome
Population: 58,145,321
Area: 116,306 sq. mi. (301,230 sq km)
Language: Italian, German, French, Slovene
Money: Euro
Government: Republic

CHECK IT OUT

Engineers successfully stopped Italy's famous Leaning Tower of Pisa from collapsing through a construction project in 2001.

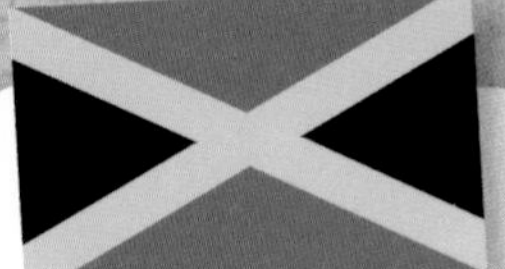

JAMAICA

Capital: Kingston
Population: 2,804,332
Area: 4,244 sq. mi. (10,991 sq km)
Language: English, English patois
Money: Dollar
Government: Constitutional monarchy with parliamentary system

CHECK IT OUT

The pirate known as Blackbeard (Edward Teach) is said to have operated out of Jamaica in the 1700s. Some stories say that he went into battle with lit matches stuck in his hat to make enemies think his head was smoking.

JAPAN

Capital: Tokyo
Population: 127,288,419
Area: 145,883 sq. mi. (337,835 sq km)
Language: Japanese
Money: Yen
Government: Constitutional monarchy with parliamentary democracy

CHECK IT OUT

Japan has four major islands—Honshu, Hokkaido, Kyushu, and Shikoku—and thousands of smaller ones.

JORDAN

Capital: Amman
Population: 6,198,677
Area: 35,637 sq. mi. (92,300 sq km)
Language: Arabic, English
Money: Dinar
Government: Constitutional monarchy

CHECK IT OUT

The points of the star on Jordan's flag stand for the first seven verses of the Koran, the holy book of Islam.

KAZAKHSTAN

Capital: Astana
Population: 15,340,533
Area: 1,049,155 sq. mi. (2,717,300 sq km)
Language: Kazakh, Russian, German
Money: Tenge
Government: Republic

CHECK IT OUT

The Caspian Sea, which borders Kazakhstan, is the largest enclosed body of water on Earth.

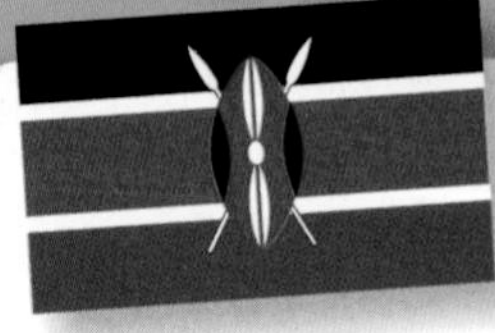

KENYA

Capital: Nairobi
Population: 37,953,838
Area: 224,962 sq. mi. (582,650 sq km)
Language: Kiswahili, English, numerous indigenous languages
Money: Shilling
Government: Republic

CHECK IT OUT

In Kenya's Lake Turkana area, scientists discovered a fossil known as Kenya Man, thought to be over three million years old.

KIRIBATI

Capital: Tawara
Population: 110,356
Area: 266 sq. mi. (719 sq km)
Language: English, I-Kiribati
Money: Dollar
Government: Republic

CHECK IT OUT

Kiribati consists of three groups of islands surrounded by coral reefs, roughly halfway between Australia and Hawaii.

KOREA, NORTH

Capital: Pyongyang
Population: 23,479,089
Area: 46,541 sq. mi. (120,540 sq km)
Language: Korean
Money: Won
Government: Communist state

CHECK IT OUT

North Korea has the fourth-largest army in the world.

KOREA, SOUTH

Capital: Seoul
Population: 48,379,392
Area: 38,023 sq. mi. (98,480 sq km)
Language: Korean, English
Money: Won
Government: Republic

CHECK IT OUT

South Korea has more than twice as many people as North Korea, but much less land area. It's one of the mostly densely populated countries in the world.

KOSOVO

Capital: Pristina
Population: 2,126,708
Area: 4,203 sq. mi. (10,887 sq km)
Language: Albanian, Serbian, Bosnian, Turkish, Roma
Money: Euro
Government: Republic

Kosovo, a country about the size of Connecticut in southeastern Europe, declared its independence from Serbia on February 17, 2008.

KUWAIT

Capital: Kuwait City
Population: 2,596,799
Area: 6,880 sq. mi. (17,820 sq km)
Language: Arabic, English
Money: Dinar
Government: Constitutional emirate

CHECK IT OUT

Summers in Kuwait are dry and extremely hot, averaging 108–115°F (42–46°C).

KYRGYZSTAN

Capital: Bishkek
Population: 5,356,869
Area: 76,641 sq. mi. (198,500 sq km)
Language: Kyrgyz, Russian, Uzbek
Money: Som
Government: Republic

CHECK IT OUT

Kyrgyzstan is one of 15 countries that became independent with the collapse of the Soviet Union in 1991.

LAOS

Capital: Vientiane
Population: 6,677,534
Area: 91,429 sq. mi. (236,800 sq km)
Language: Lao, French, English, other ethnic languages
Money: Kip
Government: Communist state

CHECK IT OUT

In 2008, cavers exploring the 6-mile-long (almost 10 km) Xe Bang Fai River cave in central Laos found huge rooms and spiders as big as dinner plates.

LATVIA

Capital: Riga
Population: 2,245,423
Area: 24,938 sq. mi. (64,589 sq km)
Language: Latvian, Lithuanian, Russian
Money: Lat
Government: Parliamentary democracy

CHECK IT OUT

Latvia has a 100 percent literacy rate.

LEBANON

Capital: Beirut
Population: 3,971,841
Area: 4,015 sq. mi. (10,400 sq km)
Language: Arabic, English, French, Armenian
Money: Pound
Government: Republic

CHECK IT OUT

Beirut is a lively pop music center, with TV music channels, yearly festivals, and talent shows such as *Star Academy* and *Superstar*.

LESOTHO

Capital: Maseru
Population: 2,128,180
Area: 11,720 sq. mi. (30,355 sq km)
Language: Sesotho, English, Zulu, Xhosa
Money: Loti
Government: Parliamentary constitutional monarchy

CHECK IT OUT

To visualize Lesotho, think of a doughnut hole—a small circle of land surrounded by the much larger nation of South Africa.

LIBERIA

Capital: Monrovia
Population: 3,334,587
Area: 43,000 sq. mi. (111,370 sq km)
Language: English, about 20 ethnic languages
Money: Dollar
Government: Republic

CHECK IT OUT

Many Liberians are descendants of American slaves who were sent to live here in freedom by a U.S. antislavery group in the 1800s.

LIBYA

Capital: Tripoli
Population: 6,173,579
Area: 679,362 sq. mi. (1,759,540 sq km)
Language: Arabic, Italian, English
Money: Dinar
Government: Jamahiriya ("state of the masses")

CHECK IT OUT

Libya has a young population. About one-third of all Libyans are under 15.

LIECHTENSTEIN

Capital: Vaduz
Population: 34,498
Area: 62 sq. mi. (160 sq km)
Language: German, Alemannic dialect
Money: Swiss franc
Government: Constitutional monarchy

CHECK IT OUT

Tiny Liechtenstein shares some services with neighboring Switzerland. Its residents use Swiss money, and Switzerland runs Liechtenstein's telephone and postal systems.

LITHUANIA

Capital: Vilnius
Population: 3,565,205
Area: 25,174 sq. mi. (65,200 sq km)
Language: Lithuanian, Russian, Polish
Money: Litas
Government: Parliamentary democracy

CHECK IT OUT

Lithuania is the largest of the Baltic States, three countries on the eastern edge of the Baltic Sea. The others are Estonia and Latvia.

LUXEMBOURG

Capital: Luxembourg-Ville
Population: 486,006
Area: 998 sq. mi. (2,586 sq km)
Language: Luxembourgish, German, French
Money: Euro
Government: Constitutional monarchy

CHECK IT OUT

Luxembourg is an industrial country known particularly for two products: steel and computers.

MACEDONIA

Capital: Skopje
Population: 2,061,315
Area: 9,781 sq. mi. (25,333 sq km)
Language: Macedonian, Albanian, Turkish
Money: Denar
Government: Parliamentary democracy

CHECK IT OUT

About 80 percent of Macedonia consists of hills and mountains, but more than half the population lives in cities.

MADAGASCAR

Capital: Antananarivo
Population: 20,042,551
Area: 226,657 sq. mi. (587,040 sq km)
Language: Malagasy, English, French
Money: Ariary
Government: Republic

CHECK IT OUT

Madagascar is the world's fourth-largest island, after Greenland, New Guinea, and Borneo. It is home to a huge variety of unique plants and animals that evolved 165 million years ago.

MALAWI

Capital: Lilongwe
Population: 13,931,831
Area: 45,745 sq. mi. (118,480 sq km)
Language: Chichewa, Chinyan'ji, Chiyao, Chitumbka
Money: Kwacha
Government: Multiparty democracy

CHECK IT OUT

Lake Malawi is nearly 9,000 square miles (23,310 sq km). It takes up about a fifth of the country's total area.

MALAYSIA

Capital: Kuala Lumpur
Population: 25,274,133
Area: 127,317 sq. mi. (329,750 sq km)
Language: Bahasa Malaysia, English, Chinese dialects, Panjabi, Thai
Money: Ringgit
Government: Constitutional monarchy

CHECK IT OUT

Malaysia's capital is the home of the 1,483-foot (452 m) Petronas Twin Towers. They were the tallest buildings in the world from 1996 to 2003.

MALDIVES

Capital: Male
Population: 385,925
Area: 116 sq. mi. (300 sq km)
Language: Maldivian Dhivehi, English
Money: Rufiyaa
Government: Republic

CHECK IT OUT

About a thousand of the 1,190 coral islands that make up Maldives, located south of India in the Indian Ocean, are uninhabited.

MALI

Capital: Bamako
Population: 12,324,029
Area: 478,767 sq. mi. (1,240,000 sq km)
Language: French, Bambara, numerous African languages
Money: CFA franc
Government: Republic

CHECK IT OUT

Most of Mali's people make their living farming or fishing around the Niger River.

MALTA

Capital: Valletta
Population: 403,532
Area: 122 sq. mi. (316 sq km)
Language: Maltese, English
Money: Euro
Government: Republic

CHECK IT OUT

This group of islands in the Mediterranean Sea south of Sicily has one of the world's healthiest populations. Average life expectancy is over 79 years.

MARSHALL ISLANDS

Capital: Majuro
Population: 63,174
Area: 70 sq. mi. (181 sq km)
Language: Marshallese, English
Money: U.S. dollar
Government: Constitutional government in free association with the United States

CHECK IT OUT

The first hydrogen bomb was exploded in the Marshall Islands in 1952. Radiation levels in some areas are still high, but improving through environmental cleanup programs.

MAURITANIA

Capital: Nouakchott
Population: 3,364,940
Area: 397,955 sq. mi. (1,030,700 sq km)
Language: Arabic, Pulaar, Soninke, Wolof, French
Money: Ouguiya
Government: Military junta

CHECK IT OUT

This western African nation has it together! It's a major producer of gum arabic, used to make glue.

MAURITIUS

Capital: Port Louis
Population: 1,274,189
Area: 788 sq. mi. (2,040 sq km)
Language: Creole, Bhojpuri, French
Money: Rupee
Government: Parliamentary democracy

CHECK IT OUT

Mauritius has the second-highest per-person income in Africa. Most of the country's money comes from sugarcane.

MEXICO

Capital: Mexico City
Population: 109,955,400
Area: 761,606 sq. mi. (1,972,550 sq km)
Language: Spanish, various Mayan, Nahuati, other regional indigenous dialects
Money: Peso
Government: Federal republic

CHECK IT OUT

Mexico has dozens of bullfighting rings, including one that holds 50,000 people—about the entire population of Biloxi, Mississippi.

MICRONESIA

Capital: Palikir
Population: 107,665
Area: 271 sq. mi. (702 sq km)
Language: English, Chuukese, Kosrean, Pohnpeian, Yapese
Money: U.S. dollar
Government: Constitutional government in free association with the United States

CHECK IT OUT

Micronesia's first settlers have been traced back more than 4,000 years.

MOLDOVA

Capital: Chisinau
Population: 4,324,450
Area: 13,067 sq. mi. (333,843 sq km)
Language: Moldovan, Russian, Gagauz
Money: Leu
Government: Republic

CHECK IT OUT

Moldova was the first former Soviet state to elect a Communist as president.

MONACO

Capital: Monaco
Population: 32,796
Area: 0.75 sq. mi. (1.95 sq km)
Language: French, English, Italian, Monegasque
Money: Euro
Government: Constitutional monarchy

Minisized Monaco covers about as much area as New York City's Central Park.

MONGOLIA

Capital: Ulan Bator
Population: 2,996,081
Area: 603,909 sq. mi. (1,564,116 sq km)
Language: Khalka Mongol, Turkic, Russian
Money: Togrog/Tughrik
Government: Mixed parliamentary/presidential

CHECK IT OUT

Mongolia's average population density is only 5 people per square mile (1.9 per sq km), although many people live in the cities.

MONTENEGRO

Capital: Podgorica
Population: 678,177
Area: 5,415 sq. mi. (14,026 sq km)
Language: Montenegrin, Serbian, Bosnian, Albanian, Croatian
Money: Euro
Government: Republic

CHECK IT OUT

Montenegro's name means "black mountain." The name comes from the dark forests on the mountains that once covered most of the country.

MOROCCO

Capital: Rabat
Population: 34,343,219
Area: 172,414 sq. mi. (446,550 sq km)
Language: Arabic, Berber dialects, French
Money: Dirham
Government: Constitutional monarchy

CHECK IT OUT

Morocco is a North African country about the size of California. Part of it is covered by the Sahara Desert, whose 3,500,000 square miles (9,064,958 sq km) make it the largest desert in the world.

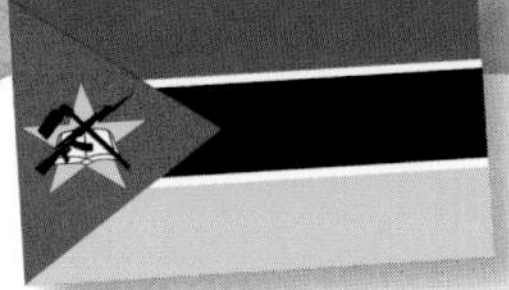

MOZAMBIQUE

Capital: Maputo
Population: 21,284,701
Area: 309,496 sq. mi. (801,590 sq km)
Language: Portuguese, Emakhuwa, Xichangana, Elomwe, Cisena
Money: Metical
Government: Republic

CHECK IT OUT

Portuguese is the official language of Mozambique. However, most residents, who are of African descent, speak a form of Bantu.

NAMIBIA

Capital: Windhoek
Population: 2,088,669
Area: 318,696 sq. mi. (825,418 sq km)
Language: Afrikaans, German, English, other indigenous languages
Money: Dollar, South African rand
Government: Republic

CHECK IT OUT

Namibia's rich diamond deposits have made it one of the world's best sources of high-quality diamonds.

NAURU

Capital: Yaren
Population: 13,770
Area: 8 sq. mi. (21 sq km)
Language: Nauruan, English
Money: Australian dollar
Government: Republic

CHECK IT OUT

Nauru joined the United Nations in 1999 as the world's smallest independent republic.

NEPAL

Capital: Kathmandu
Population: 29,519,114
Area: 56,827 sq. mi. (147,181 sq km)
Language: Nepali, Maithali, English
Money: Rupee
Government: Federal democratic republic

CHECK IT OUT

Eight of the world's ten highest mountain peaks are in Nepal, including Mount Everest, the highest of them all—29,035 feet (8,850 m).

NETHERLANDS

Capital: Amsterdam
Population: 16,645,313
Area: 16,033 sq. mi. (41,526 sq km)
Language: Dutch, Frisian
Money: Euro
Government: Constitutional monarchy

CHECK IT OUT

Most Netherlanders dress in modern clothing, but many farmers say wooden shoes known as *klompen* keep feet drier.

NEW ZEALAND

Capital: Wellington
Population: 4,173,460
Area: 103,738 sq. mi. (268,680 sq km)
Language: English, Maori, sign language
Money: Dollar
Government: Parliamentary democracy

CHECK IT OUT

New Zealand was settled by the Polynesian Maori in AD 800. Today Maori make up about 9.38 percent of the country's population.

NICARAGUA

Capital: Managua
Population: 5,785,846
Area: 49,998 sq. mi. (129,494 sq km)
Language: Spanish, English, indigenous languages on Atlantic coast
Money: Gold cordoba
Government: Republic

CHECK IT OUT

Nicaragua got its name from Nicarao, a tribal chief who lived and reigned here in the 16th century.

NIGER

Capital: Niamey
Population: 13,272,679
Area: 489,191 sq. mi. (1,267,000 sq km)
Language: French, Hausa, Djerma
Money: CFA franc
Government: Republic

CHECK IT OUT

Niger is known as the Frying Pan of the World. It can get hot enough to make raindrops evaporate before they hit the ground.

NIGERIA

Capital: Abuja
Population: 146,255,306
Area: 356,669 sq. mi. (923,768 sq km)
Language: English, Hausa, Yoruba, Igbo, Fulani
Money: Naira
Government: Federal republic

CHECK IT OUT

Nigeria is the most heavily populated country in Africa. More than half the continent's people live there.

NORWAY

Capital: Oslo
Population: 4,644,457
Area: 125,021 sq. mi. (323,802 sq km)
Language: Bokmal Norwegian, Nynorsk Norwegian, Sami
Money: Krone
Government: Constitutional monarchy

CHECK IT OUT

Moving glaciers during the Ice Age left Norway with a jagged coastline marked by long strips of water-filled fjords and thousands of islands.

OMAN

Capital: Muscat
Population: 3,311,640
Area: 82,031 sq. mi. (212,460 sq km)
Language: Arabic, English, Baluchi, Urdu, Indian dialects
Money: Rial
Government: Monarchy

CHECK IT OUT

Members of the Al Bu Said family have ruled Oman for more than 250 years.

PAKISTAN

Capital: Islamabad
Population: 172,800,051
Area: 310,403 sq. mi. (803,940 sq km)
Language: English, Urdu, Punjabi, Sindhi, Siraiki, Pashtu
Money: Rupee
Government: Federal republic

CHECK IT OUT

Pakistan is the sixth most heavily populated country in the world. The others, in order, are China, India, the United States, Indonesia, and Brazil.

PALAU

Capital: Melekeok
Population: 21,093
Area: 177 sq. mi. (458 sq km)
Language: English, Palauan, various Asian languages
Money: U.S. dollar
Government: Constitutional government in free association with the United States

CHECK IT OUT

In March 2008, thousands of human bones, some of them ancient and very small, were found by scientists in Palau.

PANAMA

Capital: Panama City
Population: 3,309,679
Area: 30,193 sq. mi. (78,200 sq km)
Language: Spanish, English
Money: Balboa
Government: Constitutional democracy

CHECK IT OUT

Spain was the first country to think of cutting a canal across the Isthmus of Panama. The French started building the 51-mile-long (82 km) canal in 1881 and the United States finished it in 1914.

PAPUA NEW GUINEA

Capital: Port Moresby
Population: 5,931,769
Area: 178,704 sq. mi. (462,840 sq km)
Language: Melanesian Pidgin, English, 820 indigenous languages
Money: Kina
Government: Constitutional parliamentary democracy

CHECK IT OUT

Living in Papua New Guinea means coping with the constant threat of active volcanoes, frequent earthquakes, mud slides, and tsunamis.

PARAGUAY

Capital: Asuncíon
Population: 6,831,306
Area: 157,047 sq. mi. (406,750 sq km)
Language: Spanish, Guarani
Money: Guarani
Government: Constitutional republic

CHECK IT OUT

Paraguay's got the power! Hydroelectric dams, including the largest one in the world, keep the country well supplied with electricity.

PERU

Capital: Lima
Population: 29,180,899
Area: 496,226 sq. mi. (1,285,220 sq km
Language: Spanish, Quechua, Aymara, numerous minor languages
Money: Nuevo sol
Government: Constitutional republic

CHECK IT OUT

The third-largest country in South America (after Brazil and Argentina), Peru is three times as big as California but has only two-thirds of that state's population.

Machu Picchu, Peru

PHILIPPINES

Capital: Manila
Population: 96,061,683
Area: 115,831 sq. mi. (300,000 sq km)
Language: Filipino, English, 8 major dialects
Money: Peso
Government: Republic

CHECK IT OUT

Almost half of all working Filipinos earn their living by farming, although the farmland itself is owned by a wealthy few.

POLAND

Capital: Warsaw
Population: 38,500,696
Area: 120,726 sq. mi. (312,679 sq km)
Language: Polish
Money: Zloty
Government: Republic

CHECK IT OUT

Physicist Marie Curie and composer Frederic Chopin are just two of the many world-famous people who came from Poland.

PORTUGAL

Capital: Lisbon
Population: 10,676,910
Area: 35,672 sq. mi. (92,391 sq km)
Language: Portuguese, Mirandese
Money: Euro
Government: Republic, parliamentary democracy

CHECK IT OUT

The national music of Portugal is called *fado*. The songs are often sad but can also be funny.

QATAR

Capital: Doha
Population: 824,789
Area: 4,416 sq. mi. (11,437 sq km)
Language: Arabic, English
Money: Rial
Government: Emirate

CHECK IT OUT

Qatar is only about as big as Los Angeles County, CA, but it holds more than 15 percent of the world's gas reserves.

ROMANIA

Capital: Bucharest
Population: 22,246,862
Area: 91,699 sq. mi. (237,500 sq km)
Language: Romanian, Hungarian, Romany (Gypsy)
Money: New leu
Government: Republic

CHECK IT OUT

Cruel 15th-century Romanian prince Vlad Tepes was the model for the horror novel *Dracula*. One of Vlad's homes, Bran Castle, is Romania's most popular tourist attraction.

RUSSIA

Capital: Moscow
Population: 140,702,094
Area: 6,592,772 sq. mi. (17,075,200 sq km)
Language: Russian, many minority languages
Money: Ruble
Government: Federation

CHECK IT OUT

Russia is the largest country in the world and contains the ninth-largest population. It was formerly the center of the Union of Soviet Socialist Republics (USSR), which broke up into 15 separate states in 1991.

RWANDA

Capital: Kigali
Population: 10,186,063
Area: 10,169 sq. mi. (26,338 sq km)
Language: Kinyarwanda, French, English, Swahili
Money: Franc
Government: Republic, presidential-multiparty system

CHECK IT OUT

Rwanda leads the world in terms of female representation in its parliamentary body. Roughly half of its legislators are women.

SAINT KITTS and NEVIS

Capital: Basseterre
Population: 39,817
Area: 101 sq. mi. (261 sq km)
Language: English
Money: Dollar
Government: Parliamentary democracy

CHECK IT OUT

These two Caribbean islands have been a single state since 1983.

SAINT LUCIA

Capital: Castries
Population: 159,585
Area: 238 sq. mi. (616 sq km)
Language: English, French patois
Money: Dollar
Government: Parliamentary democracy

CHECK IT OUT

This small Caribbean island changed hands between France and England 14 times before being given to the United Kingdom in 1814. It became independent in 1979.

SAINT VINCENT and the GRENADINES

Capital: Kingstown
Population: 118,432
Area: 150 sq. mi. (389 sq km)
Language: English, French patois
Money: Dollar
Government: Parliamentary democracy

CHECK IT OUT

These islands are the world's leading supplier of arrowroot, which is used to thicken fruit pie fillings and sauces.

SAMOA

Capital: Apia
Population: 217,083
Area: 1,137 sq. mi. (2,944 sq km)
Language: Samoan, English
Money: Tala
Government: Parliamentary democracy

CHECK IT OUT

Author Robert Louis Stevenson (*Treasure Island*, *Kidnapped*) lived in Samoa from 1890 until he died in 1894. His Polynesian neighbors called him *Tusitala*, or "storyteller."

SAN MARINO

Capital: San Marino
Population: 29,973
Area: 24 sq. mi. (61 sq km)
Language: Italian
Money: Euro
Government: Republic

CHECK IT OUT

San Marino, in central Italy, is the third-smallest state in Europe. Some historians say it was founded in AD 301, making it the world's oldest republic.

SÃO TOMÉ and PRINCIPE

Capital: São Tomé
Population: 206,178
Area: 387 sq. mi. (1,001 sq km)
Language: Portuguese
Money: Dobra
Government: Republic

CHECK IT OUT

São Tomé and Principe are the two largest islands in an African island group in the Gulf of Guinea.

SAUDI ARABIA

Capital: Riyadh
Population: 28,146,657
Area: 830,000 sq. mi. (2,149,690 sq km)
Language: Arabic
Money: Riyal
Government: Monarchy

CHECK IT OUT

Saudi Arabia is known as the birthplace of Islam.

SENEGAL

Capital: Dakar
Population: 12,853,259
Area: 75,749 sq. mi. (196,190 sq km)
Language: French, Wolof, Pulaar, Jola, Mandinka
Money: CFA Franc
Government: Republic

CHECK IT OUT

Senegal's economy depends on peanuts. In recent years the country has produced more than 800,000 tons of them, 95 percent for oil.

SERBIA

Capital: Belgrade
Population: 10,159,046
Area: 29,913 sq. mi. (77,474 sq km)
Language: Serbian, Hungarian
Money: Dinar
Government: Republic

CHECK IT OUT

Favorite foods in Serbia are *cevacici*, a grilled meatball sandwich with raw onions, and *burek*, a pastry layered with cheese, meat, or jam.

SEYCHELLES

Capital: Victoria
Population: 82,247
Area: 176 sq. mi. (455 sq km)
Language: Creole, English
Money: Rupee
Government: Republic

CHECK IT OUT

From the early 1500s to the 1700s, the Seychelles were a popular pirate hideout.

SIERRA LEONE

Capital: Freetown
Population: 6,294,774
Area: 27,699 sq. mi. (71,740 sq km)
Language: English, Mende and Temne vernaculars, Krio (English-based Creole)
Money: Leone
Government: Constitutional democracy

CHECK IT OUT

Sierra Leone is one of the wettest places in western Africa. Rainfall can reach 195 inches (495 cm) a year.

SINGAPORE

Capital: Singapore
Population: 4,608,167
Area: 241 sq. mi. (693 sq km)
Language: Mandarin, English, Malay, Hokkien, Cantonese, Teochew
Money: Dollar
Government: Republic

CHECK IT OUT

Singapore is a city-state—an independent state made up of a city and the areas around it. It is an important international business center with one of the busiest harbors in the world.

SLOVAKIA

Capital: Bratislava
Population: 5,455,407
Area: 18,859 sq. mi. (48,845 sq km)
Language: Slovak, Hungarian
Money: Koruna
Government: Parliamentary democracy

CHECK IT OUT

Following World War I, Slovaks and Czechs were joined into a single nation: Czechoslovakia. But in 1993 Czechoslovakia redivided into Slovakia and the Czech Republic.

SLOVENIA

Capital: Ljubljana
Population: 2,007,711
Area: 7,827 sq. mi. (20,273 sq km)
Language: Slovenian, Serbo-Croation
Money: Euro
Government: Parliamentary democracy

CHECK IT OUT

Big puddles and small lakes can appear and disappear suddenly in Slovenia because of underground caves and channels.

SOLOMON ISLANDS

Capital: Honiara
Population: 581,318
Area: 10,985 sq. mi. (28,450 sq km)
Language: English, Melanesian pidgin, 120 indigenous languags
Money: Dollar
Government: Parliamentary democracy

CHECK IT OUT

On April 1, 2007, a massive underwater earthquake triggered a tsunami that caused widespread destruction in the Solomon Islands.

SOMALIA

Capital: Mogadishu
Population: 9,558,666
Area: 246,201 sq. mi. (637,657 sq km)
Language: English, Arabic, Italian, English
Money: Shilling
Government: In transition

CHECK IT OUT

Each point of the flag's white star stands for a Somalia homeland.

SOUTH AFRICA

Capital: Pretoria (administrative), Cape Town (legislative), Bloemfontein (judicial)
Population: 48,782,755
Area: 471,011 sq. mi. (1,219,912 sq km)
Language: IsiZulu, IsiXhosa, Afrikaans, English, Sepedi, Setswana, Sesotho
Money: Rand
Government: Republic

CHECK IT OUT

South Africa is in a subtropical location—so how come penguins thrive there? The penguins' breeding grounds are cooled by Antarctic Ocean currents on the west coast.

SPAIN

Capital: Madrid
Population: 40,491,051
Area: 194,897 sq. mi. (504,782 sq km)
Language: Castilian Spanish, Catalan, Galician, Basque
Money: Euro
Government: Parliamentary monarchy

CHECK IT OUT

Spain's capital city is in almost the exact center of the country.

SRI LANKA

Capital: Colombo
Population: 21,128,773
Area: 25,332 sq. mi. (65,610 sq km)
Language: Sinhala, Tamil, English
Money: Rupee
Government: Republic

CHECK IT OUT

Once named Ceylon, Sri Lanka was an important port in the ancient world. Arab traders called it Serendip, the origin of the word *serendipity*, which means "a pleasing chance discovery."

SUDAN

Capital: Khartoum
Population: 40,218,455
Area: 967,499 sq. mi. (2,505,810 sq km)
Language: Arabic, Nubian, Ta Bedawie, Nilotic, Nilo-Hamitic, Sudanic dialects, English
Money: Pound
Government: Power sharing, with military dominant (elections in July 2009)

CHECK IT OUT

Sudan is the largest country in Africa. Two branches of the Nile River, the White Nile and the Blue Nile, meet in Khartoum to form the main Nile River corridor.

SURINAME

Capital: Paramaribo
Population: 475,996
Area: 63,039 sq. mi. (163,270 sq km)
Language: Dutch, English, Sranang Tongo, Caribbean Hindustani, Javanese
Money: Dollar
Government: Constitutional democracy

CHECK IT OUT

Suriname is the smallest independent country in South America. It could fit into Brazil, its massive neighbor to the south, 52 times.

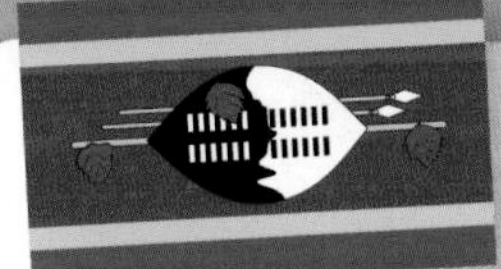

SWAZILAND

Capital: Mbabane
Population: 1,128,814
Area: 6,704 sq. mi. (17,363 sq km)
Language: English, siSwati
Money: Lilangeni
Government: Monarchy

CHECK IT OUT

Other parts of southern Africa suffer from drought, but four major rivers—the Komati, the Umbuluzi, the Ingwavuma, and the Great Usutu—keep Swaziland's water supply healthy.

SWEDEN

Capital: Stockholm
Population: 9,045,389
Area: 173,732 sq. mi. (449,964 sq km)
Language: Swedish, Finnish, Sami
Money: Krona
Government: Constitutional monarchy

CHECK IT OUT

Sweden has an army, navy, and air force, but its military can only be used in peacekeeping actions, not wars.

SWITZERLAND

Capital: Bern
Population: 7,581,520
Area: 15,942 sq. mi. (41,290 sq km)
Language: German, French, Italian, Romansch
Money: Franc
Government: Federal republic-like confederation

CHECK IT OUT

Switzerland's famous flag comes in two shapes. A square version is flown on land and a rectangular flag (like the one above) is flown at sea.

SYRIA

Capital: Damascus
Population: 19,747,586
Area: 71,498 sq. mi. (185,180 sq km)
Language: Arabic, Kurdish, Armenian, Aramaic, Circassian
Money: Pound
Government: Republic (under military regime)

CHECK IT OUT

In 2008, archaeologists excavating in the Syrian desert dug up a camel jawbone they said could be a million years old.

TAIWAN

Capital: Taipei
Population: 22,920,946
Area: 13,892 sq. mi. (35,980 sq km)
Language: Mandarin Chinese, Taiwanese, Hakka
Money: Dollar (yuan)
Government: Multiparty democracy

CHECK IT OUT

Taiwan's Palace Museum's collection of Chinese bronze, jade, calligraphy, painting, and porcelain is so big that only 1 percent of it is displayed at any one time.

TAJIKISTAN

Capital: Dushanbe
Population: 7,211,884
Area: 55,251 sq. mi. (143,100 sq km)
Language: Tajik, Russian
Money: Somoni
Government: Republic

CHECK IT OUT

When mountainous Tajikistan became independent after the breakup of the Soviet Union, it inherited a mountain called Communism Peak. The Tajiks quickly changed the name to Imeni Ismail Samani Peak.

TANZANIA

Capital: Dodoma
Population: 40,213,162
Area: 364,900 sq. mi. (945,087 sq km)
Language: Kiswahili, English, Arabic, many local languages
Money: Shilling
Government: Republic

CHECK IT OUT

Africa's highest mountain, 19,340-foot-high (5,895 m) Mount Kilimanjaro, is in Tanzania. Lions, elephants, giraffes, and other animals roam free, protected by the government, in Serengeti Park.

THAILAND

Capital: Bangkok
Population: 65,493,298
Area: 198,457 sq. mi. (514,000 sq km)
Language: Thai, English, other ethnic languages
Money: Baht
Government: Constitutional monarchy

CHECK IT OUT

Formerly Siam, this Southeast Asian country has contributed Thai food, kickboxing, and the musical *The King and I* to world culture—among many other things.

TIMOR-LESTE

Capital: Dili
Population: 1,108,777
Area: 5,794 sq. mi. (15,007 sq km)
Language: Tetum, Portuguese, Indonesian, English
Money: U.S. dollar
Government: Republic

CHECK IT OUT

Timor-Leste is a really young nation. It became independent amid protests in 1999, and in 2007 it held largely peaceful presidential and parliamentary elections for the first time.

TOGO

Capital: Lomé
Population: 5,858,673
Area: 21,925 sq. mi. (56,785 sq km)
Language: French, Ewe, Mina, Kabye, Dagomba
Money: CFA franc
Government: Republic (under transition to multiparty democratic rule)

CHECK IT OUT

Watch your step! Poisonous vipers—cobras, pythons, and green and black mambas—are abundant here. So are scorpions and spiders.

TONGA

Capital: Nuku'alofa
Population: 119,009
Area: 289 sq. mi. (748 sq km)
Language: Tongan, English
Money: Pa'anga
Government: Constitutional monarchy

CHECK IT OUT

Tonga, an archipelago of about 150 islands east of Australia, is the last remaining monarchy in the Pacific.

TRINIDAD and TOBAGO

Capital: Port of Spain
Population: 1,047,366
Area: 1,980 sq. mi. (5,128 sq km)
Language: English, Caribbean Hindustani, French, Spanish, Chinese
Money: Dollar
Government: Parliamentary democracy

CHECK IT OUT

Native animals include the quenck, a kind of wild hog, and the agouti, a rabbitlike rodent. Howler monkeys are also native, but increasing development has made them rare.

TUNISIA

Capital: Tunis
Population: 10,383,577
Area: 63,170 sq. mi. (163,610 sq km)
Language: Arabic, French
Money: Dinar
Government: Republic

CHECK IT OUT

Every *Star Wars* movie but one was filmed in Tunisia. So was *Indiana Jones: Raiders of the Lost Ark.*

TURKEY

Capital: Ankara
Population: 71,892,807
Area: 301,384 sq. mi. (780,580 sq km)
Language: Turkish, Kurdish, Dimli
Money: New lira
Government: Republican parliamentary democracy

CHECK IT OUT

Turkey gave the world the man who would become Santa Claus: St. Nicholas, a fourth-century bishop.

TURKMENISTAN

Capital: Ashgabat
Population: 5,179,571
Area: 188,456 sq. mi. (488,100 sq km)
Language: Turkmen, Russian, Uzbek
Money: Manat
Government: Republic under authoritarian presidential rule

CHECK IT OUT

Turkmenistan's stunning flag incorporates five traditional carpet designs. Each design is associated with a particular tribe.

TUVALU

Capital: Funafuti
Population: 12,177
Area: 10 sq. mi. (26 sq km)
Language: Tuvaluan, English, Samoan
Money: Australian dollar
Government: Constitutional monarchy with parliamentary democracy

CHECK IT OUT

Tuvalu is made up of nine coral atolls in the South Pacific. Eight are inhabited. The word *tuvalu* means "group of eight."

UGANDA

Capital: Kampala
Population: 31,367,972
Area: 91,136 sq. mi. (236,040 sq km)
Language: English, Ganda, Luganda
Money: Shilling
Government: Republic

CHECK IT OUT

Ugandans speak in more than 42 different dialects. In fact, no single language is understood by all Ugandans.

UKRAINE

Capital: Kyiv (Kiev)
Population: 45,994,287
Area: 233,090 sq. mi. (603,700 sq km)
Language: Ukrainian, Russian, Romanian, Polish, Hungarian
Money: Hryvnia
Government: Republic

CHECK IT OUT

Ukraine is the largest country located completely within Europe.

UNITED ARAB EMIRATES

Capital: Abu Dhabi
Population: 4,621,399
Area: 32,278 sq. mi. (83,600 sq km)
Language: Arabic, Persian, English, Hindi, Urdu
Money: Dirham
Government: Federation of emirates

CHECK IT OUT

The United Arab Emirates consists of seven independent Arab states in southwestern Asia. City dwellers live in modern buildings. Country people live in huts, and most wear long robes. Nomadic tribes roam the desert regions with camels, goats, and sheep.

UNITED KINGDOM

Capital: London
Population: 60,943,912
Area: 94,526 sq. mi. (244,820 sq km)
Language: English, Welsh, Scottish form of Gaelic
Money: Pound
Government: Constitutional monarchy

CHECK IT OUT

Today the United Kingdom (UK) consists of England, Scotland, Wales, and Northern Ireland. At one time the British Empire extended to five other continents.

UNITED STATES

Capital: Washington, DC
Population: 303,824,646
Area: 3,794,083 sq. mi. (9,826,630 sq km)
Language: English, Spanish, Hawaiian, other minority languages
Money: Dollar
Government: Federal republic with strong democratic tradition

CHECK IT OUT

What is now the United States was the first European colony to become independent from its motherland (England).

URUGUAY

Capital: Montevideo
Population: 3,477,778
Area: 68,039 sq. mi. (176,220 sq km)
Language: Spanish, Portunol, Brazilero
Money: Peso
Government: Constitutional republic

CHECK IT OUT

Uruguay's name comes from a Guarani word meaning "river of painted birds."

UZBEKISTAN

Capital: Tashkent
Population: 27,345,026
Area: 172,742 sq. mi. (447,400 sq km)
Language: Uzbek, Russian, Tajik
Money: Som
Government: Republic with authoritarian presidential rule

CHECK IT OUT

The cities of Uzbekistan—Samarkand, Bukhara, and Khiva—were well-traveled centers on the Silk Road, an ancient trade route linking Asia to Europe.

VANUATU

Capital: Port-Vila
Population: 215,446
Area: 4,710 sq. mi. (12,200 sq km)
Language: Bislama, English, French, 100 local languages
Money: Vatu
Government: Parliamentary republic

CHECK IT OUT

Vanuatu is not just one island but more than 80 volcanic islands in a South Pacific archipelago.

VENEZUELA

Capital: Caracas
Population: 26,414,815
Area: 352,144 sq. mi. (912,050 sq km)
Language: Spanish, indigenous dialects
Money: Bolivar Fuerte
Government: Federal republic

CHECK IT OUT

Venezuela is home to the largest rodents in the world—the capybaras. They measure up to 4.3 feet (1.3 m) long and weigh up to 140 pounds (about 64 kg).

VIETNAM

Capital: Hanoi
Population: 86,116,559
Area: 127,244 sq. mi. (329,560 sq km)
Language: Vietnamese, English, French, Chinese, Khmer
Money: Dong
Government: Communist state

CHECK IT OUT

Vietnam is shaped like a long, skinny *S*. It measures 1,031 miles (1,650 km) from north to south, but at its narrowest point is only 31 miles (50 km) across.

YEMEN

Capital: Sanaa
Population: 23,013,376
Area: 203,850 sq. mi. (527,970 sq km)
Language: Arabic
Money: Rial
Government: Republic

CHECK IT OUT

According to legend, coffee was discovered by a goat herder who noticed his goats got livelier after eating berries from a certain plant. The plant was brought to Yemen, where it was developed into a drink.

ZAMBIA

Capital: Lusaka
Population: 11,669,534
Area: 290,586 sq. mi. (752,614 sq km)
Language: English, numerous vernaculars
Money: Kwacha
Government: Republic

CHECK IT OUT

One of the world's highest waterfalls, the Victoria Falls is created by the Zambezi River tumbling over cliffs between Zambia and Zimbabwe. The waterfall is twice as high as Niagara Falls.

ZIMBABWE

Capital: Harare
Population: 11,350,111
Area: 150,804 sq. mi. (390,580 sq km)
Language: English, Shona, Sindebele, minor tribal dialects
Money: Dollar
Government: Parliamentary democracy

CHECK IT OUT

Zimbabwe means "stone house." Ruins of the stone palaces of African kings can be seen in many parts of the country.

States of the United States

A country's flag is an important symbol reflecting the nation's spirit and personality. Over the years, as the United States has grown and changed, so has the national flag. In 1777 the first commissioned flag had 13 red and white stripes and 13 white stars representing the original 13 colonies. Over time, as states were added, so were stars. In 1960 the 50th star was added after Hawaii became the 50th state. Today the American flag has 13 stripes and 50 stars on a blue background—showing the world where we came from and where we are now.

One Nation, Fifty Faces

Each state in America has its own capital, state bird, flower, motto, and diverse ethnic makeup. Each state also has a great deal of pride. It doesn't matter whether the state is the biggest in land area, Alaska, or the smallest, Rhode Island. It doesn't matter whether the state has the most people, California, or the least, Wyoming. Each state has a unique story to tell. And the design, colors, and patterns of its flag are one way to tell that story.

Take a peek through the flags in this section. You will see a variety of plants, animals, stars, moons, and people, reflecting a state's history and personality. You will also learn facts and statistics about each state that may surprise you.

CIRCLE OF LIFE

New Mexico's flag tells a story of its people. The colors—golden yellow and bright red—are the colors of Spain, first brought to New Mexico in the 1500s. The symbol—a circle with four rays emanating in each of four directions—is an ancient Native American sun symbol. The circle has no beginning or end and embodies life and love. The rays symbolize:

- ★ the four seasons—spring, summer, autumn, winter
- ★ the four directions—north, south, east, west
- ★ the four times of day—morning, daytime, afternoon, night
- ★ the four stages of life—childhood, young adulthood, middle years, old age

TAKE a LOOK

There are 21 state flags that feature a star or stars, 26 flags on a field of blue, 8 with birds on them, 2 with bears, and 1 with a moose! Can you find them all? (Answers are on page 271.)

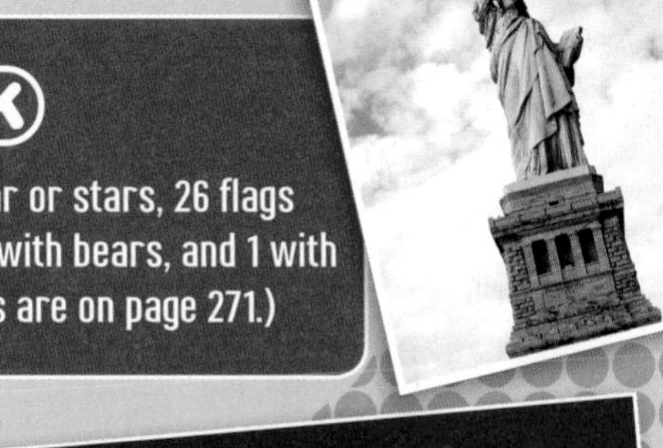

In addition to the 50 states, the United States includes 1 federal district, 2 commonwealths, 3 main territories, and several minor territories. Only one of these places is located within the continental United States. See page 105 for all the information.

Alaska
Juneau

Olympia
Washington
Montana
North Dakota
Helena
Salem
Bismarck
Oregon
Idaho
Boise
South Dakota
Pierre
Wyoming
Cheyenne
Nebraska
Sacramento
Carson City
Salt Lake City
Lincoln
Nevada
Utah
Denver
Top
Colorado
Kansas
California
Santa Fe
Oklaho
Arizona
Oklahoma
Phoenix
New Mexico
Texas
Austin
Honolulu
Hawaii

U.S. States and Their Capital Cities

New Hampshire
Maine
sota
Vermont
Augusta
Montpelier
Concord
Paul
Massachusetts
Boston
Michigan
Wisconsin
Albany
New York
Providence
Rhode Island
Madison
Lansing
Hartford
Connecticut
va
Pennsylvania
Trenton
Moines
Harrisburg
New Jersey
Ohio
Indiana
Illinois
Dover
Delaware
Columbus
West Virginia
Annapolis
Springfield
Indianapolis
Maryland
Richmond
Jefferson City
Charleston
Washington, DC
Frankfort
Virginia
Missouri
Kentucky
Raleigh
Nashville
North Carolina
Tennessee
Arkansas
Columbia
Little Rock
Atlanta
South Carolina
Alabama
Mississippi
Montgomery
Georgia
Jackson
Louisiana
Tallahassee
Baton Rouge
Florida

State Quarters by Release Date (and Statehood Dates)

Release Date   Statehood Date

Delaware
January 4, 1999
December 7, 1787

Pennsylvania
March 8, 1999
December 12, 1787

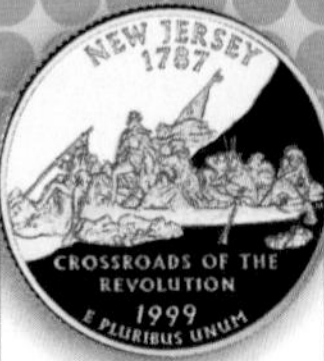

New Jersey
May 17, 1999
December 18, 1787

Georgia
July 19, 1999
January 2, 1788

Connecticut
October 12, 1999
January 9, 1788

Massachusetts
January 3, 2000
February 6, 1788

Maryland
March 13, 2000
April 28, 1788

South Carolina
May 22, 2000
May 23, 1788

New Hampshire
August 7, 2000
June 21, 1788

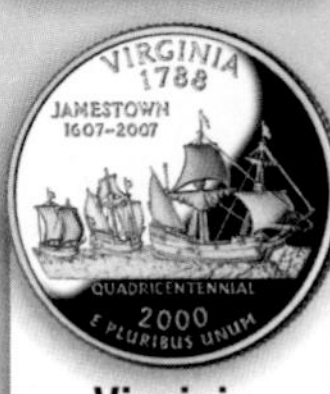

Virginia
October 16, 2000
June 25, 1788

New York
January 2, 2001
July 26, 1788

North Carolina
March 12, 2001
November 21, 1789

Rhode Island
May 21, 2001
May 29, 1790

Vermont
August 6, 2001
March 4, 1791

Kentucky
October 15, 2001
June 1, 1792

Tennessee
January 2, 2002
June 1, 1796

Ohio
March 11, 2002
March 1, 1803

Louisiana
May 20, 2002
April 30, 1812

Indiana
August 2, 2002
December 11, 1816

Mississippi
October 15, 2002
December 10, 1817

Illinois
January 2, 2003
December 3, 1818

Alabama
March 17, 2003
December 14, 1819

Maine
June 2, 2003
March 15, 1820

Missouri
August 4, 2003
August 10, 1821

Arkansas
October 20, 2003
June 15, 1836

Release Date
Statehood Date

Michigan
January 26, 2004
January 26, 1837

Florida
March 29, 2004
March 3, 1845

Texas
June 1, 2004
December 29, 1845

Iowa
August 30, 2004
December 28, 1846

Wisconsin
October 25, 2004
May 29, 1848

California
January 31, 2005
September 9, 1850

Minnesota
April 4, 2005
May 11, 1858

Oregon
June 6, 2005
February 14, 1859

Kansas
August 29, 2005
January 29, 1861

West Virginia
October 14, 2005
June 20, 1863

Nevada
January 31, 2006
October 31, 1864

Nebraska
April 3, 2006
March 1, 1867

Colorado
June 14, 2006
August 1, 1876

North Dakota
August 28, 2006
November 2, 1889

South Dakota
November 6, 2006
November 2, 1889

Montana
January 29, 2007
November 8, 1889

Washington
April 2, 2007
November 11, 1889

Idaho
June 4, 2007
July 3, 1890

Wyoming
September 3, 2007
July 10, 1890

Utah
November 5, 2007
January 4, 1896

Oklahoma
January 28, 2008
November 16, 1907

New Mexico
April 7, 2008
January 6, 1912

Arizona
June 2, 2008
February 14, 1912

Alaska
August 25, 2008
January 3, 1959

Hawaii
November 3, 2008
August 21, 1959

ALABAMA

Capital: Montgomery
Postal Code: AL
Nickname: Heart of Dixie
Flower: Camellia
Bird: Yellowhammer
Area: 52,419 sq. mi. (135,765 sq km)
Population: 4,661,900

Huntsville, Alabama, is the site where the first rocket that took people to the moon was built.

ALASKA

Capital: Juneau
Postal Code: AK
Nickname: Last Frontier
Flower: Forget-me-not
Bird: Willow ptarmigan
Area: 666,267 sq. mi. (1,726,556 sq km)
Population: 686,293

Woolly mammoth remains have been found in Alaska's frozen ground.

ARIZONA

Capital: Phoenix
Postal Code: AZ
Nickname: Grand Canyon State
Flower: Saguaro cactus blossom
Bird: Cactus wren
Area: 113,998 sq. mi. (295,253 sq km)
Population: 6,500,180

There are more species of hummingbirds in Arizona than in any other state.

ARKANSAS

Capital: Little Rock
Postal Code: AR
Nickname: Land of Opportunity
Flower: Apple blossom
Bird: Mockingbird
Area: 53,179 sq. mi. (137,733 sq km)
Population: 2,855,390

Stuttgart, Arkansas, is home to the annual World's Championship Duck Calling Contest.

CALIFORNIA

Capital: Sacramento
Postal Code: CA
Nickname: Golden State
Flower: Golden poppy
Bird: California quail
Area: 163,696 sq. mi. (423,971 sq km)
Population: 36,756,666

The highest and lowest points in the continental United States are in California—Mount Whitney (14,494 ft./4,418 m) and Badwater in Death Valley (282 ft./86 m below sea level).

COLORADO

Capital: Denver
Postal Code: CO
Nickname: Centennial State
Flower: Rocky Mountain columbine
Bird: Lark bunting
Area: 104,094 sq. mi. (269,602 sq km)
Population: 4,939,456

CHECK IT OUT

The streets in Victor, Colorado, were actually paved in a low grade of gold back in 1890 to make use of the low-quality ore that couldn't be refined.

CONNECTICUT

Capital: Hartford
Postal Code: CT
Nickname: Constitution State
Flower: Mountain laurel
Bird: American robin
Area: 5,543 sq. mi. (14,356 sq km)
Population: 3,501,252

America's first newspaper, the *Hartford Courant*, was printed in 1764 in Connecticut.

DELAWARE

Capital: Dover
Postal Code: DE
Nickname: First State
Flower: Peach blossom
Bird: Blue hen chicken
Area: 2,489 sq. mi. (6,446 sq km)
Population: 873,092

Delaware was the first state to ratify the U.S. Constitution.

FLORIDA

Capital: Tallahassee
Postal Code: FL
Nickname: Sunshine State
Flower: Orange blossom
Bird: Mockingbird
Area: 65,755 sq. mi. (170,305 sq km)
Population: 18,328,340

Florida's name comes from the Spanish word for "flowery." Ponce de Leon named it after the beautiful flowers he saw all around when he arrived there in 1513.

Florida wildflowers

GEORGIA

Capital: Atlanta
Postal Code: GA
Nickname: Empire State of the South
Flower: Cherokee rose
Bird: Brown thrasher
Area: 59,425 sq. mi. (153,910 sq km)
Population: 9,685,744

CHECK IT OUT

Georgia's top crops include peaches. The "World's Largest Peach Cobbler," which uses 75 gallons (285 L) of peaches and 150 pounds (68 kg) each of sugar and flour, is the star of the annual Georgia Peach Festival.

HAWAII

Capital: Honolulu
Postal Code: HI
Nickname: Aloha State
Flower: Yellow hibiscus
Bird: Nene or Hawaiian goose
Area: 10,931 sq. mi. (28,311 sq km)
Population: 1,288,198

CHECK IT OUT

Hawaii is made up of 132 islands. The 8 main ones are Niihau, Kauai, Oahu, Maui, Molokai, Lanai, Kahoolawe, and the Big Island of Hawaii.

IDAHO

Capital: Boise
Postal Code: ID
Nickname: Gem State
Flower: Syringa
Bird: Mountain bluebird
Area: 83,570 sq. mi. (216,445 sq km)
Population: 1,523,816

CHECK IT OUT

The largest freshwater fish ever caught in America was a white sturgeon hauled out of Idaho's Snake River in 1898. It weighed 1,500 pounds (680 kg), about as much as a grown Holstein cow.

ILLINOIS

Capital: Springfield
Postal Code: IL
Nickname: Land of Lincoln
Flower: Native violet
Bird: Cardinal
Area: 57,914 sq. mi. (149,997 sq km)
Population: 12,901,563

The tallest building in the United States is the Willis (formerly Sears) Tower in Chicago, measuring 1,725 feet (526 m) from the ground to the tip of the antenna.

INDIANA

Capital: Indianapolis
Postal Code: IN
Nickname: Hoosier State
Flower: Peony
Bird: Cardinal (sometimes called northern cardinal)
Area: 36,418 sq. mi. (94,322 sq km)
Population: 6,376,792

Santa Claus, Indiana, receives over half a million letters at Christmastime.

IOWA

Capital: Des Moines
Postal Code: IA
Nickname: Hawkeye State
Flower: Wild prairie rose
Bird: Eastern goldfinch (also called American goldfinch)
Area: 56,272 sq. mi. (145,744 sq km)
Population: 3,002,555

Iowa is the only state name in America that begins with two vowels.

KANSAS

Capital: Topeka
Postal Code: KS
Nickname: Sunflower State
Flower: Native sunflower
Bird: Western meadowlark
Area: 82,277 sq. mi. (213,096 sq km)
Population: 2,802,134

CHECK IT OUT

In 1905, the element helium was discovered at the University of Kansas.

KENTUCKY

Capital: Frankfort
Postal Code: KY
Nickname: Bluegrass State
Flower: Goldenrod
Bird: Northern cardinal
Area: 40,409 sq. mi. (104,659 sq km)
Population: 4,269,245

CHECK IT OUT

The Kentucky Derby, held the first Saturday in May, is the oldest annual horse race in the United States.

LOUISIANA

Capital: Baton Rouge
Postal Code: LA
Nickname: Pelican State
Flower: Magnolia
Bird: Eastern brown pelican
Area: 51,840 sq. mi. (134,265 sq km)
Population: 4,410,796

CHECK IT OUT

Louisiana is the only state divided into parishes instead of counties.

MAINE

Capital: Augusta
Postal Code: ME
Nickname: Pine Tree State
Flower: White pine cone and tassel
Bird: Black-capped chickadee
Area: 35,385 sq. mi. (91,647 sq km)
Population: 1,316,456

CHECK IT OUT

Eastport, Maine, is the first town in America to see the sunrise because it is the town farthest east.

MARYLAND

Capital: Annapolis
Postal Code: MD
Nickname: Old Line State
Flower: Black-eyed Susan
Bird: Baltimore oriole
Area: 12,407 sq. mi. (32,134 sq km)
Population: 5,633,597

Maryland is famous for having the first dental school in the United States.

MASSACHUSETTS

Capital: Boston
Postal Code: MA
Nickname: Bay State
Flower: Mayflower
Bird: Black-capped chickadee
Area: 10,555 sq. mi. (27,337 sq km)
Population: 6,497,967

Volleyball was invented in 1895 in Holyoke, Massachusetts, by gym teacher William Morgan. The game was originally called Mintonette. Basketball was invented in nearby Springfield.

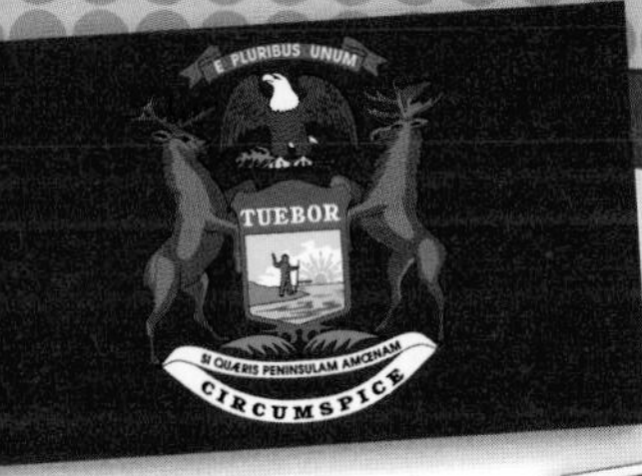

MICHIGAN

Capital: Lansing
Postal Code: MI
Nickname: Wolverine State
Flower: Apple blossom
Bird: American robin
Area: 96,716 sq. mi. (250,493 sq km)
Population: 10,003,422

With over 11,000 inland lakes and over 36,000 miles (57,936 km) of rivers and streams, Michigan has the longest freshwater shoreline in the world.

MINNESOTA

Capital: St. Paul
Postal Code: MN
Nickname: Gopher State
Flower: Pink and white lady's slipper
Bird: Common loon
Area: 86,939 sq. mi. (225,171 sq km)
Population: 5,220,393

The Mall of America in Bloomington, Minnesota, is 9.5 million square feet (8,825,780 sq m)—about the size of 78 football fields!

MISSISSIPPI

Capital: Jackson
Postal Code: MS
Nickname: Magnolia State
Flower: Magnolia
Bird: Mockingbird
Area: 48,430 sq. mi. (125,433 sq km)
Population: 2,938,618

Edward Adolf Barq, Sr., invented root beer in Biloxi, Mississippi, in 1898.

MISSOURI

Capital: Jefferson City
Postal Code: MO
Nickname: Show Me State
Flower: Hawthorn
Bird: Eastern bluebird
Area: 69,704 sq. mi. (180,533 sq km)
Population: 5,911,605

The St. Louis World's Fair in 1904 was so hot that Richard Blechyden decided to serve his tea over ice—and invented iced tea.

MONTANA

Capital: Helena
Postal Code: MT
Nickname: Treasure State
Flower: Bitterroot
Bird: Western meadowlark
Area: 147,042 sq. mi. (380,837 sq km)
Population: 967,440

The average square mile (1.6 sq km) of land in Montana contains 1.4 pronghorn antelope, 1.4 elk, and 3.3 deer. Montana has the largest number of mammal species in the United States.

NEBRASKA

Capital: Lincoln
Postal Code: NE
Nickname: Cornhusker State
Flower: Goldenrod
Bird: Western meadowlark
Area: 77,354 sq. mi. (200,346 sq km)
Population: 1,783,432

CHECK IT OUT

About 95 percent of Nebraska's area is taken up by farms and ranches—a higher percentage than any other state. The state's top crop is corn.

NEVADA

Capital: Carson City
Postal Code: NV
Nickname: Silver State
Flower: Sagebrush
Bird: Mountain bluebird
Area: 110,561 sq. mi. (286,352 sq km)
Population: 2,600,167

CHECK IT OUT

The Silver State produces more gold than any other state and is third in the world after China and South Africa.

NEW HAMPSHIRE

Capital: Concord
Postal Code: NH
Nickname: Granite State
Flower: Purple lilac
Bird: Purple finch
Area: 9,350 sq. mi. (24,216 sq km)
Population: 1,315,809

CHECK IT OUT

The winds on top of New Hampshire's Mount Washington have been recorded at speeds over 231 miles (372 km) an hour—the fastest winds on Earth!

NEW JERSEY

Capital: Trenton
Postal Code: NJ
Nickname: Garden State
Flower: Purple violet
Bird: Eastern goldfinch
Area: 8,721 sq. mi. (22,587 sq km)
Population: 8,682,661

CHECK IT OUT

The street names in Monopoly come from real street names in Atlantic City, New Jersey.

NEW MEXICO

Capital: Santa Fe
Postal Code: NM
Nickname: Land of Enchantment
Flower: Yucca flower
Bird: Roadrunner (also called greater roadrunner)
Area: 121,589 sq. mi. (314,914 sq km)
Population: 1,984,356

There are more than 110 caves in Carlsbad Caverns. One cave is 22 stories high and is home to tens of thousands of bats.

NEW YORK

Capital: Albany
Postal Code: NY
Nickname: Empire State
Flower: Rose
Bird: Eastern bluebird
Area: 54,556 sq. mi. (141,299 sq km)
Population: 19,490,297

CHECK IT OUT

More than 100 million people have visited the top of the Empire State Building in New York City. The building is 1,453 feet, 8 9/16 inches (443.2 m) from the street to the top of the lightning rod.

New York City, with th Empire State Building far right

NORTH CAROLINA

Capital: Raleigh
Postal Code: NC
Nickname: Tar Heel State
Flower: Dogwood
Bird: Cardinal
Area: 53,819 sq. mi. (139,391 sq km)
Population: 9,222,414

On March 7, 1914, in Fayetteville, North Carolina, George Herman "Babe" Ruth hit his first professional home run.

NORTH DAKOTA

Capital: Bismarck
Postal Code: ND
Nickname: Flickertail State
Flower: Wild prairie rose
Bird: Western meadowlark
Area: 70,700 sq. mi. (183,112 sq km)
Population: 641,481

Jamestown, North Dakota, is home to the World's Largest Buffalo monument. It stands 26 feet (7.9 m) high and 46 feet (14 m) long, and weighs 60 tons (54,441 kg).

OHIO

Capital: Columbus
Postal Code: OH
Nickname: Buckeye State
Flower: Scarlet carnation
Bird: Cardinal
Area: 44,825 sq. mi. (116,096 sq km)
Population: 11,485,910

The first traffic light in America began working on August 5, 1914, in Cleveland, Ohio.

OKLAHOMA

Capital: Oklahoma City
Postal Code: OK
Nickname: Sooner State
Flower: Mistletoe
Bird: Scissor-tailed flycatcher
Area: 69,898 sq. mi. (181,035 sq km)
Population: 3,642,361

Not every state has a state amphibian, but Oklahoma does—the American bullfrog.

OREGON

Capital: Salem
Postal Code: OR
Nickname: Beaver State
Flower: Oregon grape
Bird: Western meadowlark
Area: 98,381 sq. mi. (254,806 sq km)
Population: 3,790,060

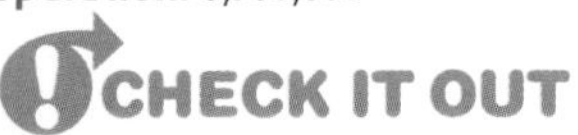

Two pioneers founded Portland, Oregon. One was from Boston, Massachusetts, and the other was from Portland, Maine. They couldn't decide what to name the city so they flipped a coin. Guess who won?

PENNSYLVANIA

Capital: Harrisburg
Postal Code: PA
Nickname: Keystone State
Flower: Mountain laurel
Bird: Ruffed grouse
Area: 46,055 sq. mi. (119,282 sq km)
Population: 12,448,279

In 1953, Dr. Jonas Salk created the polio vaccine at the University of Pittsburgh.

RHODE ISLAND

Capital: Providence
Postal Code: RI
Nickname: Ocean State
Flower: Violet
Bird: Rhode Island Red chicken
Area: 1,545 sq. mi. (4,002 sq km)
Population: 1,050,788

"I'm a Yankee Doodle Dandy" and "You're a Grand Old Flag" were written by George M. Cohan, who was born in Providence, Rhode Island, in 1878.

SOUTH CAROLINA

Capital: Columbia
Postal Code: SC
Nickname: Palmetto State
Flower: Yellow jessamine
Bird: Great Carolina wren
Area: 32,020 sq. mi. (82,931 sq km)
Population: 4,479,800

The first battle of the Civil War was fought at Fort Sumter, South Carolina.

SOUTH DAKOTA

Capital: Pierre
Postal Code: SD
Nickname: Mount Rushmore State
Flower: Pasqueflower
Bird: Ring-necked pheasant
Area: 77,116 sq. mi. (199,730 sq km)
Population: 804,194

CHECK IT OUT

The faces of George Washington, Thomas Jefferson, Theodore Roosevelt, and Abraham Lincoln are sculpted into Mount Rushmore, the world's greatest mountain carving. The carvings are taller than a four-story building.

TENNESSEE

Capital: Nashville
Postal Code: TN
Nickname: Volunteer State
Flower: Iris
Bird: Mockingbird
Area: 42,143 sq. mi. (109,150 sq km)
Population: 6,214,888

CHECK IT OUT

More than nine million people visit Smoky Mountain National Park in Tennessee every year, making it America's most visited national park. Over 30 species of salamanders and 1,500 black bears live there full-time.

TEXAS

Capital: Austin
Postal Code: TX
Nickname: Lone Star State
Flower: Bluebonnet
Bird: Mockingbird
Area: 268,581 sq. mi. (695,622 sq km)
Population: 24,326,974

CHECK IT OUT

The name *Texas* is actually derived from a misunderstanding of *tejas*, a Caddo Indian word meaning "friend."

UTAH

Capital: Salt Lake City
Postal Code: UT
Nickname: Beehive State
Flower: Sego lily
Bird: California gull
Area: 84,899 sq. mi. (219,887 sq km)
Population: 2,736,424

Utah's Great Salt Lake is several times saltier than seawater. It's so salty that you'd float on the surface of the water like a cork if you swam there!

VERMONT

Capital: Montpelier
Postal Code: VT
Nickname: Green Mountain State
Flower: Red clover
Bird: Hermit thrush
Area: 9,614 sq. mi. (24,900 sq km)
Population: 621,270

Vermont is the only New England state that doesn't border the Atlantic Ocean.

VIRGINIA

Capital: Richmond
Postal Code: VA
Nickname: Old Dominion
Flower: American dogwood
Bird: Cardinal
Area: 42,774 sq. mi. (110,784 sq km)
Population: 7,769,089

CHECK IT OUT

More U.S. presidents come from Virginia than from any other state—George Washington, Thomas Jefferson, James Madison, James Monroe, William Henry Harrison, John Tyler, Zachary Taylor, and Woodrow Wilson.

WASHINGTON

Capital: Olympia
Postal Code: WA
Nickname: Evergreen State
Flower: Coast rhododendron
Bird: Willow goldfinch (also called American goldfinch)
Area: 71,300 sq. mi. (184,666 sq km)
Population: 6,549,224

CHECK IT OUT

Washington is a hotbed of volcanic activity. Mount Rainier erupted in 1969 and Mount St. Helen's erupted in 1980.

WEST VIRGINIA

Capital: Charleston
Postal Code: WV
Nickname: Mountain State
Flower: Big rhododendron
Bird: Cardinal
Area: 24,230 sq. mi. (62,755 sq km)
Population: 1,814,468

CHECK IT OUT

Before the Civil War, West Virginia was part of Virginia. It became a separate state and remained part of the Union when Virginia decided to secede at the dawn of the war.

WISCONSIN

Capital: Madison
Postal Code: WI
Nickname: Badger State
Flower: Wood violet
Bird: American robin
Area: 65,498 sq. mi. (169,639 sq km)
Population: 5,627,967

CHECK IT OUT

Wisconsin produces 40 percent of all the cheese and 20 percent of all the butter melted, slathered, spread, and devoured in the United States. No wonder folks from Wisconsin are sometimes called "cheeseheads."

WYOMING

Capital: Cheyenne
Postal Code: WY
Nickname: Equality State
Flower: Indian paintbrush
Bird: Western meadowlark
Area: 97,814 sq. mi. (253,337 sq km)
Population: 532,668

Wyoming's Yellowstone National Park has more than 500 geysers, including Old Faithful, that regularly shoot hot water into the air.

Washington, DC
Our Nation's Capital

Every state has a capital, the city where all the state's official government business takes place. Our country's capital, Washington, DC, is the center for all national, or federal, business. But our nation's capital isn't located in a state. It's part of a federal district, the District of Columbia. Congress wanted the capital to be in a district, not a state, so as not to favor any one state above the others.

The city is named after our first president, George Washington, who chose its location in 1791. It became the capital in 1800. Before that the center of the federal government was Philadelphia, Pennsylvania.

The United States Capitol

WASHINGTON, DC

Flower: American Beauty rose
Area: 68 sq. mi. (177 sq km)
Population: 591,833
Government: Federal district under the authority of Congress; mayor and city council, elected to four-year terms, run the local government

CHECK IT OUT

The White House, at 1600 Pennsylvania Ave., is the official presidential residence. George Washington is the only U.S. president who never lived there.

PUERTO RICO

Besides the 50 states and the District of Columbia, the United States also includes a number of commonwealths and territories. A commonwealth has its own constitution and has more rights and independence than a territory, but neither one has all the rights of a state.

The largest commonwealth is Puerto Rico, which is made up of one large island and three smaller ones in the Caribbean Sea. Puerto Rico was given to the United States by Spain in 1898 and became a commonwealth in 1952.

PUERTO RICO

Capital: San Juan
Area: 3,515 sq. mi. (8,870 sq km)
Population: 3,954,037
Language: Spanish, English
Money: U.S. dollar
Goverment: U.S. territory with commonwealth status

Puerto Ricans are American citizens, but they cannot vote in U.S. presidential elections.

Other U.S. Commonwealths and Territories

The Northern Mariana Islands in the North Pacific Ocean are the only other U.S. commonwealth. U.S. territories are:

- American Samoa
- Guam
- The U.S. Virgin Islands

The United States Minor Outlying Islands:

- Midway Islands
- Johnston Atoll
- Navassa Island
- Baker, Howland, and Jarvis Islands
- Wake Island
- Kingman Reef
- Palmyra Atoll

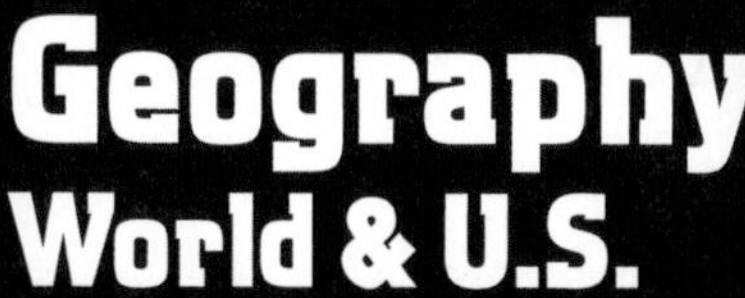

Geography World & U.S.

A Curious World

If you hung out on your street for your whole life, you'd never know anything except your own neighborhood. Can you imagine what kind of world it would be if people never left home?

Lucky for us, people have always been driven to explore. Some searched for better hunting grounds or warmer climates. Some wanted riches, spices, new kingdoms, or more land. Some were just curious to see what was around the next corner. And in leaving home these explorers found new and never-before-seen worlds.

All Over the Map

Of course, explorers couldn't take everyone along on their journeys. But such people as Marco Polo, Christopher Columbus, Meriwether Lewis, William Clark, and others captured their voyages in the form of journals and diaries. (In fact, the word *geographia* means "to describe or write about the Earth.") They also created maps showing where they had been and how they got there.

A Flat-Out Mistake

Early explorers and scientists had a lot to work through when it came to mapping the world. First of all, up until the 1500s many people believed that Earth was flat. That meant a sailing ship could sail off into the horizon and drop over the edge. An expedition led by Magellan successfully circumnavigated the world and proved that Earth was a globe.

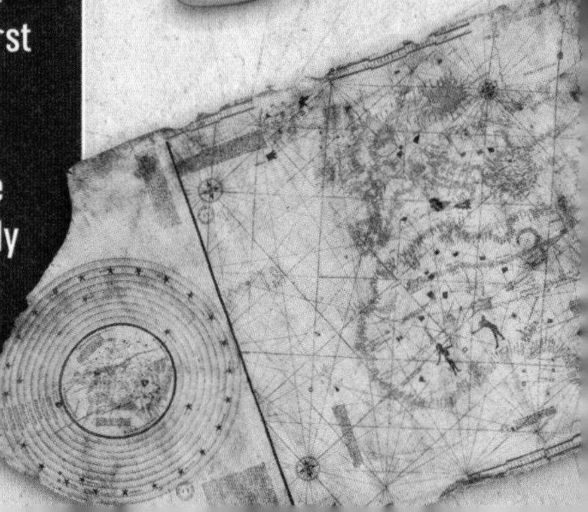

Christopher Columbus

Marco Polo

Lewis & Clark

Line Up, Please!

Navigators and mapmakers needed new tools to plot out voyages and measure distances on the globe. A system of imaginary lines was created.

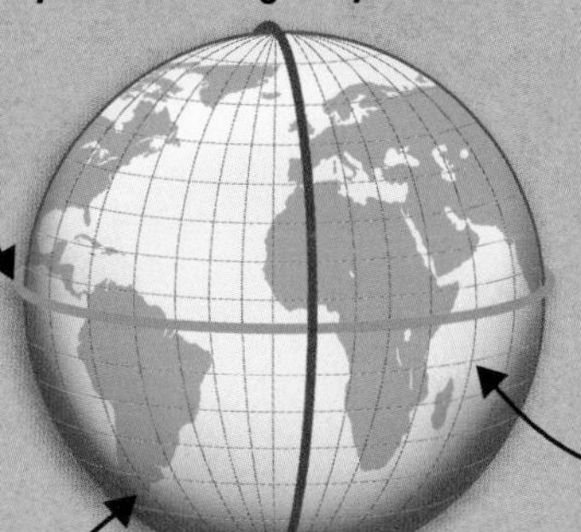

he equator circles the niddle of the globe like a iant belt. It divides the vorld in half horizontally.

Parallels run east and west, parallel to the equator. They are used to measure latitude, or distance north or south of the equator.

Meridians run north and south, looping around the poles. The prime meridian divides the world in half vertically. Meridians are used to measure longitude, or distance east or west of the prime meridian.

Ve measure longitude and latitude by degrees. The equator is at 0 degrees latitude. The orime meridian is at 0 degrees longitude.

TAKE a LOOK

Each point on a map is described by two sets of degrees depending on distance north or south of the equator and east or west of the prime meridian. For instance, Kansas City, Missouri, has a latitude of 39° N and a longitude of 94° W. On a map, find the latitude of your city and state. Then reverse the direction. (If it's north, change it to south, for example.) Next, find the longitude of your location. Subtract it from 180 and reverse its direction, too. The new location will be the place directly opposite your home on the other side of the globe.

Greenwich, England

CHECK IT OUT!

The prime meridian passes through the city of Greenwich, England. That's why it's also known as the Greenwich meridian.

How to Read a Map

Directions

When you're reading a map, how do you figure out which way is which? On most—but not all—maps:

Up means north

Down means south

Left means west

Right means east

Some maps are turned or angled so that north is not straight up. Always look for a symbol called a compass rose to show you exactly where north is on the map you're reading.

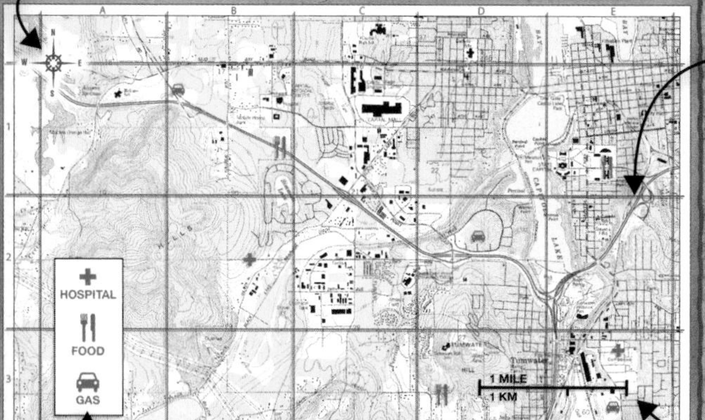

Location

Maps that show large areas such as countries and continents include lines of longitude and latitude. Maps of cities and streets are divided into blocks called grids. Grid maps have numbers on one side and letters on another. They also have an index that gives a number-letter combination for every place on the map.

Distance

You can look at a map and think it's a hop, skip and a jump from Maine to Maryland, but it's really a few million hops. The map scale shows you how many miles (or km) a certain length of map represents.

Shapes and Symbols

Every picture, object, shape, and line on a map stands for something. A tiny red airplane stands for an airport. A thick line is one kind of road and a dotted line is another. A map's legend, or key, shows these symbols and explains what they stand for.

A Map Is a Map Is a Map . . .

All maps are not created equal. There are different maps for different purposes, such as:

- A bathymetric map shows the depths and contours of the bottom of a body of water.
- A geological map shows earthquake faults, volcanoes, minerals, rock types, underground water, and landslide areas.
- A physical map shows mountains, lakes, and rivers.
- A planimetric map shows horizontal (not vertical, such as elevations) features.
- A political map shows political boundaries of cities, states, countries, and provinces.
- A relief map uses different colors to show different elevations.
- A road map shows roads, highways, cities, and towns.
- A topographic map shows elevations.
- A weather map shows temperatures, fronts, rain, snow, sleet, storms, fog, and other weather conditions.

Geographical Terms

Term	Definition
Altitude	the distance above sea level
Archipelago	a group or chain of islands clustered together in an ocean or sea
Atlas	a book of maps
Atoll	an ocean island made out of an underwater ring of coral
Bay	a body of water protected and partly surrounded by land
Cartographer	a mapmaker
Compass rose	a four-pointed design on a map that shows north, south, east, and west
Continent	one of Earth's seven largest land masses
Degree	a unit of measurement used to calculate longitude and latitude
Delta	a flat, triangular piece of land that fans out at the mouth of a river
Elevation	the height of a point on the earth's surface above sea level
Equator	an imaginary circle around the earth halfway between the North Pole and the South Pole
Globe	a 3-D spherical map of the earth
GPS	short for Global Positioning System; finds longitude and latitude by bouncing information off satellites in space
Grid	a criss-cross pattern of lines forming squares on a map
Hemisphere	one half of the world
Island	land that is surrounded by water on all sides
Isthmus	a narrow strip of land (with water on both sides) that connects two larger land areas
Latitude	distance north or south of the equator
Legend	a key to the symbols on a map
Longitude	distance east or west of the prime meridian
Map	a flat picture of a place drawn to scale
Meridian	an imaginary line running north and south and looping around the poles used to measure longitude
North Pole	the most northerly point on Earth
Ocean	the body of salt water surrounding the great land masses and divided by the land masses into several distinct portions
Parallel	an imaginary line parallel to the equator, used to measure latitude
Peninsula	a body of land surrounded by water on three sides
Scale	a tool on a map that helps calculate real distance
Sea level	the surface of the ocean
South Pole	the most southerly point on Earth
Strait	a narrow body of water that connects two larger bodies
Topography	the physical features of a place, such as mountains

Continental Drift

Maps are all well and good if things don't change. "Go east one mile and turn south and find Mt. Crumpet" works only if Mt. Crumpet doesn't decide to walk a few miles north. Sound ridiculous? Actually, the earth didn't always look like it does today. About 250 million years ago, all the continents were scrunched together in one lump called Pangaea.

Gradually the land drifted and changed into the continents we know today in a process called continental drift. And the land is still moving.

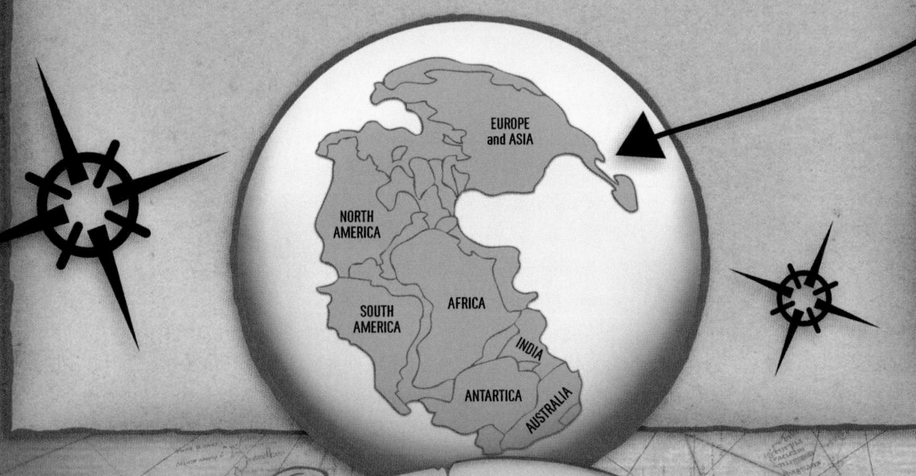

Journey to the Center of the Earth

Earth isn't just one big blue superball with the same stuff all the way through. It's made up of layers.

The part we walk around on is the crust, or lithosphere. It's only about 60 miles (100 km) deep.

Beneath the lithosphere is the mantle. It's a layer about 1,800 miles (2,897 km) deep.

Beneath that is the core, which is made of two parts.

- The outer core (1,375 miles, or 2,200 km, thick) is almost as big as the Moon and made up of soupy molten iron.
- The inner core is about 781 miles (1,250 km) thick and about as hot as the surface of the Sun.

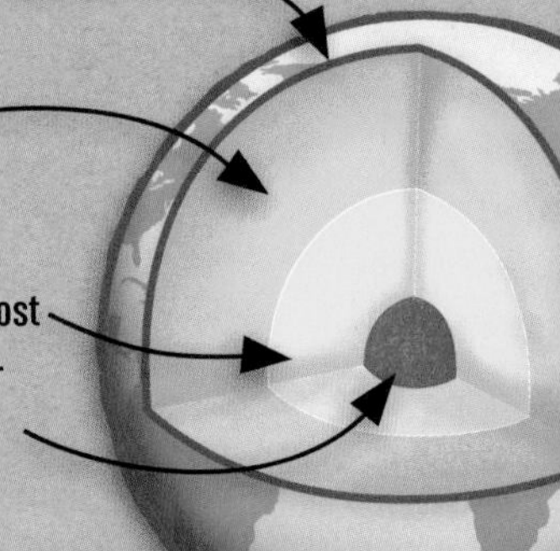

THE WORLD TODAY

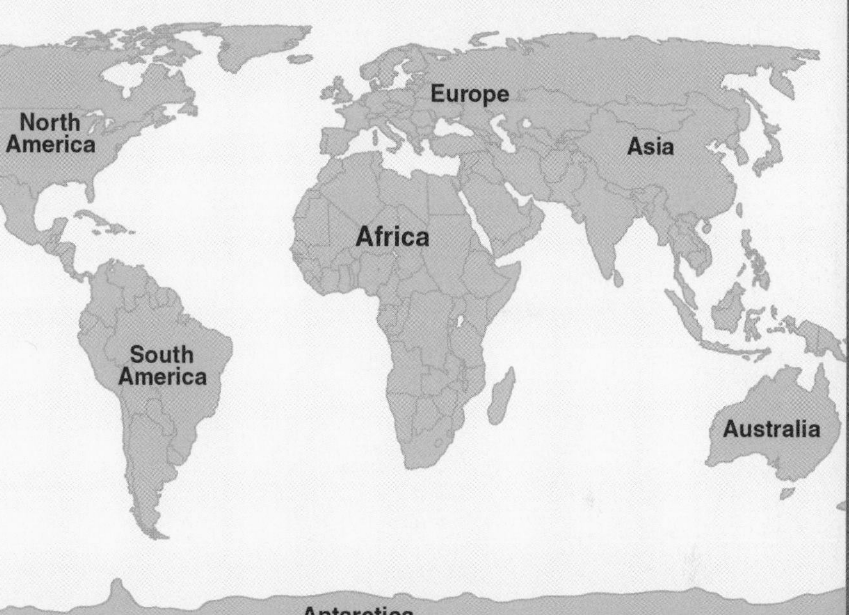

30% LAND

70% WATER

CHECK IT OUT!

The total surface area of the world is 196,937,583 square miles (510,066,000 sq km). However, about 70 percent of that is water. The area of each continent is:

Asia	11,948,911 sq. mi. (30,947,538 sq km)
Africa	11,508,043 sq. mi. (29,805,695 sq km)
Europe	8,815,510 sq. mi. (22,832,065 sq km)
North America	8,234,599 sq. mi. (21,327,514 sq km)
South America	6,731,004 sq. mi. (17,433,220 sq km)
Antarctica	5,405,430 sq. mi. (14,000,000 sq km)
Oceania (including Australia)	3,253,542 sq. mi. (8,426,635 sq km)

World's 5 Largest Oceans and Seas

Pacific Ocean
63.8 million sq. mi.
(165.3 msk*)

Atlantic Ocean
31.8 million sq. mi.
(82.4 msk)

Indian Ocean
28.3 million sq. mi.
(73.3 msk)

Arctic Ocean
5.4 million sq. mi.
(14.0 msk)

South China Sea
1.4 million sq. mi.
(3.7 msk)

*million square kilometers

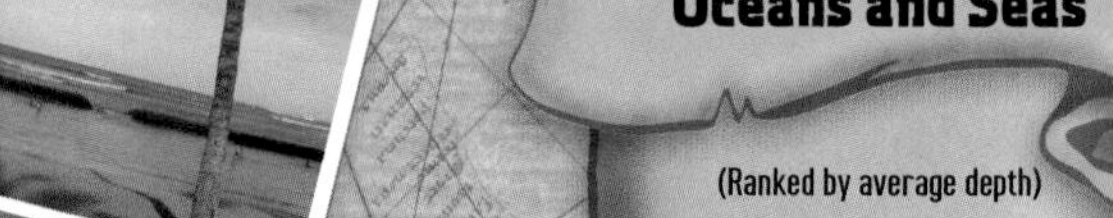

World's 5 Largest Lakes

Caspian Sea
Azerbaijan/Iran/Kazakhstan/Russia/Turkmenistan
146,101 sq. mi.
(378,401 sq km)

Lake Superior
Canada/U.S.
31,699 sq. mi.
(378,401 sq km)

Lake Victoria
Kenya/Tanzania/Uganda
26,828 sq. mi.
(69,485 sq km)

Lake Huron
Canada/U.S.
23,004 sq. mi.
(59,580 sq km)

Lake Michigan
United States
22,278 sq. mi.
(57,700 sq km)

World's 5 Deepest Oceans and Seas

(Ranked by average depth)

Pacific Ocean
14,040 ft. (4,279 m)

Indian Ocean
12,800 ft. (3,900 m)

Atlantic Ocean
11,810 ft. (3,600 m)

Caribbean Sea
8,448 ft. (2,575 m)

Sea of Japan
5,468 ft. (1,666 m)

World's 5 Highest Waterfalls

Angel
Venezuela
Tributary of Caroni River
3,212 ft. (979 m)

Tugela
South Africa
Tugela River
3,110 ft. (948 m)

Tres Hermanas
Peru
Cutivireni River
3,000 ft. (914 m)

Olo'upena
United States
2,953 ft. (900 m)

Yumbilla
Peru
2,938 ft. (896 m)

World's 5 Highest Mountains

(Height of principal peak. Lower peaks of same mountain excluded)

Everest
Nepal/Tibet
29,035 ft. (8,850 m)

K2
Kashmir/China
28,250 ft. (8,611 m)

Kanchenjunga
Nepal/Sikkim
28,208 ft. (8,598 m)

Lhotse
Tibet
27,923 ft. (8,511 m)

Makalu I
Nepal/Tibet
27,824 ft. (8,480 m)

World's 5 Longest River Systems

Nile
Tanzania/Uganda/Sudan/Egypt
4,145 mi.
(6,670 km)

Amazon
Peru/Brazil
4,007 mi.
(6,448 km)

Yangtze-Kiang
China
3,915 mi.
(6,300 km)

Mississippi-Missouri-Red
United States
3,710 mi.
(5,971 km)

Yenisey-Angara-Selenga
Mongolia/Russia
2,500 mi.
(4,000 km)

Physical Map of the United States

The total area of the United States is 3,794,083 sq. mi. (9,826,630 sq km), making it the third-largest country in the world. The Rocky Mountains form the "backbone" of the country and of the entire continent of North America. The Continental Divide passes through the Rockies, and the mighty Colorado, Missouri, and Rio Grande rivers begin there.

CHECK IT OUT!

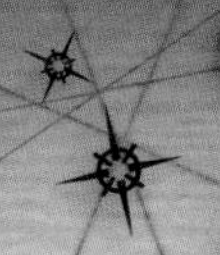

10 Largest States in Total Area

1. Alaska	663,267 sq. mi. (1,717,854 sq km)
2. Texas	268,581 sq. mi. (695,622 sq km)
3. California	163,696 sq. mi. (423,971 sq km)
4. Montana	147,042 sq. mi. (380,837 sq km)
5. New Mexico	121,589 sq. mi. (314,914 sq km)
6. Arizona	113,998 sq. mi. (295,253 sq km)
7. Nevada	110,561 sq. mi. (286,352 sq km)
8. Colorado	104,094 sq. mi. (269,602 sq km)
9. Oregon	98,381 sq. mi. (254,806 sq km)
10. Wyoming	97,814 sq. mi. (253,337 sq km)

10 Smallest States in Total Area

1. Rhode Island	1,545 sq. mi. (4,002 sq km)
2. Delaware	2,489 sq. mi. (6,446 sq km)
3. Connecticut	5,543 sq. mi. (14,356 sq km)
4. New Jersey	8,721 sq. mi. (22,587 sq km)
5. New Hampshire	9,350 sq. mi. (24,216 sq km)
6. Vermont	9,614 sq. mi. (24,900 sq km)
7. Massachusetts	10,555 sq. mi. (27,337 sq km)
8. Hawaii	10,931 sq. mi. (28,311 sq km)
9. Maryland	12,407 sq. mi. (32,134 sq km)
10. West Virginia	24,230 sq. mi. (62,755 sq km)

5 Highest U.S. Mountains

Mt. McKinley
Alaska
20,320 ft. (6,194 m)

Mt. St. Elias
Alaska-Yukon
18,008 ft. (5,489 m)

Mt. Foraker
Alaska
17,400 ft. (5,304 m)

Mt. Bona
Alaska
16,550 ft. (5,044 m)

Mt. Blackburn
Alaska
16,390 ft. (4,996 m)

10 Longest U.S. Rivers

Mississippi
2,348 mi. (3,779 km)

Missouri
2,315 mi. (3,726 km)

Yukon
1,979 mi. (3,186 km)

Rio Grande
1,900 mi. (3,058 km)

Arkansas
1,459 mi. (2,348 km)

Red
1,290 mi. (2,076 km)

Columbia
1,243 mi. (2,000 km)

Snake
1,038 mi. (1,670 km)

Ohio
981 mi. (1,579 km)

St. Lawrence
800 mi. (1,287 km)

10 Largest U.S. National Historical Parks

(By total acreage and hectares)

Chaco Culture
New Mexico
33,960 acres (13,743 h)

Cumberland Gap
Kentucky/Tennessee/Virginia
22,365 acres (9,050 h)

Jean Lafitte
Louisiana
20,001 acres (8,094 h)

Chesapeake & Ohio Canal
Maryland/West Virginia/Washington, DC
19,615 acres (7,938 h)

Klondike Gold Rush
Alaska/Washington
12,996 acres (5,259 h)

Colonial
Virginia
8,676 acres (3,511 h)

Pecos
New Mexico
6,669 acres (2,699 h)

Nez Perce
Idaho/Montana/Oregon/Washington
4,570 acres (1,849 h)

Harpers Ferry
West Virginia/Maryland/Virginia
3,647 acres (1,476 h)

Cedar Creek & Belle Grove
Virginia
3,712 acres (1,502 h)

The Great Lakes—Facts and Figures

Lake Superior

Area	31,700 sq. mi. (82,103 sq km)
Borders	Minnesota, Wisconsin, Michigan (United States); Ontario (Canada)
Major Ports	Duluth, Superior, Sault Ste. Marie (United States); Sault Ste. Marie, Thunder Bay (Canada)

Lake Huron

Area	23,000 sq. mi. (59,570 sq km)
Borders	Michigan (United States); Ontario (Canada)
Major Ports	Port Huron (United States); Sarnia (Canada)

Lake Michigan

Area	22,300 sq. mi. (57,570 sq km)
Borders	Illinois, Indiana, Michigan, Wisconsin (United States)
Major Ports	Milwaukee, Racine, Kenosha, Chicago, Gary, Muskegon (United States)

Lake Erie

Area	9,940 sq. mi. (25,745 sq km)
Borders	Michigan, New York, Ohio, Pennsylvania (United States); Ontario (Canada)
Major Ports	Toledo, Sandusky, Lorain, Cleveland, Erie, Buffalo (United States)

Lake Ontario

Area	7,340 sq. mi. (19,011 sq km)
Borders	New York (United States); Ontario (Canada)
Major Ports	Rochester, Oswego (United States); Toronto, Hamilton (Canada)

The Great Lakes from space

An easy way to remember the names of the Great Lakes is the word *HOMES*:

H URON
O NTARIO
M ICHIGAN
E RIE
S UPERIOR

National Parks by State

Alaska
Denali
Gates of the Arctic
Glacier Bay
Katmai
Kenai Fjords
Kobuk Valley
Lake Clark
Wrangell—St. Elias

Arizona
Grand Canyon
Petrified Forest
Saguaro

Arkansas
Hot Springs

California
Channel Islands
Death Valley
Joshua Tree
Kings Canyon
Lassen Volcanic
Redwood
Sequoia
Yosemite

Colorado
Black Canyon of the Gunnison
Great Sand Dunes
Mesa Verde
Rocky Mountain

Florida
Biscayne
Dry Tortugas
Everglades

Hawaii
Haleakala
Hawaii Volcanoes

Idaho
Yellowstone

Kentucky
Mammoth Cave

Maine
Acadia

Michigan
Isle Royale

Minnesota
Voyageurs

Montana
Glacier
Yellowstone

Nevada
Death Valley
Great Basin

New Mexico
Carlsbad Caverns

North Carolina
Great Smoky Mountains

North Dakota
Theodore Roosevelt

Ohio
Cuyahoga Valley

Oregon
Crater Lake

South Carolina
Congaree

South Dakota
Badlands
Wind Cave

Tennessee
Great Smoky Mountains

Texas
Big Bend
Guadalupe Mountains

Utah
Arches
Bryce Canyon
Capitol Reef
Canyonlands
Zion

Virginia
Shenandoah

Washington
Mount Rainier
North Cascades
Olympic

Wyoming
Grand Teton
Yellowstone

10 Most Visited U.S. National Parks

Park (Location)	Visitors in 2008
1. Great Smoky Mountains (Tennessee/North Carolina)	9,044,010
2. Grand Canyon (Arizona)	4,425,314
3. Yosemite (California)	3431,514
4. Olympic (Washington)	3,081,451
5. Yellowstone (Wyoming/Montana/Idaho)	3,066,580
6. Cuyahoga Valley (Ohio)	2,828,233
7. Rocky Mountain (Colorado)	2,757,390
8. Zion (Utah)	2,690,154
9. Grand Teton (Wyoming)	2,485,987
10. Acadia (Maine)	2,075,857

U.S. National Memorials

Memorial	State	Description
Arkansas Post	Arkansas	First permanent French settlement in the lower Mississippi River valley
Arlington House (Robert E. Lee Memorial)	Virginia	Lee's home overlooking the Potomac
Chamizal	Texas	Commemorates 1963 settlement of 99-year border dispute with Mexico
Coronado	Arizona	Commemorates first European exploration of the Southwest
De Soto	Florida	Commemorates 16th-century Spanish explorations
Father Marquette	Michigan	Commemorates Father Jacques Marquette, a French Jesuit missionary who helped establish Michigan's first European settlement at Sault Ste. Marie in 1668
Federal Hall	New York	First seat of U.S. government under the Constitution
Flight 93	Pennsylvania	Commemorates the passengers and crew of Flight 93, who lost their lives to bring down a plane headed to attack the nation's capital on September 11, 2001
Fort Caroline	Florida	On St. Johns River; overlooks site of a French Huguenot colony
Fort Clatsop	Oregon	Lewis and Clark encampment, 1805—1806
Franklin Delano Roosevelt	DC	Statues of President Roosevelt and First Lady Eleanor Roosevelt, as well as waterfalls and gardens; dedicated May 2, 1997
General Grant	New York	Grant's Tomb
Hamilton Grange	New York	Home of Alexander Hamilton
Jefferson National Expansion Monument	Missouri	Commemorates westward expansion
Johnstown Flood	Pennsylvania	Commemorates tragic flood of 1889
Korean War Veterans	DC	Dedicated in 1995; honors those who served in the Korean War
Lincoln Boyhood	Indiana	Site of Lincoln cabin, boyhood home, and grave of Lincoln's mother
Lincoln Memorial	DC	Marble statue of the 16th U.S. president
Lyndon B. Johnson Grove on the Potomac	DC	Honors the 36th president; overlooks the Potomac River vista of the capital
Mount Rushmore	South Dakota	World-famous sculpture of four presidents
Oklahoma City	Oklahoma	Commemorates the April 18, 1995, bombing of the Alfred P. Murrah Federal Building
Perry's Victory and International Peace Memorial	Ohio	The world's largest Doric column, constructed 1912—1915, promotes pursuit of international peace through arbitration and disarmament
Roger Williams	Rhode Island	Memorial to founder of Rhode Island
Thaddeus Kosciuszko	Pennsylvania	Memorial to Polish hero of the American Revolution
Theodore Roosevelt Island	DC	Statue of the 26th president in wooded island sanctuary
Thomas Jefferson Memorial	DC	Statue of the 3rd president in a circular, colonnaded structure
USS Arizona	Hawaii	Memorializes American losses at Pearl Harbor
Vietnam Veterans	DC	Black granite wall inscribed with names of those missing or killed in action in the Vietnam War
Washington Monument	DC	Obelisk honoring the 1st U.S. president
World War II	DC	Oval plaza with central pool commemorating those who fought and died in World War II
Wright Brothers	North Carolina	Site of first powered flight

U.S. National Battlefields

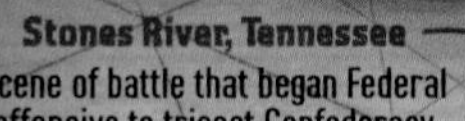

Stones River, Tennessee
Scene of battle that began Federal offensive to trisect Confederacy

Fort Donelson, Tennessee
Site of first major Union victory

Antietam, Maryland
Battle here ended first Confederate invasion of North, Sept. 17, 1862

Big Hole, Montana
Site of major battle between Nez Perce and U.S. Army

Petersburg, Virginia
Scene of 10-month Union campaigns, 1864—1865

Fort Necessity, Pennsylvania
Some of the first battles of French and Indian War

Wilson's Creek, Missouri
Scene of Civil War battle for control of Missouri

Tupelo, Mississippi
Site of crucial Civil War battle over Sherman's supply line

Cowpens, South Carolina
American Revolution battlefield

Monocacy, Maryland
Civil War battle in defense of Washington, DC, fought here July 9

Moores Creek, North Carolina
1776 battle between Patriots and Loyalists commemorated here

Stats on the Statue of Liberty

The Statue of Liberty was designed by French sculptor Frederic Auguste Bartholdi and arrived in 214 packing cases from Rouen, France, in June 1885. The completed statue was dedicated on October 28, 1886, by President Grover Cleveland. It was designated a National Monument in 1924 and is one of America's most famous symbols of freedom.

Part of Statue	Measurement
Height from heel to torch	151 ft. 1 in. (45.3 m)
Height from base of pedestal to torch	305 ft. 1 in. (91.5 m)
Length of hand	16 ft. 5 in. (5 m)
Length of index finger	8 ft. 0 in. (24 m)
Circumference at second finger joint	3 ft. 6 in. (1 m)
Size of fingernail	13 x 10 in. (33 x 25 cm)
Height of head from chin to cranium	17 ft. 3 in. (5 m)
Thickness of head from ear to ear	10 ft. 0 in. (3 m)
Distance across eye	2 ft. 6 in. (0.76 m)
Length of nose	4 ft. 6 in. (14 m)
Length of right arm	42 ft. 0 in. (12.8 m)
Thickness of right arm at thickest point	12 ft. 0 in. (3.7 m)
Thickness of waist	35 ft. 0 in. (10.7 m)
Width of mouth	3 ft. 0 in. (1 m)
Length of tablet	23 ft. 7 in. (7.2 m)
Width of tablet	13 ft. 7 in. (4.1 m)
Thickness of tablet	2 ft. 0 in. (0.6 m)

Keep it Clean!

Ever had a cold? Who hasn't? Colds and flu are spread by tiny pathogens called viruses, which like to get into your body through your eyes, nose, and mouth. They're riding around on doorknobs, pencils, desks, and faucets, just waiting for a chance to jump aboard when you reach out and touch something. The next thing you know, you're rubbing your eye, scratching your nose, or touching your lips, and *BOOM!*—the virus has an invitation. So it's really important to keep your hands germ-free at all times. Wash!

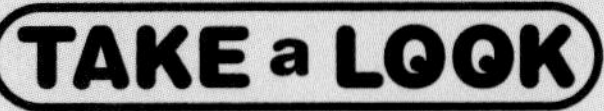

After poking around in this section—and getting up close and personal with your body systems—take a good look at your personal health habits. How do you measure up? What are some things you can do to be as healthy as possible? What are your favorite "power" foods? What's your favorite way to exercise?

CHECK IT OUT!

When you wash your hands, be sure to use warm water and lots of soap—and take your time. Health experts say you should wash your hands for 20 seconds every time you come inside. Not sure how long 20 seconds is? Try singing "Happy Birthday" when you wash your hands. (Sing it softly or to yourself if others start to object!)

The Six Systems of the Human Body

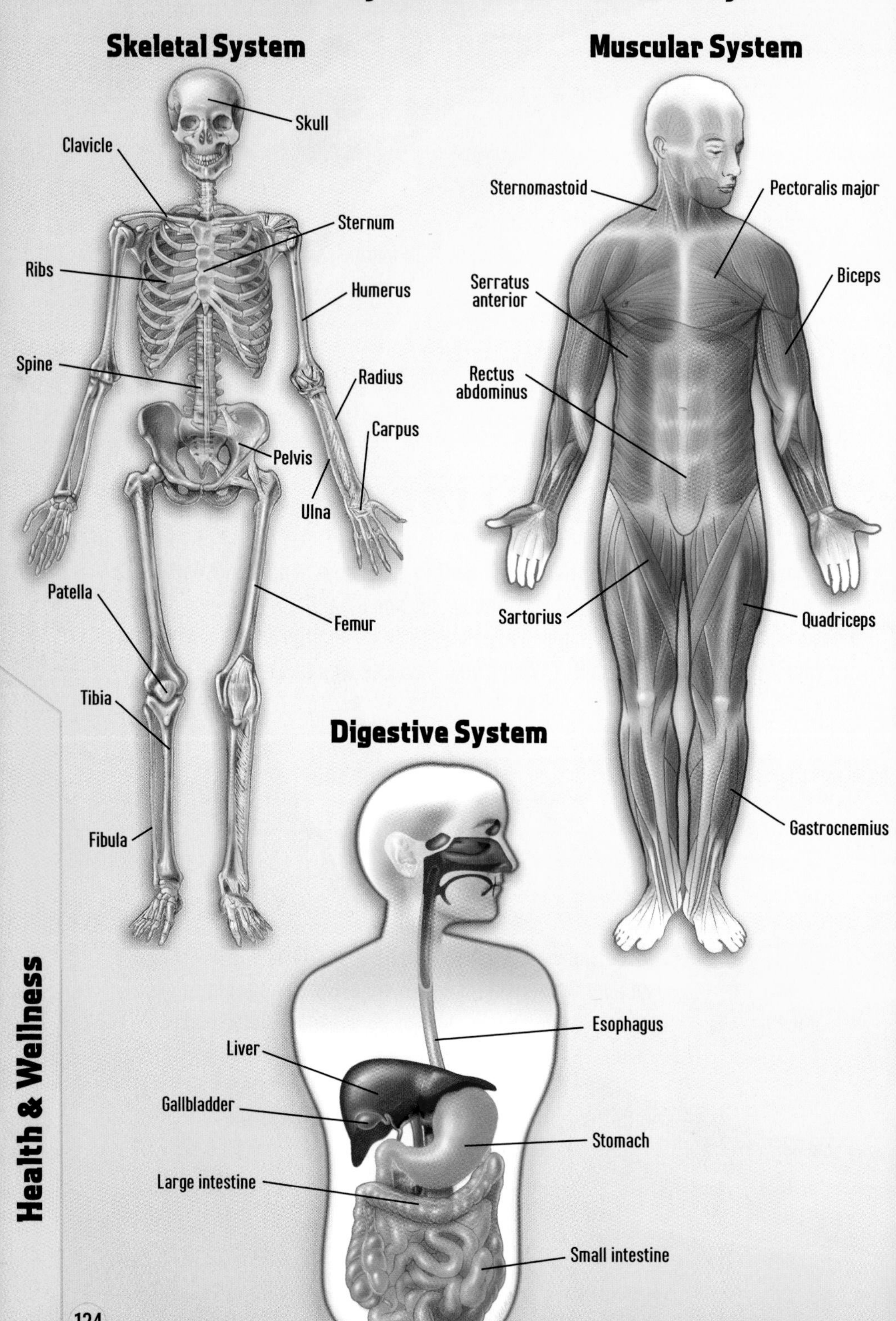

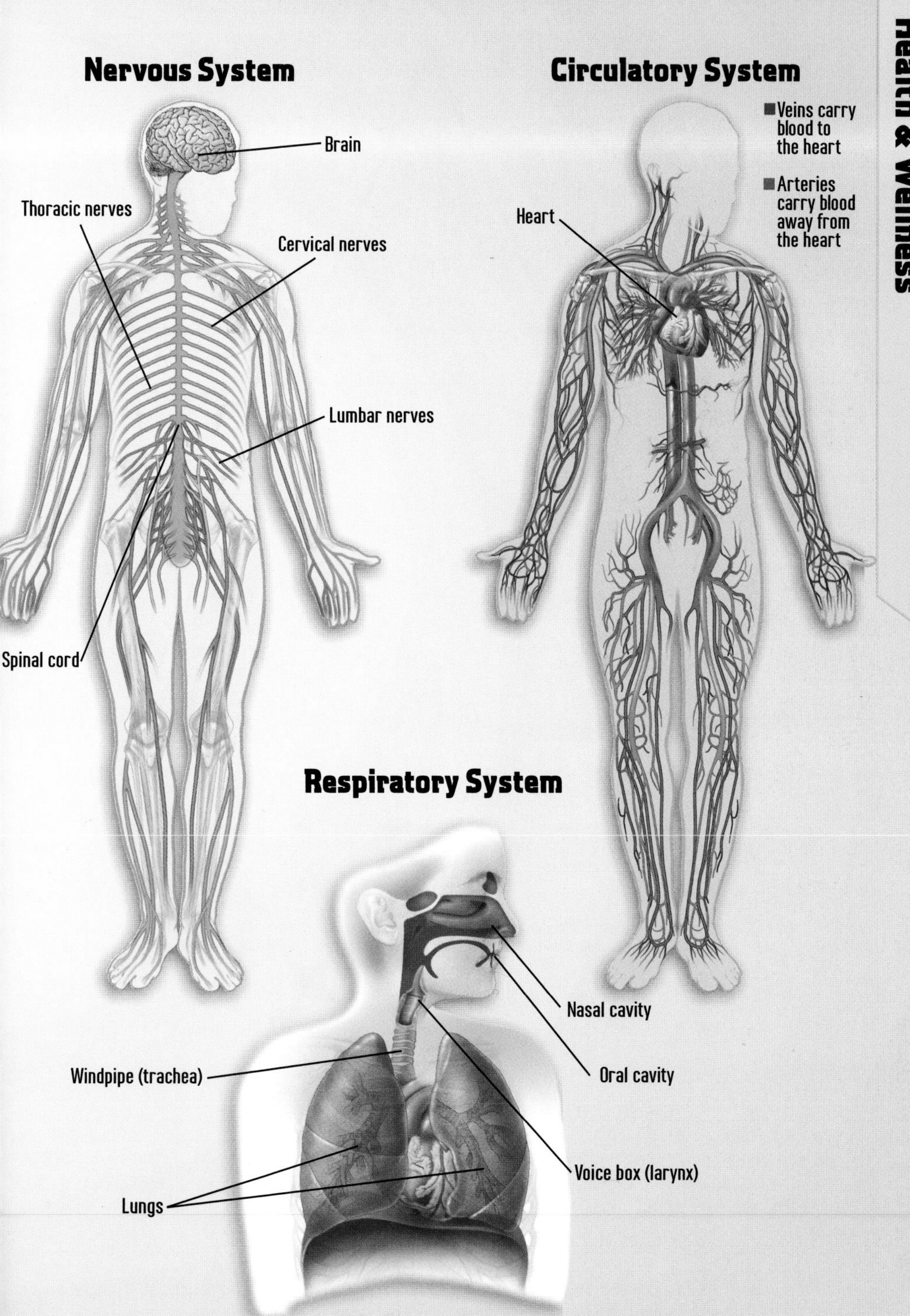
Nervous System
Brain
Thoracic nerves
Cervical nerves
Lumbar nerves
Spinal cord
Circulatory System
Veins carry blood to the heart
Arteries carry blood away from the heart
Heart
Respiratory System
Nasal cavity
Oral cavity
Windpipe (trachea)
Voice box (larynx)
Lungs

The New Food Pyramid

In 2005, the U.S. Department of Agriculture (USDA) created a new food pyramid. The colored parts of the pyramid stand for different food groups. The width of each part shows what portion of your daily diet should be from that food group.

The amounts shown below are based on what a 12-year-old boy of average height and weight who is moderately active should eat every day. To figure out your own personal food pyramid plan, go to **www.mypyramid.gov**.

The most popular fruit in the world is one you may think is a vegetable—the tomato. Scientifically speaking, a tomato is considered a fruit because it comes from a flowering plant that contains seeds. Sixty million tons of tomatoes are produced every year.

CHECK IT OUT!

Grains	Vegetables	Fruits	Milk	Meat & Beans
Seven ounces of bread, cereal, crackers, rice, or pasta every day. At least half should be whole grains.	Three cups every day, fresh or frozen. Dark green, orange, light green—mix it up!	Two cups of nature's sweet treats a day. Go easy on the fruit juice.	Three cups a day. Choose nonfat or lowfat milk products.	Six ounces of lean protein a day: meat, fish, or poultry, or nuts, seeds, beans, and peas.

Oils

Oils aren't a food group, but you need some for good health. Nuts and fish are good sources. Be sure to limit sugars and solid fats such as butter. Read the labels—you might be surprised!

Top 5 Favorite Kids' Activities

According to a survey by the Outdoor Foundation, these are the favorite activities of kids between ages 6 and 17:

1. Bicycling
2. Running Jogging Trail Running
3. Skateboarding
4. Fishing
5. Wildlife Viewing

The survey shows that the number of Americans who participated in outdoor activities increased in 2007. That's good. However, the number of kids participating decreased by 11 percent. That's bad. The sharpest drop was among kids 6 to 12. Whatever your favorite activity is, go for it!

Your Amazing Body, by the Numbers

Your heart pumps blood along 60,000 miles (97,000 km) of veins and arteries. It beats 100,000 times a day—that's 40 million times a year and more than 3 billion times in an average lifetime.

Your brain weighs only about 3 pounds (1.4 kg), but it has about 100 billion nerve cells. Nerves help you think, move, dream, feel happy or sad, and regulate unconscious activities such as digesting food and breathing.

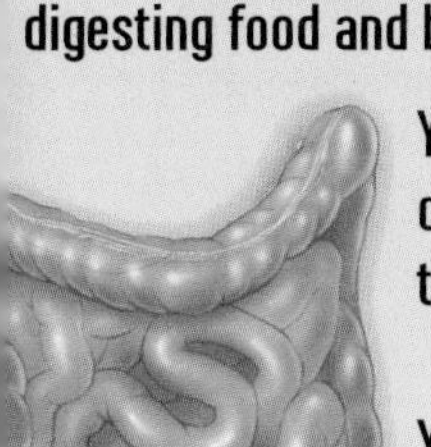

Your digestive system consists of about 30 feet (9 m) of tubes that carry food along a journey from top to bottom, squeezing out nutrients to keep you healthy and processing waste materials.

Your skin is your body's largest organ, weighing about 8 pounds (3.6 kg) and measuring about 22 square feet (2 sq m). Be good to your skin by keeping it clean and well protected from the Sun.

Inventors & Inventions

Flip a Switch and Say Thanks

From texting to snowboarding to brushing your teeth and even turning on a light, you've got an inventor to thank for almost everything you do. Sometimes you have more than one. For instance, without Benjamin Franklin, we'd still be in the dark. Franklin's famous experiment with lightning showed the world that this force was a form of electricity—a power that could be harnessed and used. Thomas Edison invented the electric lightbulb and lit up our world.

Phoning It In

Nowadays we take for granted how easy it is to chat or text on a cell phone. But someone had to invent the technology first. In this case it was Martin Cooper, in 1973. Actually, a hundred years before that you couldn't even talk on a regular telephone. Thank Alexander Graham Bell for that.

Moving Along

Some inventions made it easier for us to get from one place to another:

- Richard Trevithick of England invented the locomotive in 1803.
- Gottlieb Daimler of Germany came up with the first gas-engine motorcycle in 1885. In Germany that same year, Karl Benz came up with the first automobile with an internal combustion engine.
- American Benjamin Holt made the first tractor in 1904.
- The Wright brothers, Wilbur and Orville, gave us the first airplane in 1903. (Thankfully, France's Louis-Sébastien Lenormand had already given the world the parachute in 1783!)

SWEET SURPRISES

Percy Lebaron Spencer had a chocolate bar in his pocket as he worked on a new technology for radar called magnetrons in 1945. The magnetrons melted the chocolate and got him thinking. Many experiments and two years later, he invented the first microwave oven! (It was as big as a full-size refrigerator.)

This kind of accidental discovery happens all the time in the process of inventing. It's called serendipity. Other accidental inventions were penicillin, vulcanized rubber, Velcro—and the Popsicle. The frozen fruit treat was accidentally invented in 1905 by 11-year-old Frank Epperson. Frank left his glass of fruit punch out on the porch with a stir stick in it. The weather turned cold; the punch froze with the stick in it, and the Epsicle ice pop was created. Epperson's children named it Popsicle for their dad many years later.

TAKE a LOOK

Take a look at your day. Make a list of all the inventions that impact you every day. Then have a peek through this section to see who's responsible for making it all possible. Can you come up with any new ideas for inventions to make your life better? Tastier? Comfier?

CHECK IT OUT!

Thomas Edison was one of the most important inventors ever. He had more than 1,000 patents, including one for a motion picture viewer and one for a phonograph. He also set up the first major electric power station in the world in New York City. Edison's accomplishments were so admired that several successful female inventors were nicknamed the Lady Edisons as a compliment. One of them, Beulah Henry, held 49 patents, including one for the vacuum ice-cream freezer.

Date
Invention
Inventor

3500 BC
Wheeled vehicle
Mesopotamia

105
Paper
China

640
Windmill
Persia

900
Gunpowder
China

1447
Movable type
Johannes Gutenberg

1590
Microscope
Zacharias Jansen

1592
Thermometer
Galileo Galilei

1608
Telescope
Hans Lippershey

1656
Pendulum clock
Christian Huygens

1709
Piano
Bartolomeo Cristofori

1752
Lightning rod
Benjamin Franklin

1765
Steam engine
James Watt

1783
Hot-air balloon
Joseph-Michel and Jacques-Étienne Montgolfier

1783
Parachute
Louis-Sébastien Lenormand

1784
Bifocal lens
Benjamin Franklin

1785
Power loom
Edmund Cartwright

1793
Cotton gin
Eli Whitney

1803
Steam locomotive
Richard Trevithick

1816
Photography
Joseph Nicéphore Niépce

1821
Electric motor
Michael Faraday

1829
Braille
Louis Braille

1835
Revolver
Samuel Colt

1837
Telegraph
Samuel Morse

1839
Vulcanized rub
Charles Goody

1846
Sewing machine
Elias Howe

1865
Antiseptic
Joseph List

Eleva
Elis

D
Alf

CHECK IT OUT!

Robert Fulton launched the first commercially successful steamship in the United States, the *Clermont*, in 1807. But Fulton did not invent the steamship. Frenchman Claude de Jouffroy d'Abbans is credited with building the first boat to run successfully on steam, in 1783. In 1802, a Scottish inventor named William Symington built a steam-powered tugboat that ran on the Forth and Clyde Canal. In fact, inventors had been working with ways to use a steam engine for marine power since the early 1700s.

Important Inventions and Their Inventors

These are just a few of the inventions that have shaped our world and changed our lives. The inventors listed are either those who received patents for the invention or the ones widely credited with introducing the version of the invention we use today. But in many cases, other inventors contributed to the invention by doing experiments or making earlier versions. Do some additional research for the whole story behind these inventions and others.

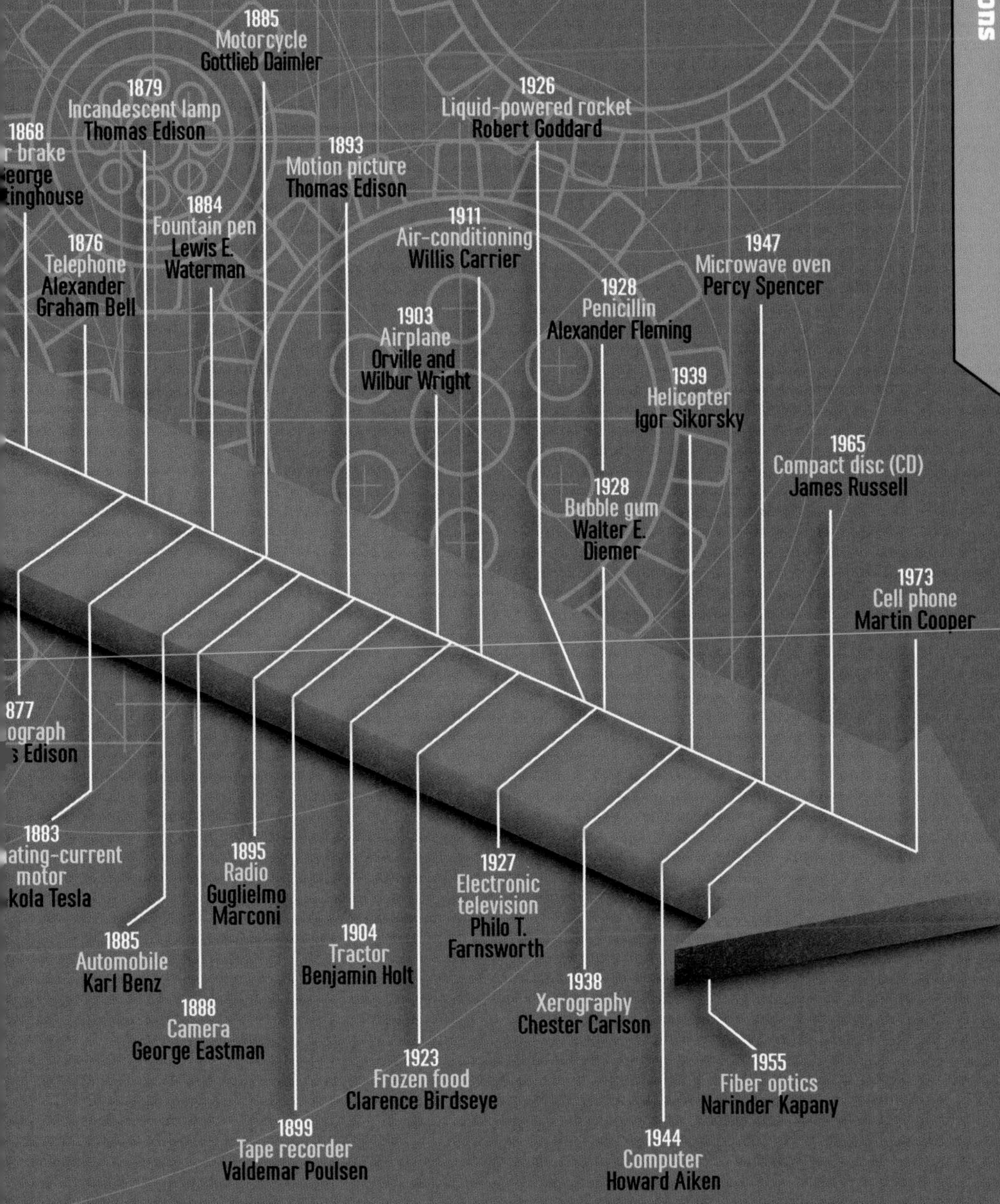

Languages

Let's Talk

There are thousands of languages spoken around the world. A language is a system of communicating by using signals, sounds, or letters that all mean something. Language lets people express written and spoken thoughts in a way that can be understood by others. Though other animals may communicate with each other and with people, strictly speaking, language is thought to be mostly a human skill.

Speak English?

William Shakespeare was a poet and playwright in the late 16th and early 17th centuries. His words still communicate thoughts and ideas, but the English language has changed a lot since his time—and it's still changing. Grammar rules come and go, new words are adopted, and common phrases and sayings evolve. A language that is developing and changing is considered a living language. A language is considered dead when it is no longer spoken as a native language.

Take a look at the following sentences by Shakespeare. Can you match them up to the modern translations? (Answers are on page 271.)

Hell

Hola

おはよう

ございま

Bonsoir

你好

Guten

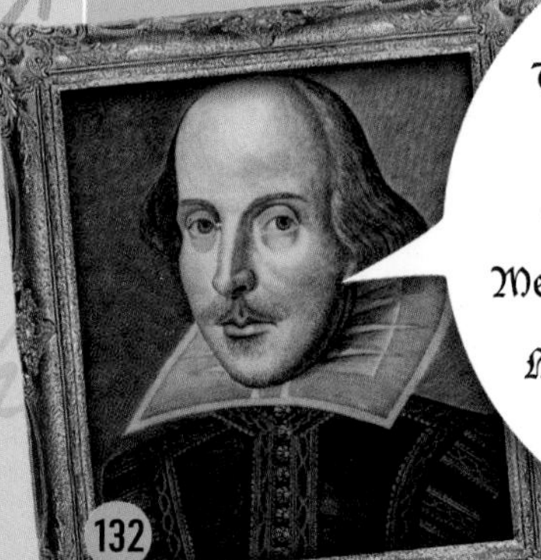

Shakespeare

They that thrive well take counsel of their friends.

Stand and unfold thyself.

Mere prattle, without practice.

Headstrong liberty is lash'd with woe.

Modern

It's all just talk.

Too much freedom can be trouble.

Tell me who you are.

It's good to get advice from your friends.

TALK AMERICA

Most Americans speak English at home, but it's certainly not the only language spoken in the United States. The history of our country begins with people coming here from all over the world. As a result, our country is a rich blend of many languages. Spanish, Chinese, French, and German are a just few of the languages being spoken in our schools and homes.

TAKE a LOOK

Hi may mean "hello" to English speakers, but to the Japanese *hai* also means "yes." Take a look at pages 135 and 136 to see if you can tell your *domo* from your *gogo*.

안녕하세요

שָׁלוֹם

Ciao

Aloha

Several times a year, the *Oxford English Dictionary* updates its entry list to include new English words. One recent addition is *achy-breaky*, which is from a song made popular in the 1990s by singer Billy Ray Cyrus, the real-life and TV dad of Miley Cyrus/Hannah Montana.

achy-breaky, adj.
Aching, hurt; (also) sad, heart-rending

Common Words and Phrases in Selected Languages

MANDARIN CHINESE

Hello	Ni hao (nee how)
Good-bye	Zài jiàn (zay GEE-en)
Yes	Shide (SURE-due)
No	Bu shi (BOO sure)
Please	Qing (ching
Thank you	Xièxiè (shieh-shieh
You're welcome	Búkèqi (boo-keh-chee
Excuse me	Duìbúqi (doo-ee-boo-chee

SPANISH

Hello	Hola (OH-lah)
Good-bye	Adiós (ah-dee-OHSS)
Good morning	Buenas días (BWAY-nahs DEE-ahs)
Good afternoon	Buenas tardes (BWAY-nahs TAHR-dehs)
Good evening	Buenas noches (BWAY-nahs NOH-chehs)
Yes	Sí (SEE)
No	No (NOH)
Please	Por favor (por fa-VOHR)
Thank you	Gracias (GRAH-see-ahs)
You're welcome	De nada (DE nada)
What's going on?	¿Qué pasa? (kay PAH-sah)
How are you?	¿Cómo está usted? (COH-mo es-TAH oo-STEHD)

GERMAN

Hello	Guten Tag (GOO-tin TAHK)
Good-bye	Auf Wiedersehen (ahf VEE-dehr-zeh-hehn)
Good morning	Guten Morgen (GOO-tin MOR-gun)
Yes	Ja (yah)
No	Nein (nain)
Please	Bitte (BIT-uh)
Thank you	Danke (DAHN-keh)
You're welcome	Bitte schön (BIT-uh shane)

Privet!

góðan dag

salut

ITALIAN

Hi, 'bye (informal)	Ciao (chow)
Good-bye	Arrivederci (ah-ree-vay-DEHR-chee)
Good morning, good afternoon, or a general hello	Buon giorno (bwohn JOOR-noh)
Yes	Sì (SEE)
No	No (NOH)
Please	Per favore (purr fa-VO-ray)
Thank you	Grazie (GRAH-tsee-ay)
You're welcome	Prego (PRAY-go)
How are you?	Come sta? (KOH-may STAH)
Fine, very well	Molto bene (MOHL-toh BAY-nay)
Excuse me	Scusi (SKOO-zee)

EGYPTIAN ARABIC

Good morning	Sabah el khair (sa-BAH el KHAIR)
Good-bye	Ma salama (MA sa-LA-ma)
Yes	Aiwa (aye-wa)
No	La (la)
Please	Min fadlak (min FAD-lak)
Thank you	Shukran (SHU-kran)
No problem	Ma fee mushkila (ma FEE mush-KI-la)
How are you?	Izzayak (iz-ZAY-ak)
What is your name?	Ismak ay? (IS-mak AY)

JAPANESE

Hi	Konnichiwa (koh-nee-chee-wah)
Good-bye	Ja mata (jahh mah-tah)
Yes	Hai (hah-ee)
No	Iie (EE-eh)
Good morning	Ohayō gozaimasu (oh-hah-yohh goh-zah-ee-mahs)
Excuse me	Sumimasen (soo-mee-mah-sehn)
Pleased to meet you	Yoroshiku (yoh-roh-shee-koo)
One	Ichi (ee-chee)
Thank you	Dōmo arigatō (dohh-moh ah-ri-gah-toh)

hoi

Common Words and Phrases in Selected Languages (continued)

FRENCH

Hello	Bonjour (bohn-zhoor)
Good-bye	Au revoir (oh reh-vwah)
Yes	Oui (wee)
No	Non (no)
Excuse me	Pardonnez-moi (par-dough-nay mwah)
Please	S'il vous plaît (see voo play)
Thank you	Merci (mare-SEE)
How are you?	Comment allez-vous? (co-mahn-tah-lay voo)

KOREAN

Hello	Anyŏng haseyo (ahn-n'yohng hah-say-yoh)
Good-bye	Anyŏng-hi kyeseyo (ahn-n'yohng-he kuh-say-yoh)
Please	Jwe-song-ha-ji-mahn (chey-song-hah-gee-mon)
Thank you	Kamsahamnida (kahm-sah-hahm-need-dah)
Excuse me	Miam hamnida (Me-ahn hahm-nee-dah)
One	Hana (hah-nah)
Ten	Yeol (yuhl)

xin chào

Hi

NIGERIAN

(four of the major Nigerian language groups)

English	Fulani	Hausa	Ibo	Yoruba
I'm fine	Jam tan (JAM-taan)	Kalau (KA-lay-U)	Adimnma (ah-DEE-mm-NMAA)	A dupe (ah-DEW-pa
one	gogo (GO-quo)	daya (DA-ya)	otu (o-TOO)	eni (EE-nee)
two	didi (DEE-dee)	biyu (BEE-you)	abua (ah-BOO-ah)	eji (EE-gee)
three	tati (TA-tea)	uku (OO-coo)	ato (ah-TOE)	eta (EE-ta)
nine	jeenayi (gee-NA-yee)	tara (TAA-ra)	iteghete (IT-egg-HE-tee)	esan (EE-san)
ten	sappo (SAP-poe)	goma (GO-ma)	iri (EE-ree)	ewa (EE-wa)

Which Languages Are Spoken Most?

The following languages have the most speakers in the world. The languages combine individual varieties and dialects that may have different names. The numbers include only first-language (mother-tongue) speakers.

Language	Estimated Number of Speakers (in millions)
Chinese	1,213
Spanish	329
English	328
Arabic	221
Hindi	182
Bengali	181
Portuguese	178
Russian	144
Japanese	122
German	90
Javanese	85
Abaza	83
Lahnda	78
Telugu	70
Vietnamese	69
French	68
Marathi	68
Korean	66
Tamil	66
Italian	62
Urdu	61

dzień dobry

talofa

hej

alô

Portugal isn't the only place where people speak Portuguese. About 150 million people speak it in Brazil, where it is the official language.

Math

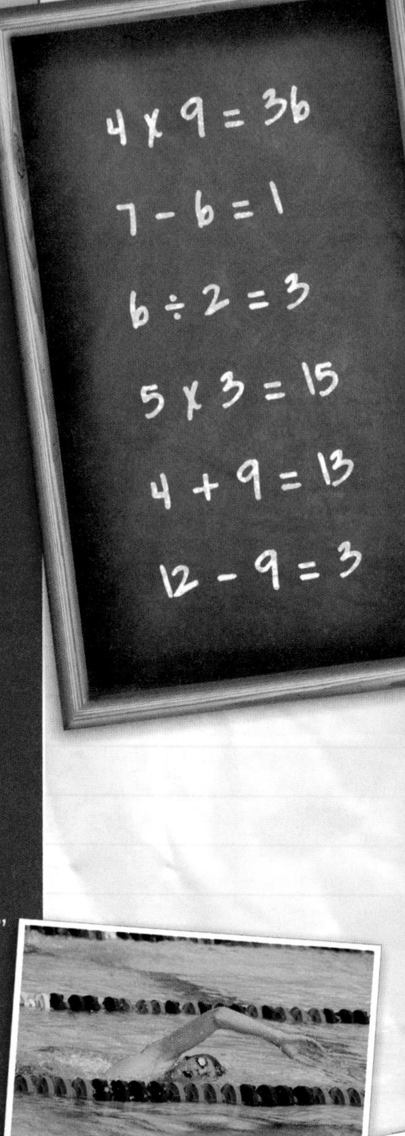

Got Your Number

Humans have been using numbers to help understand the world around them for a very long time—about 20,000 years, according to some scientists. That's the estimated age of a bone tool with three carved columns of numbers found in the Congo area of Africa in 1960. Called the Ishango bone, the relic is thought by some mathematicians to be a kind of ancient calculator—proof that even way back then, people knew how to multiply.

Give Us a Hand

Over many thousands of years, numerical systems kept developing. One ancient Egyptian system used straight lines representing small numbers and a special mark for the number ten. In the 7th century, scholars in India invented a system in which all numbers were made from only ten symbols—0, 1, 2, 3, 4, 5, 6, 7, 8, and 9. This was the basis for the decimal system we use today.

Why ten? It's the number of fingers on our two hands. In fact, another word for both numbers and fingers is "digits."

It All Adds Up

Today we use numbers all day long, in countless activities.

- "I am 12 years old."
- "When are we going to get there?"
- "Hey! Who ate three-quarters of my pizza?"

Even tiny numbers can be important. A split second can be the difference between an Olympic gold medal and a so-so finish. The circumference of an NCAA regulation basketball can't be greater than 30 inches (76.2 cm).

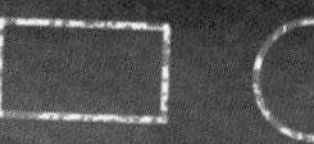

But math goes way beyond numbers. The octagon-shaped stop sign, the circular wheel on your bike, the rectangle of your desk—they're examples of a part of math called geometry. Buildings, cars, trains, planes, and even toys involve structure, which depends on math, too. And then there's logic—drawing conclusions that make sense about time, distance, money, and so many other things. We use math theories to predict and describe everything from which TV shows people will watch to where the tennis player will hit the ball to how people will spend their money. You name the process—it starts with math.

TAKE a LOOK

Browse through this chapter and then write down all the ways math enters into your daily life. Include whole numbers, fractions, decimals, minutes, hours, geometric shapes, notes on a musical scale, percentages, estimates, and so on. If you have any time left over, start counting to one million. It should take you about 12 days. If you still have time on your hands, count to one billion. Allowing one second per count, it will take about 32 years.

The googol is the number 1 followed by 100 zeros (see below). Mathematicians say that the googolplex, the number 1 followed by a googol of zeros, is the largest named number in the world.

10,000,000,000,000,000,000,000,000,000,000,
000,000,000,000,000,000,000,000,
000,000,000,000,000,000,000,000,000,
000,000,000,000,000,000,000

MULTIPLICATION TABLE

	1	2	3	4	5	6	7	8	9	10	11	12
1	1	2	3	4	5	6	7	8	9	10	11	12
2	2	4	6	8	10	12	14	16	18	20	22	24
3	3	6	9	12	15	18	21	24	27	30	33	36
4	4	8	12	16	20	24	28	32	36	40	44	48
5	5	10	15	20	25	30	35	40	45	50	55	60
6	6	12	18	24	30	36	42	48	54	60	66	72
7	7	14	21	28	35	42	49	56	63	70	77	84
8	8	16	24	32	40	48	56	64	72	80	88	96
9	9	18	27	36	45	54	63	72	81	90	99	108
10	10	20	30	40	50	60	70	80	90	100	110	120
11	11	22	33	44	55	66	77	88	99	110	121	132
12	12	24	36	48	60	72	84	96	108	120	132	144

Squares and Square Roots

Multiplying a number by itself is also called squaring it (or raising it to its second power). For example, 3 squared (3^2) is 9. By the same token, the square root of 9 is 3. The symbol for square root is called a radical sign ($\sqrt{}$).

Examples of squaring

2 squared: $2^2 = 2 \times 2 = 4$

3 squared: $3^2 = 3 \times 3 = 9$

4 squared: $4^2 = 4 \times 4 = 16$

Examples of square roots

Square root of 16: $\sqrt{16} = 4$

Square root of 9: $\sqrt{9} = 3$

Square root of 4: $\sqrt{4} = 2$

SQUARE ROOTS TO 40

$\sqrt{1} = 1$	$\sqrt{36} = 6$	$\sqrt{121} = 11$	$\sqrt{256} = 16$	$\sqrt{441} = 21$	$\sqrt{676} = 26$	$\sqrt{961} = 31$	$\sqrt{1{,}296} = 36$
$\sqrt{4} = 2$	$\sqrt{49} = 7$	$\sqrt{144} = 12$	$\sqrt{289} = 17$	$\sqrt{484} = 22$	$\sqrt{729} = 27$	$\sqrt{1{,}024} = 32$	$\sqrt{1{,}369} = 37$
$\sqrt{9} = 3$	$\sqrt{64} = 8$	$\sqrt{169} = 13$	$\sqrt{324} = 18$	$\sqrt{529} = 23$	$\sqrt{784} = 28$	$\sqrt{1{,}089} = 33$	$\sqrt{1{,}444} = 38$
$\sqrt{16} = 4$	$\sqrt{81} = 9$	$\sqrt{196} = 14$	$\sqrt{361} = 19$	$\sqrt{576} = 24$	$\sqrt{841} = 29$	$\sqrt{1{,}156} = 34$	$\sqrt{1{,}521} = 39$
$\sqrt{25} = 5$	$\sqrt{100} = 10$	$\sqrt{225} = 15$	$\sqrt{400} = 20$	$\sqrt{625} = 25$	$\sqrt{900} = 30$	$\sqrt{1{,}225} = 35$	$\sqrt{1{,}600} = 40$

Some Mathematical Formulas

To find the CIRCUMFERENCE of a:

- Circle—Multiply the diameter by π

To find the AREA of a:

- Circle—Multiply the square of the radius by π
- Rectangle—Multiply the base by the height
- Sphere (surface)—Multiply the square of the radius by π and multiply by 4
- Square—Square the length of one side
- Trapezoid—Add the two parallel sides, multiply by the height, and divide by 2
- Triangle—Multiply the base by the height and divide by 2

To find the VOLUME of a:

- Cone—Multiply the square of the radius of the base by π, multiply by the height, and divide by 3
- Cube—Cube (raise to the third power) the length of one edge
- Cylinder—Multiply the square of the radius of the base by π and multiply by the height
- Pyramid—Multiply the area of the base by the height and divide by 3
- Rectangular prism—Multiply the length by the width by the height
- Sphere—Multiply the cube of the radius by π, multiply by 4, and divide by 3

π (pi) = 3.1416

LARGE NUMBERS AND HOW MANY ZEROS THEY CONTAIN

million	6	1,000,000
billion	9	1,000,000,000
trillion	12	1,000,000,000,000
uadrillion	15	1,000,000,000,000,000
uintillion	18	1,000,000,000,000,000,000
sextillion	21	1,000,000,000,000,000,000,000
septillion	24	1,000,000,000,000,000,000,000,000
octillion	27	1,000,000,000,000,000,000,000,000,000
nonillion	30	1,000,000,000,000,000,000,000,000,000,000
decillion	33	1,000,000,000,000,000,000,000,000,000,000,000

NUMBERS GLOSSARY

COUNTING NUMBERS

Counting numbers, or natural numbers, begin with the number 1 and continue into infinity.

WHOLE NUMBERS

Whole numbers are the same as counting numbers, except that the set of whole numbers begins with 0.

INTEGERS

Integers include 0, all counting numbers (called positive whole numbers), and all whole numbers less than 0 (called negative whole numbers).

RATIONAL NUMBERS

Rational numbers include any number that can be written in the form of a fraction (or a ratio), as long as the denominator (the bottom number of the fraction) is not equal to 0. All counting numbers and whole numbers are also rational numbers because all counting numbers and whole numbers can be written as fractions with a denominator equal to 1.

PRIME NUMBERS

Prime numbers are counting numbers that can be divided by only two numbers: 1 and themselves.

Prime numbers between 1 and 1,000

2, 3, 5, 7, 11, 13, 17, 19, 23, 29, 31, 37, 41, 43, 47, 53, 59, 61, 67, 71, 73, 79, 83, 89, 97, 101, 103, 107, 109, 113, 127, 131, 137, 139, 149, 151, 157, 163, 167, 173, 179, 181, 191, 193, 197, 199, 211, 223, 227, 229, 233, 239, 241, 251, 257, 263, 269, 271, 277, 281, 283, 293, 307, 311, 313, 317, 331, 337, 347, 349, 353, 359, 367, 373, 379, 383, 389, 397, 401, 409, 419, 421, 431, 433, 439, 443, 449, 457, 461, 463, 467, 479, 487, 491, 499, 503, 509, 521, 523, 541, 547, 557, 563, 569, 571, 577, 587, 593, 599, 601, 607, 613, 617, 619, 631, 641, 643, 647, 653, 659, 661, 673, 677, 683, 691, 701, 709, 719, 727, 733, 739, 743, 751, 757, 761, 769, 773, 787, 797, 809, 811, 821, 823, 827, 829, 839, 853, 857, 859, 863, 877, 881, 883, 887, 907, 911, 919, 929, 937, 941, 947, 953, 967, 971, 977, 983, 991, 997

COMPOSITE NUMBERS

Composite numbers are all counting numbers that are not prime numbers. In other words, composite numbers are numbers that have more than two factors. The number 1, because it has only one factor (itself), is not a composite number.

Composite numbers between 1 and 100

4, 6, 8, 9, 10, 12, 14, 15, 16, 18, 20, 21, 22, 24, 25, 26, 27, 28, 30, 32, 33, 34, 35, 36, 38, 39, 40, 42, 44, 45, 46, 48, 49, 50, 51, 52, 54, 55, 56, 57, 58, 60, 62, 63, 64, 65, 66, 68, 69, 70, 72, 74, 75, 76, 77, 78, 80, 81, 82, 84, 85, 86, 87, 88, 90, 91, 92, 93, 94, 95, 96, 98, 99, 100

Roman Numerals

I	1	XI	11	CD	400
II	2	XIX	19	D	500
III	3	XX	20	CM	900
IV	4	XXX	30	M	1,000
V	5	XL	40	$\overline{V}$	5,000
VI	6	L	50	$\overline{X}$	10,000
VII	7	LX	60	$\overline{L}$	50,000
VIII	8	XC	90	$\overline{C}$	100,000
IX	9	C	100	$\overline{D}$	500,000
X	10	CC	200	$\overline{M}$	1,000,000

Fractions, Decimals, and Percents

To find the equivalent of a fraction in decimal form, divide the numerator (top number) by the denominator (bottom number). To change from a decimal to a percent, multiply by 100. To change from a percent to a decimal, divide by 100.

Fraction	Decimal	Percent
1/16 (= 2/32)	0.0625	6.25
1/8 (= 2/16)	0.125	12.5
3/16 (= 6/32)	0.1875	18.75
1/4 (= 2/8; = 4/12)	0.25	25.0
5/16 (= 10/32)	0.1325	31.25
1/3 (= 2/6; = 4/12)	0.333	33.3
3/8 (= 6/16)	0.375	37.5
7/16 (= 14/32)	0.4375	43.75
1/2 (= 2/4; = 4/8; = 8/16)	0.5	50.0
9/16 (= 18/32)	0.5625	56.25
5/8 (= 10/16)	0.625	62.5
2/3 (= 4/6; = 8/12)	0.666	66.6
11/16 (= 22/32)	0.6875	68.75
3/4 (= 6/8; = 12/16)	0.75	75.0
13/16 (= 26/32)	0.8125	81.25
7/8 (= 14/16)	0.875	87.5
15/16 (= 30/32)	0.9375	93.75
1 (= 2/2; = 4/4; = 8/8; = 16/16)	1.0	100.0

Geometry Glossary

Acute angle	Any angle that measures less than 90°
Angle	Two rays that have the same endpoint form an angle
Area	The amount of surface inside a closed figure
Chord	A line segment whose endpoints are on a circle
Circumference	The distance around a circle
Congruent figures	Geometric figures that are the same size and shape
Degree (angle)	A unit for measuring angles
Diameter	A chord that passes through the center of a circle
Endpoint	The end of a line segment
Line of symmetry	A line that divides a figure into two identical parts if the figure is folded along the line
Obtuse angle	Any angle that measures greater than 90°
Perimeter	The distance around the outside of a plane figure
Pi (π)	The ratio of the circumference of a circle to its diameter; when rounded to the nearest hundredth, pi equals 3.14
Polygon	A simple closed figure whose sides are straight lines
Protractor	An instrument used to measure angles
Quadrilateral	A polygon with four sides
Radius	A straight line that connects the center of a circle to any point on the circumference of the circle
Ray	A straight line with one endpoint
Rectangle	A four-sided figure with four right angles
Right angle	An angle that measures 90°
Square	A rectangle with congruent sides and 90° angles in all four corners
Surface area	The total outside area of an object
Symmetrical	A figure that, when folded along a line of symmetry, has two halves that superimpose exactly on each other
Triangle	A three-sided figure
Vertex	The common endpoint of two or more rays that form angles
Vertices	The plural of vertex

All About Polygons

Polygons are two-dimensional, or flat, shapes, formed from three or more line segments.

Examples

Triangles

Triangles are polygons that have three sides and three vertices; the common endpoints of two or more rays form angles.

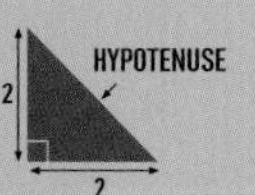

- **Right triangles** are formed when two of three line segments meet in a 90° angle. In a right triangle, the longest side has a special name: the hypotenuse.

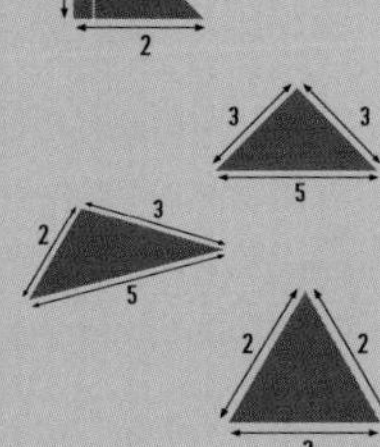

- **Isosceles triangles** have two sides of equal length.
- **Scalene triangles** have no sides of equal length.
- **Equilateral triangles** have three sides of equal length.

Quadrilaterals

Quadrilaterals are polygons that have four sides and four vertices.

- **Trapezoids** are quadrilaterals that have one pair of parallel sides.
- **Parallelograms** are quadrilaterals that have parallel line segments in both pairs of opposite sides.
- **Rectangles** are parallelograms formed by line segments that meet at right angles. A rectangle always has four right angles.
- **Squares** are rectangles that have sides of equal length and four 90° angles.
- **Rhombuses** are parallelograms that have sides of equal length but don't meet at right angles.

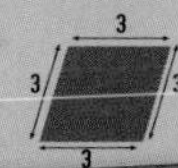

Circles

A circle is a set of points within a plane. Each point on the circle is at an equal distance from a common point inside the circle called the center.

The distance from the center of the circle to any point on the circle is called the radius. (r = radius)

A line segment drawn through the center of the circle to points on either side of the circle is called the diameter. The circle is bisected, or cut in two equal parts, along the diameter line. Diameter is equal to two times the radius. (2r = diameter)

The distance around the circle is called the circumference. (πd or π2r = circumference)

Plants

Silent Partners

Take a breath. Let it out. Do it again—and again—and again. Humans inhale and exhale about 14 times a minute. It may seem as if we're going through this process alone, but we're not. When it comes to the air we breathe, plants and people are a natural partnership.

Give and Take

Through a process called photosynthesis, plants convert energy from the Sun into sugars they store as food. Photosynthesis releases oxygen, which humans breathe in. When we breathe out, we give something back to plants. We release carbon dioxide, a waste gas needed for photosynthesis to work. This cycle goes on and on countless times a day, all over the earth.

Let's Eat

Of the 275,000—300,000 plant species on Earth, not all get their food through photosynthesis. About 4,000 species are parasites, which feed on other plants. Another 400 or so plants are meat-eaters. Plants such as the pitcher plant and sundew have hairs that trap insects inside their leaves. Then the plants' digestive juices help them consume their victims. Other carnivorous plants even eat frogs, birds, and mice!

Extreme Plants

The smallest plants are duckweeds, which can measure only 0.01–0.04 inches (0.5–1.2 mm). The rafflesia plant in Southeast Asia has the largest flowers in the world. It has a reddish-brown blossom that can measure up to 3 feet (91 cm) wide and weigh up to 15 pounds (7 kg). This plant is commonly known as the stinking corpse lily because it smells like a rotting carcass! But don't turn up your nose. The foul odor has a purpose—it attracts flies, which pollinate the flower.

TAKE a LOOK

Explore the plant variety outside your school or home. How many different kinds of plants can you find? Draw pictures and write descriptions of your plants in a notebook, and try to figure out where they fit into the plant kingdom, shown on the next page. (Don't pick any plants that aren't on your property, and don't eat any, regardless of where you find them. Many plants are poisonous.)

CHECK IT OUT!

Plants don't have to be big to be deadly. The tiny bladderwort is the fastest killer of the carnivorous plants. It can suck in prey in less than 1⁄50 of a second.

Biological Classification of Plants

PLANT KINGDOM

Filicinophyta FERNS

Lycopodophyta CLUB MOSSES

Ginkgophyta GINKGO

Gnetophyta WELWITSCHIA, EPHEDRA, GNETUM

Psilophyta WHISKFERNS

Cycadophyta CYCADS

Bryophyta BRYOPHYTES

Sphenophyta HORSETAILS

Coniferophyta CONIFERS

Angiospermophyta FLOWERING PLANTS

Hepaticae LIVERWORTS

Musci MOSSES

Anthocerotae HORNWORTS

Monocotyledoneae MONOCOTYLEDONS

Dicotyledoneae DICOTYLEDONS

KEY

These colors show the classification groupings in the chart.

- **PHYLUM or DIVISION**
- **CLASS**
- **ORDER**

Liliaceae	LILY, TULIP
Orchidaceae	ORCHIDS
Poaceae	WHEAT, BAMBOO
Iridaceae	IRIS, GLADIOLUS
Arecaceae	COCONUT PALM, DATE PALM
Bromeliaceae	BROMELIAD, PINEAPPLE
Cyperaceae	SEDGES
Juncaceae	RUSHES
Musaceae	BANANA
Amaryllidaceae	DAFFODIL, AMARYLLIS
Ranunculaceae	BUTTERCUP, DELPHINIUM
Brassicaceae	CABBAGE, TURNIP
Roasceae	APPLE, ROSE
Fabaceae	BEAN, PEANUT
Magnoliaceae	MAGNOLIA, TULIP TREE
Apiaceae	CARROT, PARSLEY
Solonaceae	POTATO, TOMATO
Lamiaceae	MINT, LAVENDER
Asteraceae	SUNFLOWER, DANDELION
Salicaceae	WILLOW, POPLAR
Cucurbitaceae	MELON, CUCUMBER
Malvaceae	HIBISCUS, HOLLYHOCK
Cactaceae	CACTUS

Where Do Plants Grow?

Plants grow everywhere in the world, except where there is permanent ice. However, different types of plants grow best in different regions. A region's plant life depends on the climate, the amount of water and sun, the type of soil, and other features. For instance, plants in the tundra grow close to the ground, away from the region's icy winds. Desert plants have thick skins to hold in every drop of water. This map shows five major regions where certain kinds of plants grow best, and the areas where the climate is too harsh for any plant life at all.

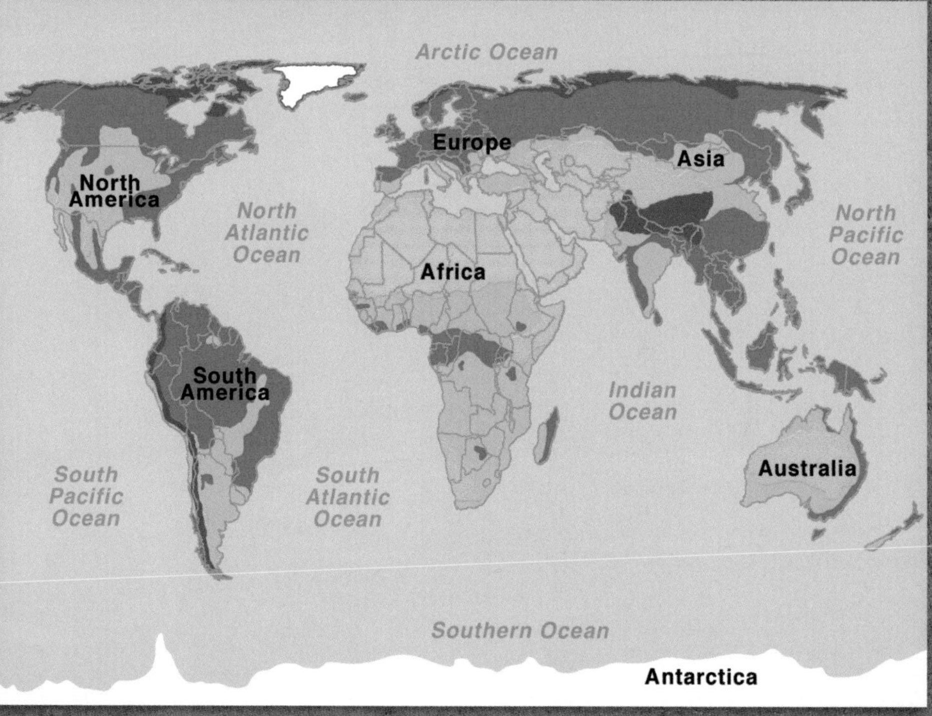

Region	Types of Plants
Aquatic	Cattails, seaweed
Grassland	Short and tall grasses
Forest	Trees, shrubs, ferns, wildflowers
Tundra	Small shrubs, mosses
Desert	Many kinds of cacti
Permanent ice	No plant life

Pop Culture

What's Hot? What's Not?

Every era has a different idea of what's "cool." In the 1800s, Charles Dickens was a big celebrity. In the 1950s, poodle skirts and hula hoops were the craze. Today, it's *American Idol* and *High School Musical*. Pop culture, short for popular culture, is made up of the celebrities, movies, TV shows, toys, fads, and video games the public can't get enough of.

The Ultimate Fan

Whether you're a fan of a particular movie character, TV show, band, book, or celebrity, there's probably a fan club for you. Fan clubs all over the world create communities to support different groups and ideas people are passionate about. As of April 2008, the largest fan club in the world was Cassiopeia, supporters of the South Korean boy band Dong Bang Shin Ki. Cassiopeia has over 800,000 members in Korea alone.

Book It!

Have you seen the Harry Potter movies or *Twilight*? How about a Narnia movie? All of these big-screen blockbusters began as bestselling books. As you'll see on page 152, half of the top-grossing movies in 2008 were adapted from books or comics! How many have you read?

American I

Jonas Brothers

Taylor Swift

All in the Family

Billy Ray Cyrus became a pop culture phenomenon in 1992 with the release of his debut album, *Some Gave All*, which included the smash hit "Achy-Breaky Heart." That same year, his daughter Destiny Hope Cyrus was born. Her smiling face earned her the nickname Miley, short for Smiley. Thirteen years later, Billy Ray and Miley Cyrus stepped into the spotlight together when they signed on for Disney's show *Hannah Montana*. Since then Miley Cyrus has conquered TV, music, and movies to become her own pop culture phenomenon.

Miley Cyrus

TAKE a LOOK

Want to know what's going on in pop culture? Take a look at the magazine racks the next time you're in a grocery store or bookstore. Browse through celebrity blogs and fan sites. You'll likely see a few of the faces featured on the following pages.

CHECK IT OUT!

Seventeen magazine first appeared on newsstands in 1944 and is the oldest teen publication still in circulation. The oldest teen fan magazine is *Tiger Beat*, launched in 1965.

Movies

10 Top-Grossing Movies of 2008

Movie	Box-Office Receipts
*The Dark Knight**	$530,936,438
*Iron Man**	$318,313,199
Indiana Jones and the Kingdom of the Crystal Skull	$317,023,851
Hancock	$227,946,274
Wall-E	$223,799,741
Kung Fu Panda	$215,434,591
Madagascar: Escape 2 Africa	$176,058,413
*Twilight**	$172,274,208
*Quantum of Solace**	$165,690,358
*Horton Hears a Who**	$154,529,439

*Movies based on books or comic books

Heath Ledger

2009 Oscar Winners

Best Picture: *Slumdog Millionaire*
Best Director: Danny Boyle, *Slumdog Millionaire*
Best Actor: Sean Penn, *Milk*
Best Actress: Kate Winslet, *The Reader*
Best Supporting Actor: Heath Ledger, *The Dark Knight*
Best Supporting Actress: Penélope Cruz, *Vicky Cristina Barcelona*
Best Animated Film: *Wall-E*
Best Foreign Film: *Departures*, Japan
Best Original Screenplay: *Milk*, Dustin Lance Black
Best Adapted Screenplay: *Slumdog Millionaire*, Simon Beaufoy

CHECK IT OUT!

"Your Choice, Your Voice." This motto was announced by Britney Spears in 1999 when she hosted the first Teen Choice Awards. Each year teens have awarded a surfboard to their favorite actors, singers, and celebrities in TV, movies, and music. Some winners—like Jennifer Love Hewitt, Aaron Carter, Serena and Venus Williams, and Zac Efron—actually use their award to surf.

2009 Golden Globe Winners

Best Picture, Drama: *Slumdog Millionaire*
Best Actor, Drama: Mickey Rourke, *The Wrestler*
Best Actress, Drama: Kate Winslet, *Revolutionary Road*
Best Picture, Comedy or Musical: *Vicky Cristina Barcelona*
Best Actor, Comedy or Musical: Colin Farrell, *In Bruges*
Best Actress, Comedy or Musical: Sally Hawkins, *Happy-Go-Lucky*
Best Director: Danny Boyle, *Slumdog Millionaire*
Best Supporting Actor: Heath Ledger, *The Dark Knight*
Best Supporting Actress: Kate Winslet, *The Reader*
Best Animated Film: *Wall-E*
Best Foreign Film: *Waltz with Bashir* (Israel)
Best Screenplay: *Slumdog Millionaire*, Simon Beaufoy

2009 Nickelodeon Kids' Choice Awards Movie Winners

Favorite Movie: *High School Musical 3*
Favorite Movie Actor: Will Smith
Favorite Movie Actress: Vanessa Hudgens
Favorite Animated Movie: *Madagascar: Escape 2 Africa*
Favorite Voice from an Animated Movie: Jack Black

Ashley Tisdale

2008 Teen Choice Awards Movie Winners

Will Smith

Breakout Female: Ellen Page
Breakout Male: Drake Bell
Villain: Johnny Depp
Actress, Horror/Thriller: Jessica Alba
Actor, Horror/Thriller: Will Smith
Actress, Comedy: Ellen Page
Actor, Comedy: Ashton Kutcher
Actress, Action Adventure: Rachel Bilson
Actor, Action Adventure: Shia LaBeouf
Actress, Drama: Keira Knightley
Actor, Drama: Channing Tatum
Horror/Thriller: *I Am Legend*
Comedy: *Juno*
Action Adventure: *The Chronicles of Narnia: Prince Caspian*
Drama: *Step Up 2: The Streets*
Bromantic Comedy: *What Happens in Vegas*
Chick Flick: *27 Dresses*

Television

Most Watched TV Shows of 2008

American Idol
Dancing with the Stars
The Mentalist
NBC Sunday Night Football
CSI
NCIS
60 Minutes
Survivor: Gabon

David Cook

2008 Emmy Award Winners

Ouststanding Series, Drama: *Mad Men*
Outstanding Series, Comedy: *30 Rock*
Outstanding Reality Program, Competition: *The Amazing Race*
Outstanding Actor, Drama: Bryan Cranston, *Breaking Bad*
Outstanding Actress, Drama: Glenn Close, *Damages*
Outstanding Actor, Comedy: Alec Baldwin, *30 Rock*
Outstanding Actress, Comedy: Tina Fey, *30 Rock*
Outstanding Supporting Actor, Drama: Zeljko Ivanek, *Damages*
Outstanding Supporting Actress, Drama: Dianne Wiest, *In Treatment*
Outstanding Supporting Actor, Comedy: Jeremy Piven, *Entourage*
Outstanding Supporting Actress, Comedy: Jean Smart, *Samantha Who?*

2009 Nickelodeon Kids' Choice Awards TV Winners

Favorite TV Show: *iCarly*
Favorite Reality Show: *American Idol*
Favorite TV Actor: Dylan Sprouse
Favorite TV Actress: Selena Gomez
Favorite Cartoon: *SpongeBob SquarePants*

Dylan and Cole Sprouse

2008 Teen Choice Awards TV Winners

Breakout Female: Blake Lively
Breakout Male: Chace Crawford
Breakout Show: *Gossip Girl*
Villain: Ed Westwick
Personality: Tyra Banks
Actress, Comedy: Miley Cyrus
Actor, Comedy: Steve Carell
Actress, Action Adventure: Hayden Panettiere
Actor, Action Adventure: Milo Ventimiglia
Actress, Drama: Blake Lively
Actor, Drama: Chad Michael Murray
Female, Reality/Variety: Lauren Conrad
Male, Reality/Variety: David Cook
Comedy: *Hannah Montana*
Action Adventure: *Heroes*
Drama: *Gossip Girl*
Reality Competition: *Oprah's Big Give*
Looking for Love: *The Bachelor*
Celebrity Reality: *The Hills*
Reality Music Competition: *American Idol*
Reality Dance Competition: *America's Best Dance Crew*
Game Show: *Deal or No Deal*
Animated Show: *Family Guy*

Blake Lively

CHECK IT OUT!

For Blake Lively, star of *Gossip Girl*, acting is a family matter. Her mom, dad, and four siblings are all in show business. In fact, Blake's dad, Ernie Lively, played her movie dad in *The Sisterhood of the Traveling Pants*.

Music

Top 10 Albums of 2008

Album	Artist
As I Am	Alicia Keys
Noel	Josh Groban
Tha Carter III	Lil Wayne
Long Road Out of Eden	Eagles
Taylor Swift	Taylor Swift
Rock n Roll Jesus	Kid Rock
Viva La Vida	Coldplay
NOW 26	Various artists
Carnival Ride	Carrie Underwood
The Ultimate Hits	Garth Brooks

Top 10 Digitally Downloaded Songs of 2008

Song	Artist
"Low"	Flo Rida featuring T-Pain
"Bleeding Love"	Leona Lewis
"Lollipop"	Lil Wayne featuring Static Major
"I Kissed a Girl"	Katy Perry
"Viva La Vida"	Coldplay
"Love Song"	Sara Bareilles
"Apologize"	Timbaland featuring OneRepublic
"No Air"	Jordin Sparks and Chris Brown
"Disturbia"	Rihanna
"4 Minutes"	Madonna featuring Justin Timberlake

2009 Nickelodeon Kids' Choice Awards Music Winners

Favorite Music Group: Jonas Brothers

Favorite Song: "Single Ladies," Beyoncé Knowles

Favorite Male Singer: Jesse McCartney

Favorite Female Singer: Miley Cyrus

The Jonas Brothers—Kevin, Joe, and Nick—began playing together when the youngest, Nick, signed his own solo record deal and needed help rehearsing. The brothers joined together and a couple of years later, in 2006, released their first album, *It's About Time*.

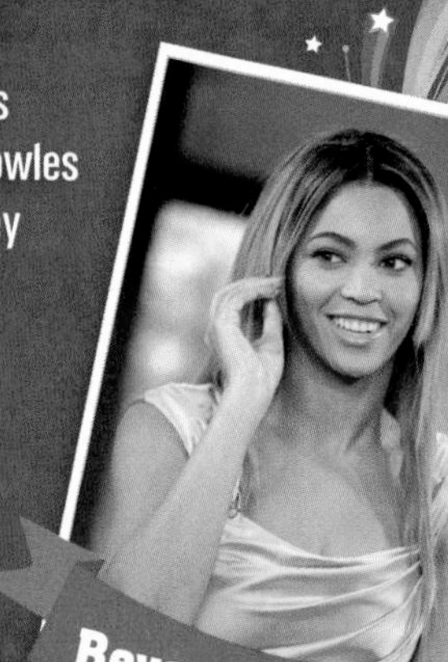

nifer
son

2009 Grammy Award Winners

Record of the Year: "Please Read the Letter," Robert Plant and Alison Krauss
Album of the Year: *Raising Sand*, Robert Plant and Alison Krauss
Song of the Year: "Viva La Vida," Coldplay
Best New Artist: Adele
Best Rap Album: *Tha Carter III*, Lil Wayne
Best Rap Song: "Lollipop," Dwayne Carter, Darius Harrison, James Scheffer, Stephen Garrett, and Rex Zamor
Best R&B Album: *Jennifer Hudson*, Jennifer Hudson
Best R&B Song: "Miss Independent," Mikkel S. Eriksen, Tor Erik Hermansen, and Shaffer Smith
Best Rock Album: *Viva La Vida or Death and All His Friends*, Coldplay
Best Rock Song: "Girls in Their Summer Clothes," Bruce Springsteen
Best Alternative Music Album: *In Rainbows*, Radiohead
Best Pop Vocal Album: *Rockferry*, Duffy
Best Country Song: "Stay," Sugarland

American Idol Winners and Runners-Up

Year	Winner	Runner-up
2002 (Season 1)	Kelly Clarkson	Justin Guarini
2003 (Season 2)	Ruben Studdard	Clay Aiken
2004 (Season 3)	Fantasia Barrino	Diana DeGarmo
2005 (Season 4)	Carrie Underwood	Bo Bice
2006 (Season 5)	Taylor Hicks	Katharine McPhee
2007 (Season 6)	Jordin Sparks	Blake Lewis
2008 (Season 7)	David Cook	David Archuleta
2008 (Season 8)	Kris Allen	Adam Lambert

2008 Teen Choice Awards
Music

Rock Track: "Crushcrushcrush," Paramore
Rock Group: Paramore
Rap/Hip-Hop Track: "Shawty Get Loose," Lil Mama, Chris Brown, and T-Pain
R&B Track: "Forever," Chris Brown
Love Song: "When You Look Me in the Eyes," Jonas Brothers
Breakout Group: Jonas Brothers
Breakout Artist: Taylor Swift
R&B Artist: Chris Brown
Rap Artist: Kanye West
Female Artist: Miley Cyrus
Male Artist: Chris Brown
Hook Up: "No Air," Jordin Sparks and Chris Brown
Single: "When You Look Me in the Eyes," Jonas Brothers

Books

Top-Selling Young Adult Fiction Books of 2008

Chains, Laurie Halse Anderson
Kingdom on the Waves, M. T. Anderson
The Penderwicks on Gardam Street, Jeanne Birdsall
Masterpiece, Elise Broach
Graceling, Kristin Cashore
The Hunger Games, Suzanne Collins
Little Brother, Cory Doctorow
Bog Child, Siobhan Dowd
Dark Dude, Oscar Hijuelos
Tender Morsels, Margo Lanagan
Savvy, Ingrid Law
The Disreputable History of Frankie Landau-Banks, E. Lockhart
Sunrise Over Fallujah, Walter Dean Myers
Nation, Terry Pratchett

2009 Children's Book Award Winners

Caldecott Medal: *The House in the Night*, illustrated by Beth Krommes, written by Susan Marie Swanson
Newbery Award: *The Graveyard Book*, Neil Gaiman
National Book Award: *What I Saw and How I Lied*, Judy Blundell*
Printz Award: *Jellicoe Road*, Melina Marchetta
Coretta Scott King Award: *We Are the Ship: The Story of Negro League Baseball*, Kadir Nelson

*2008 winner

Stephenie Meyer
Author of *Twilight*

2009 Nickelodeon Kids' Choice Awards Book Winner

Favorite Book: *Twilight*

Harry Potter and the Deathly Hallows sold 72.1 million copies the first weekend it was released in July 2007—8.3 million of those copies were sold in the first 24 hours it was on sale in the United States. *Breaking Dawn*, the final book in the Twilight series, sold 1.3 million copies on its first day in August 2008. Both books have sold millions of copies around the world, but neither compares to the bestselling book of all time—the Bible, which has sold over a billion copies.

Video Games

Top 10 PC Games in 2008

(Ranked by average minutes played per week)

World of Warcraft
Call of Duty 4: Modern Warfare
Halo: Combat Evolved
The Sims
The Sims 2
RuneScape
Diablo II
Team Fortress 2
Counter-Strike
Counter-Strike: Source

Top Video Game Console Usage in 2008

Console	Usage Minutes (%)*
PlayStation 2	31.7
Xbox 360	17.2
Wii	13.4
Xbox	9.7
PlayStation	7.3
GameCube	4.6
Other	16.1

*Percent of all measured console minutes

Population
World & U.S.

See How We've Grown

We live in a big world, and it's getting bigger all the time. Earth isn't expanding, but more and more people are calling it home. There are about 6.75 billion people on the planet today. Since 1959 the population has more than doubled. In your lifetime the population is expected to grow by at least another 50 percent.

Two at the Top

Where do all those people live? China and India top the population charts with over a billion people apiece. That means about two out of every five people in the world are Chinese or Indian. Researchers predict that India will overtake China in population within the next twenty-five years.

Born in the USA—or Not

Although the United States is far behind India and China in population, it ranks third in the world. Our country's population is more than 300 million people, and we've added about 100 million since 1970. In 1790, the entire population was only about four million.

More and more of the U.S. population gain comes from immigrants, continuing an American tradition. The United States was founded by immigrants from Europe. Today our culture, ideas, languages, and lives are still being enriched by people who come from other places. In fact, almost one in five Americans speaks a language other than English at home.

Hispanic Americans: A Major Minority

Hispanics are people from Spanish or Central or South American cultures. As of 2007, there were about 45.5 million Hispanics in the United States. Most Hispanics come from Mexico, with others from Colombia, Cuba, Dominican Republic, El Salvador, and Guatemala.

TAKE a LOOK

Everybody's from somewhere! Where are you from? How about the people you know? Ask classmates, friends, and neighbors about the towns, states, or countries where they were born. Then make a chart or graph that shows the diversity of the place you all now call home.

CHECK IT OUT!

Do you speak a language other than English? According to the U.S. Census Bureau, more than 55 million Americans do. Spanish is the top language. Chinese is second, and Tagalog, a major language of the Philippines, is number three.

Population by Continent

Continent	Population
Asia	4,053,868,153
Africa	972,752,366
Europe	729,553,228
North America	527,831,687
South America	388,619,456
Oceania, including Australia	34,368,042

CHECK IT OUT!

The continent of Antarctica is not listed above because it has no permanent population. Scientists and researchers come and go at various times.

5 Most Populous Countries

Country	Population
China	1,330,044,605
India	1,147,995,898
United States	303,824,646
Indonesia	237,512,355
Brazil	196,342,587

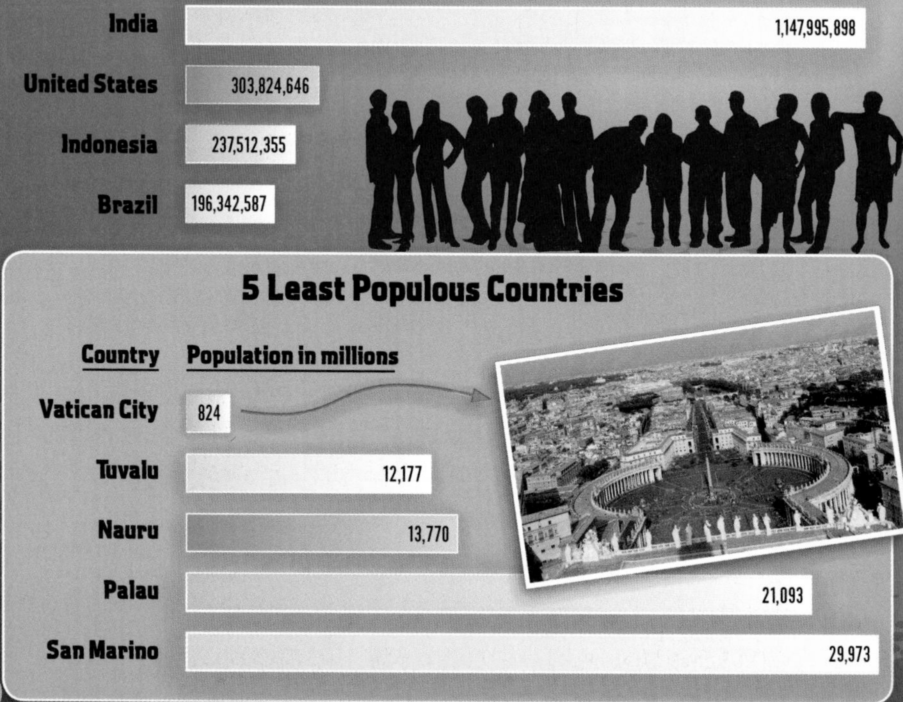

5 Least Populous Countries

Country	Population in millions
Vatican City	824
Tuvalu	12,177
Nauru	13,770
Palau	21,093
San Marino	29,973

5 Most Densely Populated Countries

Country	Persons per sq. mi. (persons per sq km)
Monaco	43,559.6 (16,818.5)
Singapore	17,482.2 (6,749.9)
Vatican City	4,850.3 (1,872.7)
Maldives	3,331.8 (1,286.4)
Malta	3,307.4 (1,277.0)

5 Most Sparsely Populated Countries

Country	Persons per sq. mi. (persons per sq km)
Mongolia	5.0 (1.9)
Namibia	6.6 (2.5)
Australia	7.1 (2.8)
Suriname	7.6 (2.9)
Iceland	7.9 (3.0)

5 Largest World Cities

City	Population (includes surrounding densely populated areas)
Tokyo, Japan	35,676,000
New York City, United States	19,040,000
Mexico City, Mexico	19,028,000
Mumbai, India	18,978,000
Sao Paulo, Brazil	18,845,000

CHECK IT OUT!

You can figure out population density by dividing the population by the land area. Land areas for all countries can be found on pages 50 to 81. Land areas for each state of the United States and Washington, DC, can be found on pages 88 to 105.

10 Most Populous States

State	Population
California	36,756,666
Texas	24,326,974
New York	19,490,297
Florida	18,328,340
Illinois	12,901,563
Pennsylvania	12,448,279
Ohio	11,485,910
Michigan	10,003,422
Georgia	9,685,744
North Carolina	9,222,414

10 Least Populous States

State	Population
Wyoming	532,668
Vermont	621,270
North Dakota	641,481
Alaska	686,293
South Dakota	804,194
Delaware	873,092
Montana	967,440
Rhode Island	1,050,788
Hawaii	1,288,198
New Hampshire	1,315,809

U.S. Population Growth 1790–2008

Year	Population (in millions)
1790	3.9
1830	12.9
1870	38.6
1890	62.9
1910	92.2
1930	123.2
1950	151.3
1970	203.2
1990	248.7
2000	281.4
2008	304.1

10 Largest U.S. Cities

City	Population
New York, NY	8,274,527
Los Angeles, CA	3,834,340
Chicago, IL	2,836,658
Houston, TX	2,208,180
Phoenix, AZ	1,552,259
Philadelphia, PA	1,449,634
San Antonio, TX	1,328,984
San Diego, CA	1,266,731
Dallas, TX	1,240,499
San Jose, CA	939,899

10 Fastest-Growing Major U.S. Cities

City	Percent increase from 2006 to 2007
New Orleans, LA	13.8
Victorville, CA	9.5
McKinney, TX	8.0
North Las Vegas, NV	7.4
Cary, NC	7.3
Killeen, TX	6.5
Port St. Lucie, FL	6.3
Gilbert, AZ	5.8
Clarksville, TN	4.8
Denton, TX	4.7

U.S. Racial Makeup

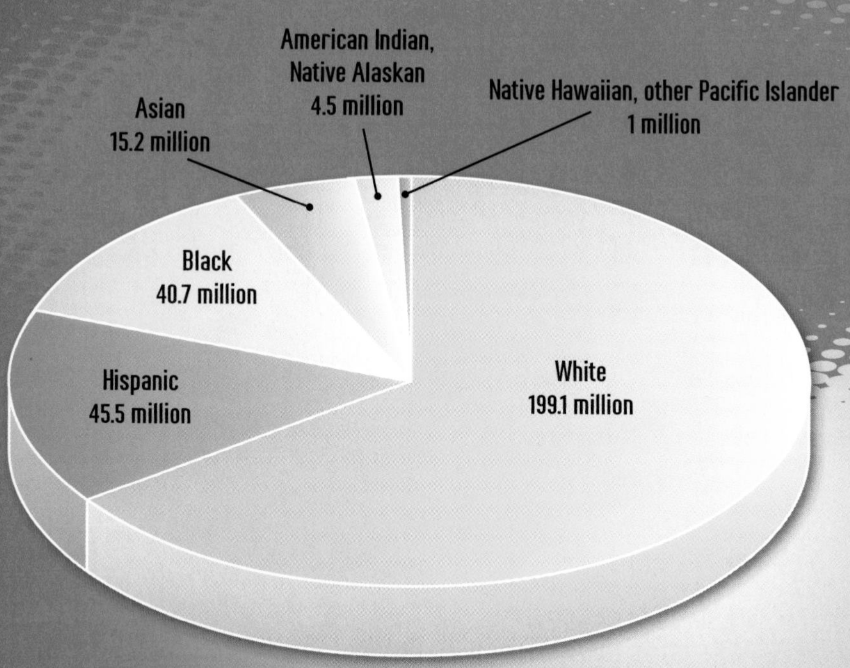

States with the Highest Population by Race

White

State	Population
California	15.6 million
New York	11.6 million
Texas	11.4 million

Hispanic

State	Population
California	13.2 million
Texas	8.6 million
Florida	3.8 million

Black

State	Population
New York	3.5 million
Florida	3 million
Texas	3 million

Asian

State	Population
California	5 million
New York	1.4 million
Texas	915,000

American Indian, Native Alaskan

State	Population
California	689,000
Oklahoma	394,000
Arizona	335,000

Native Hawaiian, other Pacific Islander

State	Population
Hawaii	269,000
California	262,000
Washington	50,000

tates with the Highest Percentage of Foreign-Born Residents

State	Percentage
California	27.4
New York	21.8
New Jersey	19.9
Nevada	19.4
Florida	18.9

In Los Angeles, CA, and Miami, FL, about half the residents speak a language other than English at home. Los Angeles and Miami also have the highest percentage of foreign-born residents. St. Louis, MO, has the lowest percentage.

Racial Makeup of 10 Largest U.S. Cities

New York, NY

White	44.7%
Black	26.6%
Hispanic	27.8%
Asian	9.8%
American Indian, Native Alaskan	0.5%
Native Hawaiian, other Pacific Islander	0.1%

Los Angeles, CA

White	46.9%
Black	11.2%
Hispanic	46.5%
Asian	10.0%
American Indian, Native Alaskan	0.8%
Native Hawaiian, other Pacific Islander	0.2%

Chicago, IL

White	42.0%
Black	36.8%
Hispanic	26.0%
Asian	4.3%
American Indian, Native Alaskan	0.4%
Native Hawaiian, other Pacific Islander	0.1%

Houston, TX

White	49.3%
Black	25.3%
Hispanic	37.4%
Asian	5.3%
American Indian, Native Alaskan	0.4%
Native Hawaiian, other Pacific Islander	0.1%

Phoenix, AZ

White	71.1%
Black	5.1%
Hispanic	34.1%
Asian	2.0%
American Indian, Native Alaskan	2.0%
Native Hawaiian, other Pacific Islander	0.1%

Philadelphia, PA

White	45.0%
Black	43.2%
Hispanic	8.5%
Asian	4.5%
American Indian, Native Alaskan	0.3%
Native Hawaiian, other Pacific Islander	0%

San Antonio, TX

White	32.1%
Black	6.8%
Hispanic	58.7%
Asian	1.6%
American Indian, Native Alaskan	0.8%
Native Hawaiian, other Pacific Islander	0.1%

San Diego, CA

White	60.2%
Black	7.9%
Hispanic	25.4%
Asian	13.6%
American Indian, Native Alaskan	0.6%
Native Hawaiian, other Pacific Islander	0.5%

Dallas, TX

White	50.8%
Black	25.9%
Hispanic	35.6%
Asian	2.7%
American Indian, Native Alaskan	0.5%
Native Hawaiian, other Pacific Islander	0%

San Jose, CA

White	47.5%
Black	3.5%
Hispanic	30.2%
Asian	26.9%
American Indian, Native Alaskan	0.8%
Native Hawaiian, other Pacific Islander	0.4%

Religion

Looking for Answers

A religion is a system of beliefs and holy practices, called rituals, that help guide people in their lives. Today there are about 20 major religions in the world, with thousands of other, smaller religious groups. At the heart of most religions is a desire to find answers to important questions such as: How should I live my life? What happens when you die? Why do some people suffer? In most religions, people seek these answers with guidance from one or more supreme beings or forces.

Supreme Beings

A supreme being or force offers people a perspective from beyond the physical world. Christians, Jews, and Muslims believe in one supreme being, or god. Practitioners of Hinduism believe in one divine principle, known as Brahman, and various gods who represent parts of that principle.

Major Religions

Christians make up the largest religious group in the world, numbering more than two billion. About half of all Christians belong to the Roman Catholic Church, whose spiritual leader is the Pope. Muslims are the second-largest group, with almost 1.4 billion members. With more than three-quarters of a billion believers, Hindus are the third-largest group. See pages 170 and 171 for detailed information.

Holy Places

Most religions have specific places on the planet that are considered holy. Christians, Jews, and Muslims may make trips to their Holy Lands in Egypt, Israel, or Jordan. Hindus sprinkle the ashes of their dead relatives in the Ganges River. The Bighorn Medicine Wheel in Wyoming is sacred to many Native Americans, and members of the Buddhist and Shinto faith believe Mount Fuji in Japan to be a sacred place.

TAKE a LOOK

Take a look at the information in this section and explore how other people approach the mysteries of life. How do you answer the big questions? What kinds of things are important to you on a spiritual level?

CHECK IT OUT!

Most major religions have five features in common: belief in a god or supreme force, a doctrine of salvation, a code of conduct, rituals, and the telling of sacred stories.

Major Religions of the World

Buddhism

Buddhism began about 525 BC, reportedly in India. This religion is based on the teachings of Gautama Siddhartha, the Buddha, who achieved enlightenment through intense meditation. The Buddha taught that though life is full of pain, you can break the cycle and achieve peace by being mindful, meditating, and doing good deeds. There are Buddhists all over the world, but mostly in Asia. The Buddha's teachings can be read in spiritual texts, or scriptures, called sutras.

Christianity

Christianity is the world's biggest religion, with over 2 billion worshippers in the world. It is based on the teachings of Jesus Christ, who lived between 8 BC and AD 29. The Old and New Testaments of the Bible are the key scriptures. Christians believe that Jesus Christ is the son of God, who died on the cross to save humankind and later rose from the dead.

Hinduism

To Hindus, there is one overarching divine principle, with a variety of gods such as Vishnu, Shiva, and Shakti representing different parts of it. Hindus believe that by being mindful and doing good deeds you can break meaningless cycles and improve the purity of your actions, known as your karma. Hinduism was founded about 1500 BC. The main scriptures are called Vedas.

Islam

Islam was founded in AD 610 by Muhammad. People who practice Islam are called Muslims. They believe in one god, Allah, who gave the spiritual writings of the Qur'an (also known as the Koran) to Muhammad so he could teach truth and justice to all people. There are two major Muslim groups, the Shiites and the Sunni.

Judaism

Judaism was founded about 2000 BC. The prophet Abraham is recognized as the founder. Jews believe in one god. They believe God created the universe, and they believe in being faithful to God and in following God's laws as outlined in key scriptures such as the Torah and the Hebrew Bible. There are people practicing Judaism all over the world. Many of them are in Israel and the United States.

5 Largest World Religions

Religion	Members
Christianity	2,199,817,400
Islam	1,387,454,500
Hinduism	875,726,000
Chinese Universists	385,621,500
Buddhism	385,609,000

CHECK IT OUT!

Most religions celebrate holy days throughout the year, including at least one day dedicated to their founder or a leading deity. Christians celebrate the birth of Christ on December 25, but in other religions exact dates change from year to year. Buddhists mark the birth of Buddha in April or May. In February or March, Muslims celebrate the birthday of Muhammad, and Hindus hold a festival dedicated to Shiva.

Science

I Wonder Why

Scientists like to look at things. They also like to ask questions. The way scientists observe, question, come up with a possible answer, and then test that answer, or hypothesis, is called the scientific process.

Let's Get Physical

Physical scientists study invisible forces such as light and sound. One of the most famous physical scientists was Sir Isaac Newton, who came up with theories that explained mysteries such as motion and gravity.

That's Life

Life scientists are also called biologists. They study animals, plants, ecology, diseases, and more, observing in a lab or in the wild. Biologist Anton von Leeuwenhoek discovered bacteria, which he called "wee creatures," when he saw them through a microscope. Jane Goodall lived in Africa with chimpanzees for many years. Through her observations we know that chimps can use tools and have individual personalities.

Rock Stars

If you want to know when an earthquake is coming, or how the Grand Canyon was formed, ask an earth scientist. Earth scientists study geography, weather, the ocean, rocks, earthquakes, and volcanoes.

IT'S A CRIME

Today, many types of science overlap. For instance, forensic scientists, such as crime scene investigators, apply knowledge from chemistry and physics to re-create crime scenes and study evidence. Because of TV shows like *CSI*, interest in criminal justice careers has skyrocketed.

TAKE a LOOK

Carry around a notebook and observe plants, people, the weather, or anything that catches your eye. Write down what you see. Draw pictures. Observe changes over time and make a hypothesis about what caused the change. Then try to prove it with an experiment.

CHECK IT OUT!

In addition to the life, earth, and physical branches of science, there is a fourth branch called the social sciences. Social scientists study people, governments, and cultures in fields such as sociology and psychology.

The 5 Kingdoms of Life

Life scientists classify all living things into one of five kingdoms: animals, plants, fungi, protista, and monera. Here are some (not all) of the types of life forms within each kingdom. (For a more detailed look at the animal kingdom, see pages 8 and 9. For more information about the plant kingdom, see page 148.)

Kingdom	Life forms
ANIMAL KINGDOM	Vertebrates (such as mammals, birds, and reptiles), sponges, worms, insects and arthropods, crustaceans, and jellyfish
PLANT KINGDOM	Ferns, mosses, ginkgos, horsetails, conifers, flowering plants, liverworts, and bladderworts
FUNGI KINGDOM	Molds, mildews, blights, smuts, rusts, mushrooms, puffballs, stinkhorns, lichens, dung fungi, yeasts, morels, and truffles
PROTISTA KINGDOM	Yellow-green algae, golden algae, protozoa, green algae, brown algae, and red algae
MONERA KINGDOM	Bacteria and blue-green algae

Scientific Classification

The five kingdoms are the biggest groups of life forms in the system biologists use, which is called classification. The system starts with the most general groups and moves down to the most specific.

Most general

Category	Example: Human Being
Kingdom	Animal
Phylum	Chordate
Subphylum	Vertebrate (animals with backbones)
Superclass	Vertebrate with jaws
Class	Mammal
Subclass	Advanced mammal
Infraclass	Placental mammal
Order	Primate
Family	Hominid
Genus	Homo
Species	Homo sapiens

Most specific

Some Major Discoveries in Life Science

Year	Discovery
400 BC	Aristotle classifies 500 species of animals into 8 classes
AD 1628	William Harvey discovers how blood circulates in the human body
1683	Anton van Leeuwenhoek observes bacteria
1735	Carolus Linnaeus introduces the classification system
1859	Charles Darwin publishes *On the Origin of Species*, which explains his theories of evolution
1860	Gregor Mendel discovers the laws of heredity through experiments with peas and fruit flies
1861	Louis Pasteur, the "father of bacteriology," comes up with a theory that certain diseases are caused by bacteria
1953	James D. Watson and Francis H. Crick develop the double helix model of DNA, which explains how traits are inherited
1953	Jonas Salk invents the polio vaccine
1981	Chinese scientists successfully clone a goldfish
1996	Dolly the sheep is cloned in Scotland

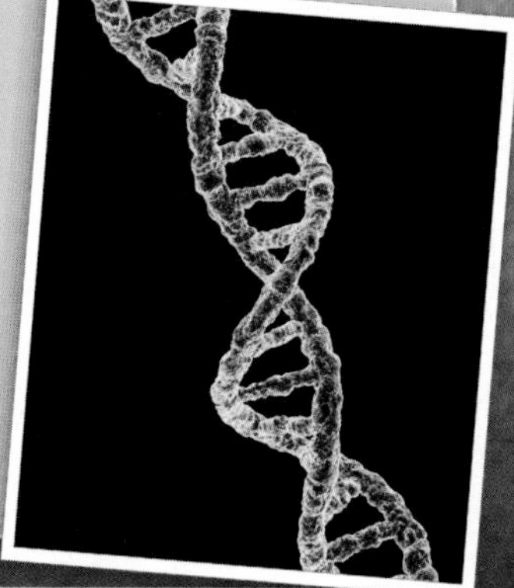

HECK OUT!

Every living thing is made of cells, and every cell contains DNA. No two organisms except clones and identical twins have the same DNA. Portions of DNA molecules called genes are passed on from parents to children. Whether you have straight hair or curly, blue eyes or brown, depends on your genes.

What Makes a Volcano?

A volcano is an opening in Earth's surface that allows hot, melted rock, called magma, to escape from below the surface. Scientists say there are about 550 historically active volcanoes.

Gently curved shield volcanoes build up over thousands of years. Mauna Loa is a shield volcano on the island of Hawaii. It rises about 56,000 feet (17 km) above the ocean floor.

Some of the most famous volcanoes in the world are stratovolcanoes, including Mount Vesuvius, Krakatau, and Mount Mayon, the most active volcano in the Philippines.

3 Types of Rocks

Geologists, scientists who study rocks, divide them into three groups.

Igneous

Forms when the melted rock, or magma, beneath Earth's surface erupts and cools

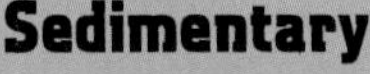

Sedimentary

Forms when loose deposits of rocky material are squeezed together into layers

Metamorphic

Forms when other rocks are changed by heat and pressure

10 Deadliest Volcanic Eruptions

Date	Volcano	Number of Deaths
April 10—12, 1815	Mt. Tambora, Indonesia	92,000
Aug. 26—28, 1883	Krakatau, Indonesia	36,000
May 8, 1902	Mt. Pelee, Martinique	28,000
Nov. 13, 1985	Nevado del Ruiz, Colombia	23,000
Aug. 24, AD 79	Mt. Vesuvius, Italy	16,000
May 21, 1792	Mt. Unzen, Japan	14,500
1586 (month and day unknown)	Kelut, Indonesia	10,000
June 8, 1783	Laki, Iceland	9,350
May 19, 1919	Mt. Kelut, Indonesia	5,000
Dec. 15, 1631	Mt. Vesuvius, Italy	4,000

What Makes an Earthquake?

At certain places there are breaks in the rocks that make up Earth's surface. These places are called faults. An earthquake is a shock wave that occurs when the tectonic plates beneath a fault rub or crash together.

10 Deadliest Earthquakes

Date	Place	Number of Deaths
Jan. 24, 1556	Shaanxi, China	830,000
Oct. 11, 1737	Calcutta, India	300,000
July 28, 1976	Tangshan, China	255,000
May 20, AD 526	Antioch, Syria	250,000
Aug. 9, 1138	Aleppo, Syria	230,000
Dec. 26, 2004	Near Sumatra, Indonesia	226,328
Dec. 22, AD 856	Damghan, Iran	200,000
Dec. 16, 1920	Gansu, China	200,000
May 22, 1927	Tsinghai, China	200,000
Sept. 1, 1923	Yokohama, Japan	143,000

CHECK IT OUT!

Ash from the eruption of Mount Tambora changed weather patterns and colored sunsets around the world for more than a year. Mary Shelley came up with the idea for *Frankenstein* in the summer of 1816, when she was staying in Switzerland with friends. The cold, dreary weather kept everyone indoors, where they amused themselves by telling ghost stories. Shelley later turned hers into a book.

Periodic Table of Elements

Everything in the world is made of elements, which are found in nature or made by scientists. The first element discovered was phosphorus, in 1669. Since then 110 elements have been added. Some elements are named for scientists. Some are named for places or characters in mythology. Others are named after a certain feature of the element. Scientists put elements in groups called periods on the periodic table.

Period	IA	IIA		IVB	VB	VIB	VIIB		
1	1 **H** Hydrogen 1.00794								
2	3 **Li** Lithium 6.941	4 **Be** Beryllium 9.012182							
3	11 **Na** Sodium 22.989770	12 **Mg** Magnesium 24.3050							
4	19 **K** Potassium 39.0983	20 **Ca** Calcium 40.078	21 **Sc** Scandium 44.955910	22 **Ti** Titanium 47.867	23 **V** Vanadium 50.9415	24 **Cr** Chromium 51.9961	25 **Mn** Manganese 54.938049	26 **Fe** Iron 55.845	27 58
5	37 **Rb** Rubidium 85.4678	38 **Sr** Strontium 87.62	39 **Y** Yttrium 88.90585	40 **Zr** Zirconium 91.224	41 **Nb** Niobium 92.90638	42 **Mo** Molybdenum 95.94	43 **Tc** Technetium (98)	44 **Ru** Ruthenium 101.07	45
6	55 **Cs** Cesium 132.90545	56 **Ba** Barium 137.327		72 **Hf** Hafnium 178.49	73 **Ta** Tantalum 180.9479	74 **W** Tungsten 183.84	75 **Re** Rhenium 186.207	76 **Os** Osmium 190.23	77
7	87 **Fr** Francium (223)	88 **Ra** Radium (226)		104 **Rf** Rutherfordium (261)	105 **Db** Dubnium (262)	106 **Sg** Seaborgium (266)	107 **Bh** Bohrium (264)	108 **Hs** Hassium (277)	10

Lanthanides	57 **La** Lanthanum 138.9055	58 **Ce** Cerium 140.116	59 **Pr** Praseodymium 140.90765	60 **Nd** Neodymium 144.24	61 **Pm** Promethium (145)	62
Actinides	89 **Ac** Actinium (227)	90 **Th** Thorium 232.0381	91 **Pa** Protactinium 231.03588	92 **U** Uranium 238.02891	93 **Np** Neptunium (237)	94

Key:

Atomic Number — 58
Symbol — **Ce**
Name — Cerium
Atomic Weight — 140.116

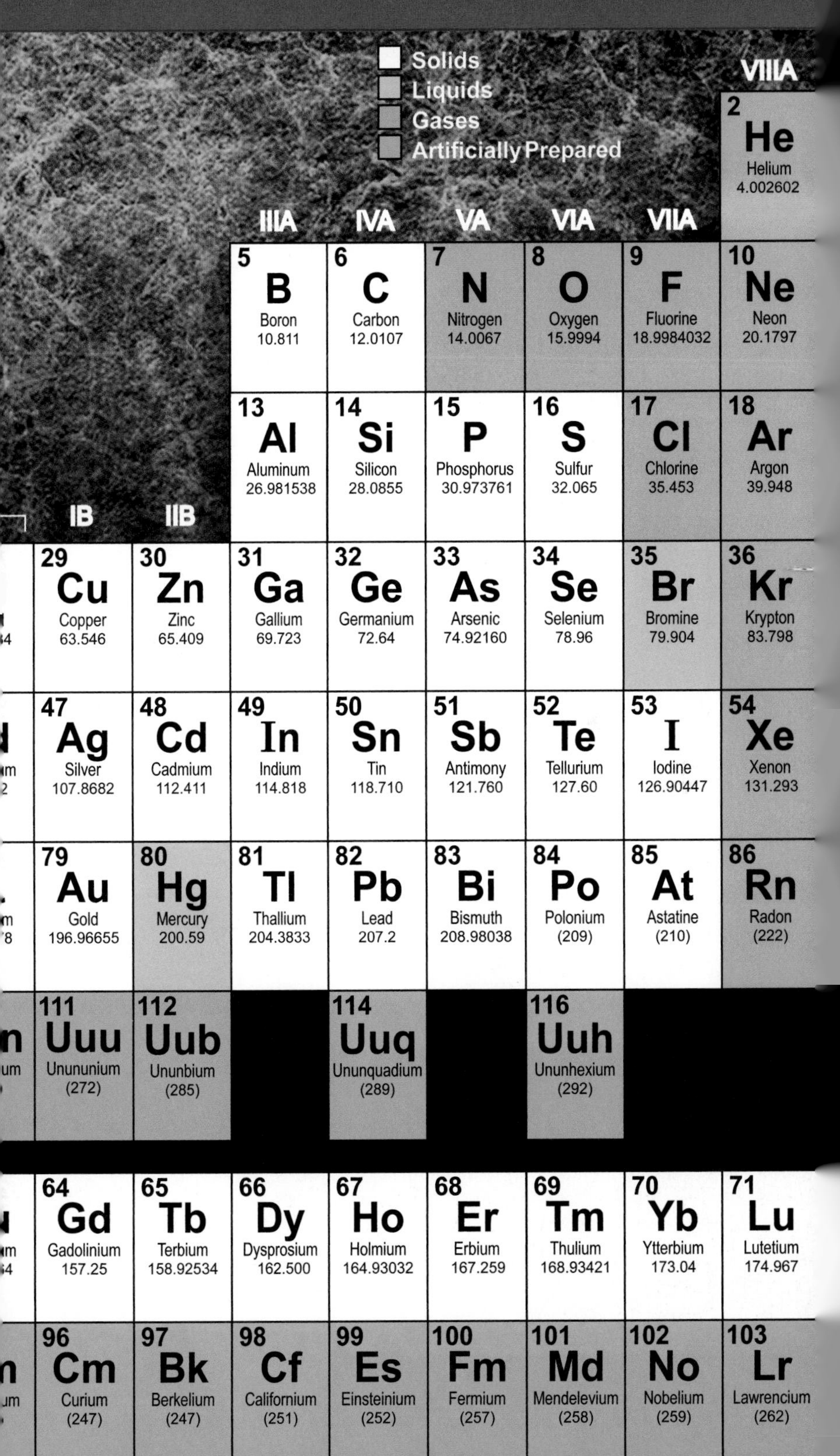

Solids
Liquids
Gases
Artificially Prepared
VIIIA
2 He Helium 4.002602
IIIA
IVA
VA
VIA
VIIA
5 B Boron 10.811
6 C Carbon 12.0107
7 N Nitrogen 14.0067
8 O Oxygen 15.9994
9 F Fluorine 18.9984032
10 Ne Neon 20.1797
13 Al Aluminum 26.981538
14 Si Silicon 28.0855
15 P Phosphorus 30.973761
16 S Sulfur 32.065
17 Cl Chlorine 35.453
18 Ar Argon 39.948
IB
IIB
29 Cu Copper 63.546
30 Zn Zinc 65.409
31 Ga Gallium 69.723
32 Ge Germanium 72.64
33 As Arsenic 74.92160
34 Se Selenium 78.96
35 Br Bromine 79.904
36 Kr Krypton 83.798
47 Ag Silver 107.8682
48 Cd Cadmium 112.411
49 In Indium 114.818
50 Sn Tin 118.710
51 Sb Antimony 121.760
52 Te Tellurium 127.60
53 I Iodine 126.90447
54 Xe Xenon 131.293
79 Au Gold 196.96655
80 Hg Mercury 200.59
81 Tl Thallium 204.3833
82 Pb Lead 207.2
83 Bi Bismuth 208.98038
84 Po Polonium (209)
85 At Astatine (210)
86 Rn Radon (222)
111 Uuu Unununium (272)
112 Uub Ununbium (285)
114 Uuq Ununquadium (289)
116 Uuh Ununhexium (292)
64 Gd Gadolinium 157.25
65 Tb Terbium 158.92534
66 Dy Dysprosium 162.500
67 Ho Holmium 164.93032
68 Er Erbium 167.259
69 Tm Thulium 168.93421
70 Yb Ytterbium 173.04
71 Lu Lutetium 174.967
96 Cm Curium (247)
97 Bk Berkelium (247)
98 Cf Californium (251)
99 Es Einsteinium (252)
100 Fm Fermium (257)
101 Md Mendelevium (258)
102 No Nobelium (259)
103 Lr Lawrencium (262)

Signs & Symbols

Getting the Message

Signs and symbols are an important part of communication, especially in a fast-moving world. A sign uses some combination of shapes, colors, pictures, and words to deliver information quickly. Symbols are visual representations of something bigger, such as a country, a brand, an emotion, or an organization. Signs and symbols are a universal language all their own.

Signs of the Times

The best signs are clear and easy to recognize and understand. Some give directions: NO PARKING, DO NOT ENTER. Others tell where to find important places such as hospitals, restrooms, and public telephones. Street signs help us find our way around a city or neighborhood, and danger signs alert us to poison, explosives, or icy roads.

Color Code

The color of a sign can indicate what kind of information it gives. On a highway, blue and white signs often point the way to services such as restaurants, lodging, gas stations, and rest areas. Signs that warn against danger are black, white, and red. Traffic signs can be red and white, like STOP, or black on yellow for SCHOOL AHEAD or YIELD.

SYMBOLS

Symbols are like shortcuts. They're quick ways to express a bigger idea. When someone gives you a thumbs-up, you know it means agreement or approval. A heart stands for love. A four-leaf clover stands for luck. In U.S. politics, the elephant symbolizes the Republican Party and the donkey stands for Democrats. Symbols are probably one of the oldest human inventions, and there are thousands of them in use today. How many symbols do you use or see every day?

TAKE a LOOK

Scientists say that the strongest color contrast seen by the human eye is black and yellow. Many important traffic signs have black writing on a yellow background so people can read them easily. Check out the signs on page 182 and then take a look around your city or neighborhood. What color are the signs that catch your eye?

YIELD

CHECK IT OUT!

Can gorillas speak? Koko the Gorilla can't speak any human languages. However, she has learned to communicate with humans through the use of American Sign Language, a series of hand gestures that represent letters, words, and ideas. She expresses her feelings, names things, and asks questions. Using the alphabet on page 183, how many things can you "say" without speaking?

Basic Signs

Fire extinguisher

Women's room

Men's room

First aid

Elevator

Information

Disabled (parking, restrooms, access)

Bus

Recycle

Fallout shelter

No smoking

No admittance

No parking

Danger

Poison

Stop

Yield

Do not enter

No left turn

Falling rock

Stop ahead

Bicycle path

Traffic light ahead

Railroad crossing

Pedestrian crossing

Intersection ahead

Left turn

Right turn

Two-way traffic

Slippery when wet

American Sign Language

In the manual alphabet of the hearing impaired, the fingers of the hand are moved to positions that represent the letters of the alphabet. Whole words and ideas are also expressed in sign language.

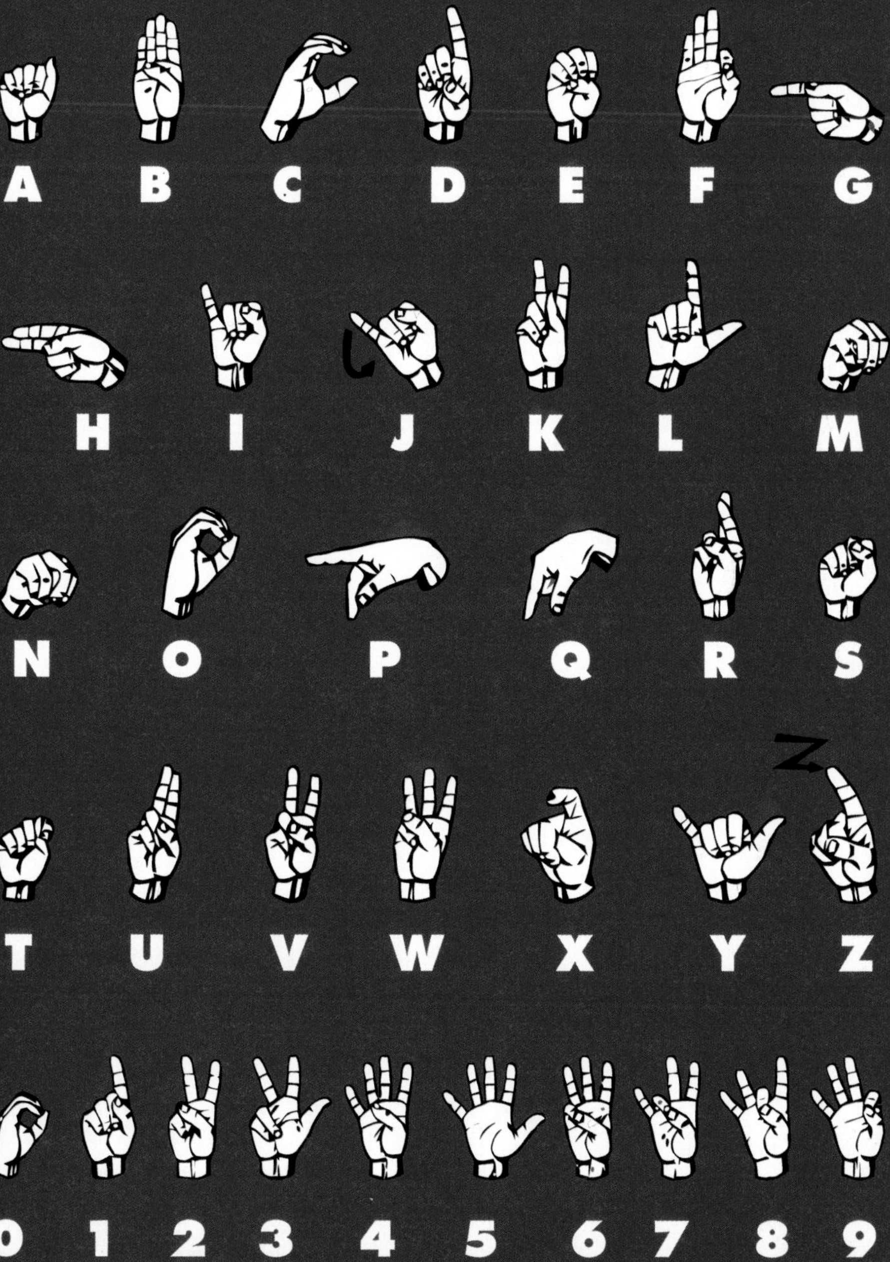

Space

Welcome to the Neighborhood

Go outside and look up. What do you see? Whether it's the clear blue sky, the Moon, the Sun, stars, planets, or just deep, inky blackness, you're looking at space. Within the vastness of space, Earth's solar system is one tiny neighborhood in a very big community.

The Star of the Show

The word *solar* means "of the sun," and the Sun is the star of our little corner of the universe. It's the closest star to Earth, which is why we can see it clearly and be warmed by its light. (Compared to other stars, our Sun is only average size.) Eight major planets and five dwarf planets revolve around our Sun.

All the major planets except Mercury and Venus have one or more moons orbiting around them, with a grand total of 166. Also spinning around the Sun are trillions of comets, tens of thousands of asteroids, and countless spheres of space dust and ice.

Spin City

Our entire solar system spins around the center of the Milky Way galaxy. It takes about 230 million years to make one orbit! The Milky Way includes roughly 400 billion stars. Could these other stars also have planets orbiting around them? In fact, scientists have discovered about 70 other solar systems in the Milky Way. There could be many more.

IT'S A BIG, BIG WORLD

The Milky Way is one of many galaxies bunched together to form a group called the Local Group. The Local Group is a small part of a bigger group called Virgo Cluster. Virgo Cluster and other galaxy clusters are all strung together like a huge web. Scientists estimate that there are more than 100 billion galaxies scattered throughout the visible universe. Well, you get the picture—space is one big place.

TAKE a LOOK

For as long as humans have been on Earth, we've wanted to explore the huge mystery known as space. Over the years we've developed telescopes and increasingly sophisticated tools to send images and information back. We've also sent people in space shuttles and rocket ships. As you explore this section and discover planets, stars, and moons and learn about the scientists and explorers who have brought that information to us, make a list of the kinds of questions that are still unanswered. Maybe you'll be the one to find the answers.

Pluto was considered a major planet until scientists reclassified it as a dwarf on August 24, 2006. Why was Pluto demoted? One of the judging standards was the ability to "clear the neighborhood." That means a planet must have a strong enough gravitational force to pull nearby space "junk" such as particles of ice and dust down to its surface. Pluto's gravitational field didn't have enough muscle. The other dwarf planets are Ceres, Haumes, Makemake, and Eris.

The Solar System

(with distances from the Sun*)

*Distances rounded to nearest tenth

Neptune
2.8 billion miles
(4.5 billion km)

Uranus
1.8 billion miles
(2.9 billion km)

Saturn
885.9 million miles
(14 billion km)

Jupiter
483.7 million miles
(7784 million km)

The Sun is the closest star to Earth. It is 270,000 times closer than the next-nearest star.

Basic Facts About the Planets in Our Solar System

Planet	Average distance from Sun	Rotation period (hours)	Period of revolution (in Earth days)	Diameter relative to Earth	Average surface or effective temperature	Planetary satellites (moons)
Mercury	36.0 million miles (57.9 million km)	1407.5 hours	88 days	38.2%	332°F (166°C)	0
Venus	67.2 million miles (108.2 million km)	-5,832.2 hours*	224.7 days	94.9%	864°F (462°C)	0
Earth	92.9 million miles (149.6 million km)	23.9 hours	365.24 days	100%	59°F (15°C)	1
Mars	141.6 million miles (227.9 million km)	24.6 hours	687 days	53.2%	-80°F (-62°C)	2
Jupiter	483.7 million miles (778.4 million km)	9.9 hours	4,330.6 days	1,121%	-234°F (-148°C)	62
Saturn	885.9 million miles (1.4 billion km)	10.7 hours	10,755.7 days	944%	-288°F (-178°C)	61
Uranus	1.8 billion miles (2.9 billion km)	-17.2 hours*	30,687.2 days	401%	-357°F (-216°C)	27
Neptune	2.8 billion miles (4.5 billion km)	16.1 hours	60,190 days	388%	-353°F (-214°C)	13

*Retrograde rotation; rotates backward, or in the opposite direction from most other planetary bodies.

Basic Facts About the Sun

Position in the solar system	center
Average distance from Earth	92,955,820 miles (149,597,891 km)
Distance from center of Milky Way galaxy	27,710 light-years
Period of rotation	25.38 days
Equatorial diameter	864,400 miles (1,391,117 km)
Diameter relative to Earth	109 times larger
Temperature at core	27,000,000°F (15,000,000°C)
Temperature at surface	10,000°F (5,538°C)
Main components	hydrogen and helium
Expected life of hydrogen fuel supply	64 billion years

Top 10 Largest Bodies in the Solar System

Ranked by size in equatorial diameter

1. Sun
864,400 miles
(1,391,117 km)

2. Jupiter
88,846 miles
(142,984 km)

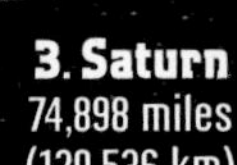

3. Saturn
74,898 miles
(120,536 km)

4. Uranus
31,764 miles
(51,118 km)

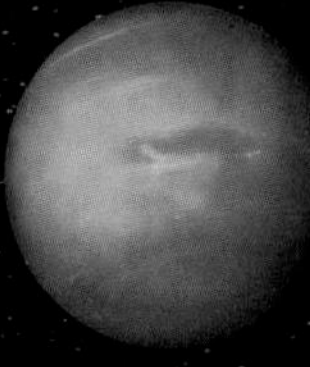

5. Neptune
30,776 miles
(49,528 km)

6. Earth
7,926 miles
(12,755 km)

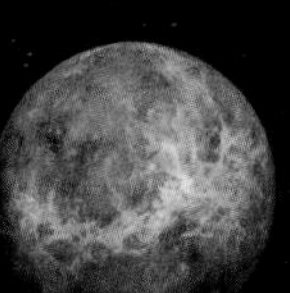

7. Venus
7,521 miles
(12,104 km)

8. Mars
4,222 miles
(6,794 km)

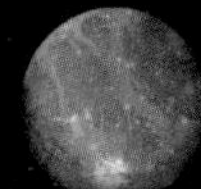

9. Ganymede
(moon of Jupiter)
3,280 miles
(5,262 km)

10. Titan
(moon of Saturn)
3,200 miles
(5,149 km)

Astronomy Terms and Definitions

Light-year (distance traveled by light in one year)	5.880 trillion miles (9.462 trillion km)
Velocity of light (speed of light)	186,000 miles/second (299,338 km/s)
Mean distance, Earth to Moon	238,855 miles (384,400 km)
Radius of Earth (distance from Earth's center to the equator)	3,963.19 miles (6,378 km)
Equatorial circumference of Earth (distance around the equator)	24,901 miles (40,075 km)
Polar circumference of Earth (distance around the poles)	24,860 miles (40,008 km)
Earth's mean velocity in orbit (how fast it travels)	18.5 miles/second (29.8 km/sec)

Fast Facts About the Moon

Age	4.6 billion years
Location	solar system
Avg. distance from Earth	238,900 miles (384,400 km)
Diameter	2,160 miles (3,476 km)
Period of revolution	27 Earth days

Interesting features:
The Moon has no atmosphere or magnetic field. Most rocks on the surface of the Moon seem to be between 3 and 4.6 billion years old. Thus the Moon provides evidence about the early history of our solar system.

Top 10 Closest Comet Approaches to Earth Prior to 2006

(ranked by lunar distance (LD*))

5. **Halley**
April 10, 837
13.0 LD

6. **Biela**
Dec. 9, 1805
14.2 LD

4. **IRAS-Araki-Alcock**
May 11, 1983
12.2 LD

7. **Comet of 1743**
Feb. 8, 1743
15.2 LD

3. **Tempel-Tuttle**
October 26, 1366
8.9 LD

8. **Pons-Winnecke**
June 26, 1927
15.3 LD

2. **Lexell**
July 1, 1770
5.9 LD

9. **Comet of 1014**
Feb. 24, 1014
15.8 LD

1. **Comet of 1491**
July 1, 1770
5.9 LD

10. **Comet of 1702**
April 20, 1702
17.0 LD

*1 LD = ~384,000 km

The Phases of the Moon

The Moon's appearance changes as it moves in its orbit around Earth.

Major Constellations

Latin	English	Latin	English
Aries	Ram	Lynx	Lynx
Camelopardalis	Giraffe	Lyra	Harp
Cancer	Crab	Microscopium	Microscope
Canes Venatici	Hunting Dogs	Monoceros	Unicorn
Canis Major	Big Dog	Musca	Fly
Canis Minor	Little Dog	Orion	Orion
Capricornus	Sea-goat	Pavo	Peacock
Cassiopeia	Queen	Pegasus	Pegasus
Centaurus	Centaur	Phoenix	Phoenix
Cetus	Whale	Pictor	Painter
Chamaeleon	Chameleon	Pisces	Fish
Circinus	Compass	Piscis Austrinus	Southern Fish
Columba	Dove	Sagitta	Arrow
Corona Australis	Southern Crown	Sagittarius	Archer
Corona Borealis	Northern Crown	Scorpius	Scorpion
Corvus	Crow	Sculptor	Sculptor
Crater	Cup	Scutum	Shield
Crux	Southern Cross	Serpens	Serpent
Cygnus	Swan	Sextans	Sextant
Delphinus	Dolphin	Taurus	Bull
Dorado	Goldfish	Telescopium	Telescope
Draco	Dragon	Triangulum	Triangle
Equuleus	Little Horse	Triangulum Australe	Southern Triangle
Gemini	Twins	Tucana	Toucan
Grus	Crane	Ursa Major	Big Bear
Hercules	Hercules	Ursa Minor	Little Bear
Horologium	Clock	Virgo	Virgin
Lacerta	Lizard	Volans	Flying Fish
Leo	Lion	Vulpecula	Little Fox
Leo Minor	Little Lion		

Galaxies Nearest to the Sun

1. Canis Major Dwarf Galaxy
25,000 light-years

2. Sagittarius Dwarf Elliptical Galaxy
70,000 light-years

3. Large Magellanic Cloud
179,000 light-years

4. Small Magellanic Cloud
210,000 light-years

CHECK IT OUT!

It would take the spacecraft *Voyager* about 749,000,000 years to get to Canis Major Dwarf Galaxy, the closest galaxy to ours.

Top 10 Closest Stars to the Sun

1. Proxima Centauri
4.22 light-years

2. Barnard's Star
5.97 light-years

3. Wolf 359
7.7 light-years

4. Sirius A
8.6 light-yea

5. Epsilon Eridani
10.5 light-years

6. Ross 128
10.8 light-years

7. Procyon
11.4 light-years

8. Tau Ceti
11.9 light-years

9. Altair
16.3 light-years

10. Eta Cassiopeiae
19 light-years

Sports

Outstanding in Their Fields

Do you wish you could bend it like Beckham? Ever since there have been sports to play, there have been players who stand out and inspire. Some remarkable athletes have worked especially hard to overcome great odds. Lance Armstrong won seven Tour de France bicycle races in a row (1999—2005) after battling cancer. Rachel Scdoris became the first legally blind athlete to race the grueling 1,100-mile (1,770 km) Iditarod Trail Sled Dog Race.

FAN-tastic!

Millions of fans follow the games, seasons, and statistics of their favorite teams and athletes. Most major cities have professional football, baseball, basketball, hockey, or soccer teams. Tennis, golf, and race car competitions also draw huge numbers of fans and bring in big bucks through ticket sales and team merchandise.

X Marks the Spot

What if you love skateboarding, street luging, or speed climbing? Before 1995, there was no national competition for these extreme action sports. Then ESPN executive Ron Semiao founded the X Games, in which athletes compete in events such as bicycle stunt, in-line skating, snowboarding, and skateboarding. Snowboarding superstar Shaun White (also known as the "Flying Tomato") holds the record for Winter X Game gold medals, with a total of nine.

PHENOMS FOREVER

Every generation has its heroes—athletes whose talents and star power leave a permanent mark in history. Baseball legend Babe Ruth was the superstar of the 1920s. Boxing champ Muhammad Ali reigned in the '60s. The '90s had basketball phenom Michael Jordan and hockey idol Wayne Gretzky. Today, powerhouses Venus and Serena Williams and Rafael Nadal rock the tennis court. Tiger Woods dominates the greens and LeBron James tears up the basketball court. Who will the heroes be next year?

TAKE a LOOK

Whether you're playing a pickup game of hoops or running around the block, sports are a great way to play, stay healthy, and have fun. What gets you up and at 'em? Take a look through this section and see how your favorite sports measure up. Maybe you'll be inspired to try something new.

Which athletes do kids admire most? At the 2009 Nickelodeon Kids' Choice Awards, quarterback Peyton Manning of the Indianapolis Colts scored for Favorite Male Athlete. Candace Parker of the WNBA's Los Angeles Sparks was named Favorite Female Athlete.

PRO FOOTBALL

League Leaders 2008

Passing Yards
Drew Brees, New Orleans Saints 5,059

Rushing Yards
Adrian Peterson, Minnesota Vikings 1,760

Receiving Yards
Andre Johnson, Houston Texans 1,575

Touchdowns
DeAngelo Williams, Carolina Panthers 20

Kick Returns
Josh Wilson, Seattle Seahawks 69 returns, 1,753 yards

Super Bowl XLIII

The Super Bowl is the professional football championship game staged annually by the National Football League. Participants include champions of the league's American Football Conference (AFC) and National Football Conference (NFC). Super Bowl XLIII was played on February 1, 2009, at the Raymond James Stadium in Tampa, Florida, between the Pittsburgh Steelers and the Arizona Cardinals. Steelers wide receiver Santonio Holmes, who made the game-winning touchdown catch with 35 seconds remaining, was named Most Valuable Player.

Pittsburgh Steelers (AFC) 27
Arizona Cardinals (NFC) 23

The game's not over till it's over! The greatest comeback in NFL history happened in a cold January game between the Buffalo Bills and the Houston Oilers in 1993. The Oilers were so far ahead in the third quarter at 35—3 that many Bills fans gave up and went home. But in that last quarter, the Bills scored five straight touchdowns and eventually won in overtime with a score of 41—38.

COLLEGE FOOTBALL

Bowl Championship Series (BCS)

National Championship Game 2008

Florida 24, Oklahoma 14

Major Bowl Games 2008–2009

Game	Location	Teams/Score
CHICK-FIL-A BOWL	Atlanta, GA	LSU 38, Georgia Tech 3
COTTON BOWL	Dallas, TX	Ole Miss 47, Texas Tech 34
EMERALD BOWL	San Francisco, CA	California 24, Miami 17
FIESTA BOWL	Glendale, AZ	Texas 24, Ohio State 21
GATOR BOWL	Jacksonville, FL	Nebraska 26, Clemson 21
LIBERTY BOWL	Memphis, TN	Kentucky 25, East Carolina 19
ORANGE BOWL	Miami, FL	Virginia Tech 20, Cincinnati 7
ROSE BOWL	Pasadena, CA	USC 38, Penn State 24
SUGAR BOWL	New Orleans, LA	Utah 31, Alabama 17
SUN BOWL	El Paso, TX	Oregon State 3, Pittsburgh 0

Heisman Trophy 2008

On December 13, 2008, University of Oklahoma quarterback Sam Bradford won the 74th Heisman Trophy. The award is presented annually to the top college football player in the United States.

BASEBALL

Top Players 2008

Rookies of the Year	
American League	Evan Longoria, Tampa Bay Rays
National League	Geovany Soto, Chicago Cubs
Managers of the Year	
American League	Joe Maddon, Tampa Bay Rays
National League	Lou Piniella, Chicago Cubs
Most Valuable Player Awards	
American League	Dustin Pedroia, Boston Red Sox
National League	Albert Pujols, St. Louis Cardinals
Cy Young Awards	
American League	Cliff Lee, Cleveland Indians
National League	Tim Lincecum, San Francisco Giants

Golden Glove Winners 2008
(selected by managers and players)

American League

Pitcher	Mike Mussina, New York Yankees
Catcher	Joe Mauer, Minnesota Twins
First Baseman	Carlos Pena, Tampa Bay Rays
Second Baseman	Dustin Pedroia, Boston Red Sox
Third Baseman	Adrien Beltre, Seattle Mariners
Shortstop	Michael Young, Texas Rangers
Outfielders	Torii Hunter, Los Angeles Angels Grady Sizemore, Cleveland Indians Ichiro Suzuki, Seattle Mariners

National League

Pitcher	Greg Maddux, Los Angeles Dodgers
Catcher	Yadier Molina, St. Louis Cardinals
First Baseman	Adrian Gonzalez, San Diego Padres
Second Baseman	Brandon Phillips, Cincinnati Reds
Third Baseman	David Wright, New York Mets
Shortstop	Jimmy Rollins, Philadelphia Phillies
Outfielders	Nate McLouth, Pittsburgh Pirates Carlos Beltran, New York Mets Shane Victorino, Philadelphia Phillies

League Leaders 2008

American League

Batting Average	Joe Mauer (.328), Minnesota Twins
Home Runs	Miguel Cabrera (37), Detroit Tigers
Runs Batted In	Josh Hamilton (130), Texas Rangers
Wins	Cliff Lee (22), Cleveland Indians
Earned Run Average	Cliff Lee (2.54), Cleveland Indians
Saves	Francisco Rodriguez (62), Los Angeles Angels

National League

Batting Average	Chipper Jones (.364), Atlanta Braves
Home Runs	Ryan Howard (48), Philadelphia Phillies
Runs Batted In	Ryan Howard (146), Philadelphia Phillies
Wins	Brandon Webb (22), Arizona Diamondbacks
Earned Run Average	Johan Santana (2.53), New York Mets
Saves	Jose Valverde (44), Houston Astros

World Series 2008

The Philadelphia Phillies won the World Series championship by defeating the Tampa Bay Rays 4—3 in Game 5 of the best-of-seven fall classic. Left-handed pitcher Cole Hamels was named Most Valuable Player of the series. The Phillies had gone undefeated at home (7—0) in the postseason run-up, the first team to do so since the New York Yankees in 1999.

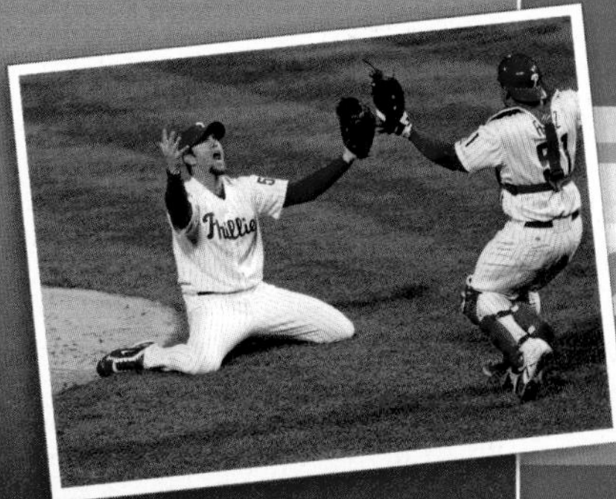

Little League World Series 2008

The Waipio Little League of Waipahu, Hawaii, defeated the Mexico Matamoros by a score of 12—3 in a tournament game played at the neutral site of Lamade Stadium in Williamsburg, Pennsylvania. It was the fourth straight win for the United States. The Hawaiians' 12 runs were the most scored by one team since the U.S. beat Japan in 1998.

NBA Championship Finals 2008

The Boston Celtics defeated the Los Angeles Lakers in the sixth game of the best-of-seven series on their home court, TD Banknorth Garden in Boston, on June 17 to win their first NBA (National Basketball Association) title since 1986. The games represented a renewal of a longstanding rivalry, matching the two teams for the 11th time in the NBA finals. The Celtics' Paul Pierce was named Most Valuable Player, averaging a team-high 21.8 points per game for the series.

NBA Top Scorers 2008

NAME	TEAM	GAMES	AVG. POINTS
1. LeBron James	Cleveland Cavaliers	75	30.0
2. Kobe Bryant	Los Angeles Lakers	82	28.3
3. Allen Iverson	Denver Nuggets	82	26.4
4. Carmelo Anthony	Denver Nuggets	77	25.7
5. Amare Stoudmire	Phoenix Suns	79	25.2

WNBA Championship Finals 2008

The Detroit Shock dominated the best-of-five championship series of the Women's National Basketball Association (WNBA), shutting out the San Antonio Silver Stars 3–0. Detroit won the first two games 77–69 and 69–61 on the Silver Stars' home court, then cinched the title with a decisive 76–60 win on their own court in Ypsilanti, Michigan. High-scoring forward/guard Katie Smith won the Most Valuable Player award for the series.

WNBA Top Scorers 2008

NAME	TEAM	GAMES	AVG. POINTS
1. Diana Taurasi	Phoenix Mercury	34	24.1
2. Cappie Pondexter	Phoenix Mercury	32	21.2
3. Lauren Jackson	Seattle Storm	21	20.2
4. Seimone Augustus	Minnesota Lynx	31	19.1
5. Candace Parker	Los Angeles Sparks	33	18.5

COLLEGE BASKETBALL

NCAA Men's Division I Championship 2009

The University of North Carolina Tar Heels defeated the Michigan State Spartans 89—72 in the title game of the NCAA (National Collegiate Athletic Association) Men's Division I Basketball Tournament. The game was played April 6, 2009, at Ford Field in Detroit, Michigan, concluding a single-elimination tournament involving 65 college teams that began on March 17. Although UNC's Wayne Ellington ranked third in scoring at 16 for the game, he racked up a combined 39 points against Villanova in the national semifinals and in the championship game, and was named Most Outstanding Player of the tournament. UNC's Ty Lawson, the game's high scorer with 21 points, was voted Player of the Year for the Atlantic Coast Conference.

NCAA Championship Game Leaders

	North Carolina		Michigan State	
Points	Ty Lawson	21	Goran Suton	17
Rebounds	Ed Davis	8	Goran Suton	11
Assists	Ty Lawson	6	Kalin Lucas	7
Steals	Ty Lawson	8	Draymond Green	1

NCAA Women's Division I Championship 2009

In the 2009 finals, held at the Scottrade Center in St. Louis, Missouri, on April 7, the University of Connecticut Huskies captured their sixth title by beating the Louisville Cardinals 76—54. UConn finished the 2008—09 season 39—0, the third time the team racked up a perfect season. Center Tina Charles, a junior, led the championship game in scoring (25 points) and rebounds (19), and was named Most Outstanding Player. The winning coach was Geno Auriemma.

TENNIS

2008 Grand Slam Singles Title Winners

	Men's	Women's
Australian Open	Novak Djokovic	Maria Sharapova
French Open	Rafael Nadal	Ana Ivanovic
Wimbledon	Rafael Nadal	Venus Williams
U.S. Open	Roger Federer	Serena Williams

HOCKEY

Stanley Cup Playoffs 2008

The Detroit Red Wings won their 11th Stanley Cup (they won their first in 1936) by defeating the Pittsburgh Penguins 3—2 in the sixth game of the National Hockey League championship. Red Wings left wing Henrik Zetterberg won the Conn Smythe Trophy as the most valuable player in the playoffs.

Hockey Teams with the Most Stanley Cup Championships

Team	No. of Championships	Years
Montreal Canadiens	23	1924, 30, 31, 44, 46, 53, 56—60, 65, 66, 68, 69, 71, 73, 76—79, 86, 93
Toronto Maple Leafs	13	1918, 22, 32, 42, 45, 47—49, 51, 62—64, 67
Detroit Red Wings	11	1936, 37, 43, 50, 52, 54, 55, 97, 98, 2002, 08

GOLF

Top Ten Golfers of 2008

(Based on tournament ranking points)

Male	Female
1. Tiger Woods, USA	1. Lorena Ochoa, Mexico
2. Sergio Garcia, Spain	2. Yani Tseng, Taiwan
3. Philip Alfred Mickelson, USA	3. Annika Sörenstam, Sweden
4. Padraig Harrington, Ireland	4. Paula Creamer, USA
5. Vijay Singh, Fiji	5. Suzann Pettersen, Norway
6. Robert Karlsson, Sweden	6. Ji-Yai Shin, Korea
7. Camilo Villegas, Colombia	7. Cristie Kerr, USA
8. Henrik Stenson, Sweden	8. Helen Alfredsson, Sweden
9. Ernie Els, Australia	9. Angela Stanford, USA
10. Lee John Westwood, UK	10. Karrie Anne Webb, Australia

Based on the estimates of sports industry experts, Tiger Woods will be worth one billion dollars by 2010. A much bigger portion of his earnings comes from product endorsements than from tournament prize money.

SOCCER

World Cup

The 2008 FIFA (Fédération Internationale de Football Association) Club World Cup was held December 11 to December 21, 2008, in Japan. Manchester United of England defeated Liga de Quito of Ecuador 1—0 in the final, becoming the first British team to win in the competition's 79-year history.

NASCAR Champions

NASCAR stands for the National Association for Stock Car Auto Racing, which was founded by Bill France in 1947. In 1949, the first championship, called Grand National, was held. The championship is now known as the Nextel Cup series and includes the Daytona 500, the Coca-Cola 600, and the Brickyard 400.

Championship Winners 1988–2008

Year	Winner	Year	Winner
2008	Jimmie Johnson	1997	Jeff Gordon
2007	Jimmie Johnson	1996	Terry Labonte
2006	Jimmie Johnson	1995	Jeff Gordon
2005	Tony Stewart	1994	Dale Earnhardt
2004	Kurt Busch	1993	Dale Earnhardt
2003	Matt Kenseth	1992	Alan Kulwicki
2002	Tony Stewart	1991	Dale Earnhardt
2001	Jeff Gordon	1990	Dale Earnhardt
2000	Bobby Labonte	1989	Rusty Wallace
1999	Dale Jarrett	1988	Bill Elliott
1998	Jeff Gordon		

Indianapolis 500

Held every Memorial Day weekend since 1911, the Indianapolis 500 is a 500-mile race around the Indianapolis Motor Speedway in Speedway, Indiana. Helio Castroneves of Brazil was the 2009 winner, with a time of 3:19:34.

In 2008, Danica Patrick became the first woman to win an Indy Car race when she won the Indy Japan 300.

OLYMPICS

The first recorded Olympic Games, held in Greece in 776 BC, consisted of one event—a running race of 210 yards (192 m). Over time, wrestling, boxing, jumping, discus, and javelin throwing were added. Eventually the Romans conquered Greece. The Games lost their significance and were banned in AD 393. In the 1800s, archaeologists uncovered the remains of the Olympic stadium and were inspired to organize a modern Olympic event. In 1896, the first modern Olympics were held in Athens. There were nine events: cycling, fencing, gymnastics, lawn tennis, shooting, swimming, track and field, weightlifting, and wrestling. Today the Olympics include 33 sports and nearly 400 events. The Olympics are held every two years, alternating between winter and summer.

Locations of the Modern-Day Summer Olympics

Year	Location
1896	Athens, Greece
1900	Paris, France
1904	St. Louis, Missouri, USA
1906	Athens, Greece
1908	London, England
1912	Stockholm, Sweden
1916	Canceled
1920	Antwerp, Belgium
1924	Paris, France
1928	Amsterdam, Holland

Year	Location
1932	Los Angeles, California, USA
1936	Berlin, Germany
1940	Canceled
1944	Canceled
1948	London, England
1952	Helsinki, Finland
1956	Melbourne, Australia
1960	Rome, Italy
1964	Tokyo, Japan
1968	Mexico City, Mexico

Year	Location
1972	Munich, Germany
1976	Montreal, Quebec, Canada
1980	Moscow, USSR
1984	Los Angeles, California, USA
1988	Seoul, South Korea
1992	Barcelona, Spain
1996	Atlanta, Georgia, USA
2000	Sydney, Australia
2004	Athens, Greece
2008	Beijing, China
2012	London, UK

Locations of the Modern-Day Winter Olympics

Year	Location
1924	Chamonix, France
1928	St. Moritz, Switzerland
1932	Lake Placid, New York, USA
1936	Garmisch-Partenkirchen, Germany
1940	Canceled
1944	Canceled
1948	St. Moritz, Switzerland
1952	Oslo, Norway
1956	Cortina d'Ampezzo, Italy
1960	Squaw Valley, California, USA
1964	Innsbruck, Austria

Year	Location
1968	Grenoble, France
1972	Sapporo, Japan
1976	Innsbruck, Austria
1980	Lake Placid, New York, USA
1984	Sarajevo, Yugoslavia
1988	Calgary, Alberta, Canada
1992	Albertville, France
1994	Lillehammer, Norway
1998	Nagano, Japan
2002	Salt Lake City, Utah, USA
2006	Turin, Italy
2010	Vancouver, Canada

Phenomenal swimmer Michael Phelps ruled the pool in Beijing at the 2008 Summer Olympics, winning an unprecedented 8 gold medals. His performance brought his career gold medal haul to a whopping 14—more than any other athlete in the history of the Games.

Technology & Computers

High-Tech World

Computers and technology have changed the way we communicate, work, learn, and play. For instance, phones are no longer just for talking. They can search the Internet, play music, navigate, and display movies and videos. We can gather news from every country in the world at the touch of a finger.

Let's Be Social

Our world has become interconnected by online communities such as Facebook and Twitter. We can watch videos or upload our own on YouTube. We can communicate with friends around the world on Skype.

Size Matters

Times have certainly changed since 1945, when a very expensive room-sized computer called ENIAC (Electronic Numerical Integrator and Computer) was invented. These days, computers are small enough to fit in the palm of your hand. Actually, the technology of microprocessors has created computers smaller than your fingernail. Computers can be found in an iPod nano, a computer mouse, even a car key.

Needle in a Haystack

The Internet is a huge network of computers where you can find just about anything that interests you. Companies and search engines such as Google were created to help you filter information by matching up keywords with news links, images, maps, and other related items. To represent the vast amount of information available on the Web, Google is named after the mathematical term *googol*, which is a huge number (1 followed by 100 zeros).

TAKE a LOOK

From their use in cell phones to refrigerators, GPS devices to TVs, computers have changed the way we get news, find our way around, and communicate. How many things in your everyday life are driven by computer technology?

CHECK IT OUT!

In 1969, ARPA (Advanced Research Projects Agency) began to connect computers in universities throughout the United States, creating the first online network. Since then the Internet has expanded, connecting people in every country and allowing people all over the world to access limitless information. How do you use the Internet in your daily life? Check out page 210 and see what others are doing online.

How Many Americans Use Technology?

Technology	Percentage Using
Cell phone	79%
Desktop computer	68%
Digital camera	55%
Video camera	43%
Laptop computer	36%
MP3 player	26%
Webcam	13%
Personal digital assistant (PDA)	11%

Where Are Americans Accessing the Internet?

Location	Percentage Accessing
At school	68.7%
At home	68.1%
At work	55.8%
By cell phone/mobile devices	11.1%
By wireless computer	10.7%

U.S. Internet Users by Age

Age Group	Percentage Using
18—29	87%
30—49	83%
50—64	65%
65+	32%

U.S. Internet Users by Gender

Gender	Percentage Using
Male	71%
Female	70%

Top 10 Countries with the Most Cell Phones per 100 People

Hong Kong, China	146.41
Italy	135.14
Czech Republic	128.36
Portugal	126.26
Ukraine	119.55
United Kingdom	118.47
Saudi Arabia	114.74
Russia	114.60
Sweden	113.73
Spain	110.24

Top 5 Countries with the Most Personal Computers

United States	251.7 million
China	85.5 million
Japan	82.1 million
Germany	58.3 million
United Kingdom	44.3 million

Top 5 Countries with the Most Internet Users

United States	222.5 million
China	166.1 million
Japan	95.3 million
India	91.4 million
Germany	53.4 million

CHECK IT OUT!

The first cellular phones were mobile car phones, created in 1947. Motorola invented the first real cell phone in 1973. These first cell phones were large and expensive, but advances in microtechnology have allowed cell phones to shrink in both size and cost. Now there are over three billion cell phones in use around the world.

What Are U.S. Internet Users Doing Online?

Activity	%
E-mailing	91%
Looking up health or medical information	80%
Reading news	72%
Visiting government sites	66%
Using a search engine	41%
Reading a journal or blog	39%
Uploading photos to a Web site to share	37%
Participating in a chat room or online discussion	22%
Creating content for the Internet	19%
Downloading video files	19%
Using a social networking site	16%
Making a phone call	8%

Top 10 Most Visited Web Sites

Google sites (YouTube; Blogger)
Yahoo! sites (Flickr; del.icio.us)
Microsoft sites
America Online sites
Fox Interactive Media sites (MySpace; Photobucket)
eBay sites (PayPal; Shopping.com; Skype)
Ask Network sites (Bloglines; Excite; iWon)
Wikimedia Foundation sites (Wikipedia)
Amazon sites (IMDb)
Glam Media sites

Top 10 Social Networking Sites

MySpace
Blogger
Facebook
Wordpress
Flickr
Classmates.com sites
Six Apart sites
Yahoo! Geocities
Reunion.com
Buzznet

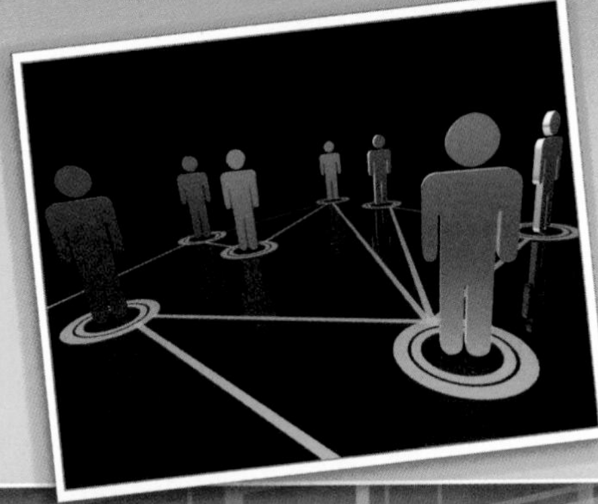

Internet and Texting Lingo

BTW	By the way
CBLO	See below
F2F	Face to face; a personal meeting
FCOL	For crying out loud
FWIW	For what it's worth
GTG	Got to go
HHOK	Ha-ha, only kidding
IMHO	In my humble opinion
IMO	In my opinion
LOL	Laughing out loud
PLS	Please
ROTFL	Rolling on the floor laughing
TAFN	That's all for now
TTFN	Ta-ta for now

Emoticons (Smileys)

:-)	Smile	:O	Surprise
;-)	Wink	:-/	Annoyed or skeptical
:-D	Laugh	:-@	Angry
:-*	Kiss	:'(	Crying
:-(	Frown	:-b...	Drooling

CHECK IT OUT!

The social networking site Facebook was founded by Mark Zuckerberg in 2004. He created the site as a college student at Harvard University. He dropped out of school after his second year and now works as the company's CEO.

U.S. Government

We, the People

Government is a system under which a nation, state, organization, or other group of people is managed. Different countries have different kinds of government. A nation may be ruled by a king or queen (monarchy). A single person can rule by himself or herself (dictatorship). In some rare instances, a country has no government at all (anarchy). The United States government is a representative democracy, ruled by the people themselves through their elected leaders. But this wasn't always the case.

Birth of a Nation

Before the United States were either united or states, they were colonies controlled largely by the English monarchy. The colonists wanted a different kind of government—one in which the people had a voice. After successfully fighting a revolutionary war of independence, they formed a new nation of their own. In 1787, they adopted the U.S. Constitution, a set of organizational rules and individual rights that serve as the foundation of our government to this day. It established three branches—the executive (president), the legislative (Congress) and the judicial (Supreme Court). The three branches work together while keeping a balance of political power among them.

Form a Line

The United States has had 44 presidents. Four of them died in office of natural causes:

- William Henry Harrison (1841)—of pneumonia
- Zachary Taylor (1849—1850)—of cholera
- Warren G. Harding (1921—1923)—of pneumonia
- Franklin D. Roosevelt (1933—1945)—of a cerebral hemorrhage

And four were assassinated:

- Abraham Lincoln (1861—1865)
- James Garfield (1881)
- William McKinley (1897—1901)
- John F. Kennedy (1961—1963)

If a president dies or can't complete his/her term, the vice president steps in. But what happens if the vice president can't take on the job either? You may be surprised at how many officials are in line for the job. (See page 218.)

TAKE a LOOK

If a picture is worth a thousand words, then whose picture is worth a thousand bucks? The faces of U.S. presidents and other leaders appear on our money, but do you know who's on what? If you had four Ulysses S. Grants, two Andrew Jacksons, a William McKinley, and five Abe Lincolns in your pocket, how much money would you have? Take a look at page 222 and count 'em up.

How can a presidential candidate win the election without getting the most votes from the people? Rutherford B. Hayes in 1876, Benjamin Harrison in 1888, and George W. Bush in 2000 are all proof that it can happen. (See page 220.)

The Branches of Government

Executive

The President

- Symbol of our nation and head of state
- Shapes and conducts foreign policy and acts as chief diplomat
- Chief administrator of federal government
- Commander-in-chief of armed forces
- Has authority to pass or veto congressional bills, plans, and programs
- Appoints and removes nonelected officials
- Leader of his or her political party

Legislative

The Congress:
The Senate
The House of Representatives

- Chief lawmaking body
- Conducts investigations into matters of national importance
- Has power to impeach or remove any civil officer from office, including the president
- Can amend Constitution
- The Senate is made up of 100 senators—2 from each state
- The House of Representatives is made up of 435 congressional representatives, apportioned to each state according to population

Judicial

The Supreme Court

- Protects Constitution
- Enforces commands of executive and legislative branches
- Protects rights of individuals and shields citizens from unfair laws
- Defines laws of our nation
- Can declare laws unconstitutional

Highest Federal Salaries

Official	Salary
President	$400,000
Vice President	$227,300
Speaker of the House	$223,500
Chief Justice of the Supreme Court	$223,500
Associate justices	$213,900
President Pro Tempore of the Senate	$193,400
Senate majority and minority leaders	$193,400
House majority and minority leaders	$193,400
Appeals court judges	$184,500
Senators	$174,000
Representatives	$174,000
District judges	$174,000

For most of the years between 1789 and 1855, members of Congress received no yearly salary at all. Instead they were paid $6.00 to $8.00 a day when Congress was in session. Benjamin Franklin proposed that elected government officials not be paid anything for their service, but his proposal didn't win much support.

How a Bill Introduced in the House of Representatives Becomes a La

How a Bill Originates

The executive branch inspires much legislation. The president usually outlines broad objectives in the yearly State of the Union address.

Members of the president's staff may draft bills and ask congresspersons who are friendly to the legislation to introduce them.

Other bills originate independently of the administration, perhaps to fulfill a campaign pledge made by a congressperson.

How a Bill Is Introduced

Each bill must be introduced by a member of the House. The Speaker then assigns the bill to the appropriate committee.

The committee conducts hearings during which members of the administration and others may testify for or against the bill.

If the committee votes to proceed, the bill goes to the Rules Committee, which decides whether to place it before the House.

The House Votes

A bill submitted to the House is voted on, with or without a debate. If a majority approves it, the bill is sent to the Senate.

Senate Procedure

The Senate assigns a bill to a Senate committee, which holds hearings and then approves, rejects, rewrites, or shelves the bill.

If the committee votes to proceed, the bill is submitted to the Senate for a vote, which may be taken with or without a debate.

Results

If the Senate does not change the House version of the bill and a majority approves it, the bill goes to the president for signing.

If the bill the Senate approves differs from the House version, the bill is sent to a House-Senate conference for a compromise solution.

If the conference produces a compromise bill and it is approved by both the House and Senate, the bill goes to the president for signing.

When a Bill Becomes Law

The bill becomes law if the president signs it. If the president vetoes the bill, two-thirds of both the House and Senate must approve it again before it can become law. If the bill comes to the president soon before Congress adjourns, the president may not do anything at all. If the bill is not signed before Congress adjourns, the bill dies. This is called the president's "pocket veto."

(A similar procedure is followed for bills introduced in the Senate.)

State and Federal Court Systems

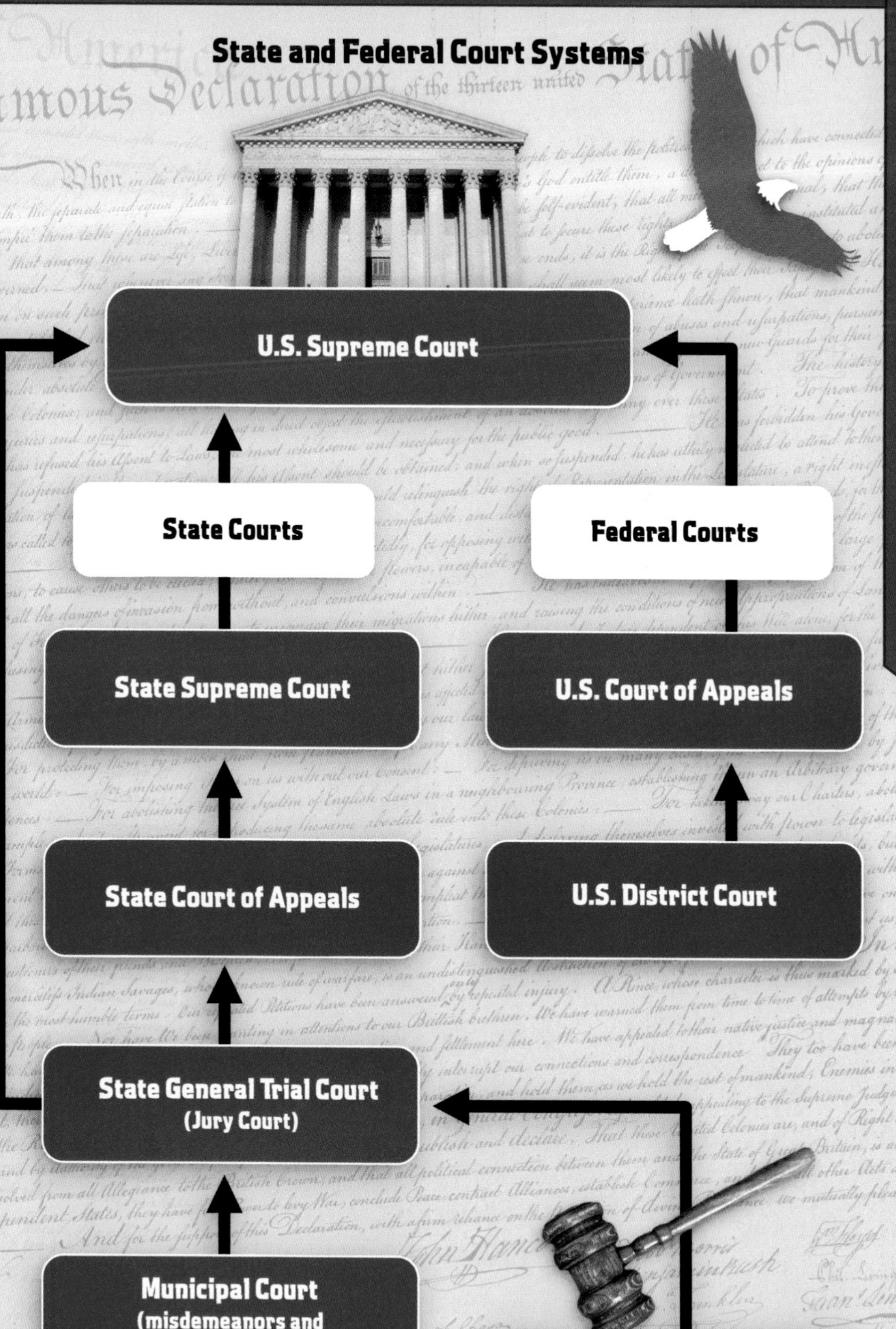

The Sequence of Presidential Succession

If the president dies, resigns, is removed from office, or can't carry out his or her duties, the vice president assumes the president's duties. If the vice president dies or becomes unable to serve, who is next in line? The order of presidential replacements is below.

1. Vice President
2. Speaker of the House
3. President Pro Tempore of the Senate
4. Secretary of State
5. Secretary of the Treasury
6. Secretary of Defense
7. Attorney General
8. Secretary of the Interior
9. Secretary of Agriculture
10. Secretary of Commerce
11. Secretary of Labor
12. Secretary of Health and Human Services
13. Secretary of Housing and Urban Development
14. Secretary of Energy
15. Secretary of Education

Voting

Basic Laws and Requirements

- You must be 18 years of age or older before an election in order to vote in it.
- You must be an American citizen to vote.
- You must register before voting.
- You must show proof of residence in order to register.

How to Register

- Registering often only requires filling out a simple form.
- It does not cost anything to register.
- You need not be a member of any political party to register.
- To find out where to register, you can call your town hall or city board of elections.
- You can find out more about voting and registering at:

www.eac.gov/voter

Voter Turnout: 1960–2008

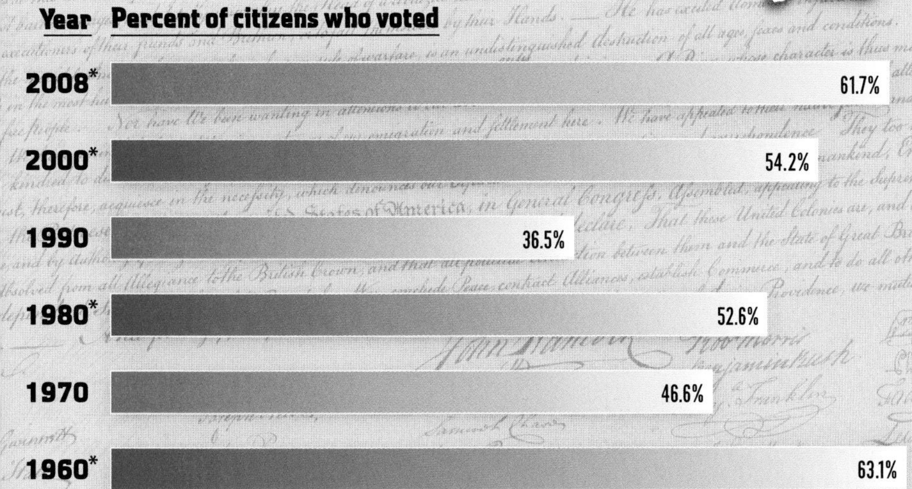

Year	Percent of citizens who voted
2008*	61.7%
2000*	54.2%
1990	36.5%
1980*	52.6%
1970	46.6%
1960*	63.1%

*Presidential election year

The Electoral College

Although people turn out on Election Day and cast their votes for president, the president and vice president are only indirectly elected by the American people. In fact, the president and vice president are the only elected federal officials not chosen by direct vote of the people. These two officials are elected by the Electoral College, which was created by the framers of the Constitution.

Here is a basic summary of how the Electoral College works:

- There are 538 electoral votes.
- The votes are divided among the 50 states and the District of Columbia. The number of votes that each state has is equal to the number of senators and representatives for that state. (California has 53 representatives and 2 senators; it has a total of 55 electoral votes.)
- During an election, the candidate who wins the majority of popular votes in a given state wins all the electoral votes from that state.
- A presidential candidate needs 270 electoral votes to win.

You may have heard that it is possible for a presidential candidate who has not won the most popular votes to win an election. This can happen if a candidate wins the popular vote in large states (ones with lots of electoral votes) by only a slim margin and loses the popular votes in smaller states by a wide margin.

Electoral Votes for President

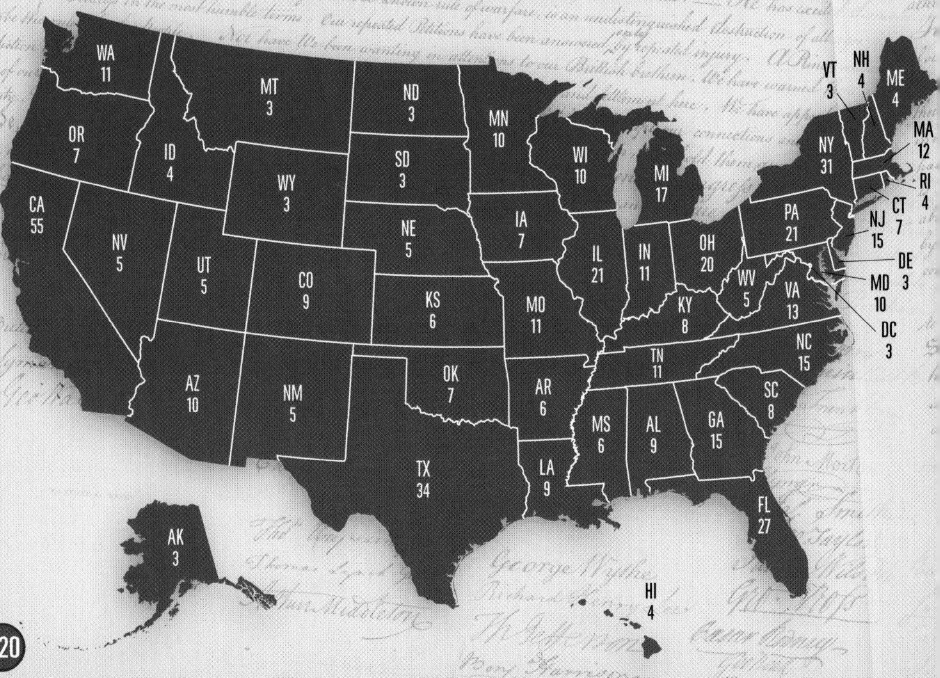

WA 11
OR 7
CA 55
ID 4
NV 5
MT 3
WY 3
UT 5
AZ 10
CO 9
NM 5
ND 3
SD 3
NE 5
KS 6
OK 7
TX 34
MN 10
IA 7
MO 11
AR 6
LA 9
WI 10
IL 21
MI 17
IN 11
OH 20
KY 8
TN 11
MS 6
AL 9
GA 15
FL 27
SC 8
NC 15
VA 13
WV 5
PA 21
NY 31
VT 3
NH 4
ME 4
MA 12
RI 4
CT 7
NJ 15
DE 3
MD 10
DC 3
AK 3
HI 4

U.S. Presidents with the Most Electoral Votes

President	Party	Year	Number of electoral votes
Ronald Reagan	Republican	1984	525
Franklin D. Roosevelt	Democrat	1936	523
Richard Nixon	Republican	1972	520
Ronald Reagan	Republican	1980	489
Lyndon B. Johnson	Democrat	1964	486
Franklin D. Roosevelt	Democrat	1932	472
Dwight D. Eisenhower	Republican	1956	457
Franklin D. Roosevelt	Democrat	1940	449
Herbert Hoover	Republican	1928	444
Dwight D. Eisenhower	Republican	1952	442

= Republican

= Democrat

U.S. Presidents with the Most Popular Votes

President	Party	Year	Number of popular votes
Ronald Reagan	Republican	1984	54,455,075
George H. W. Bush	Republican	1988	48,886,097
Richard Nixon	Republican	1972	47,169,911
Bill Clinton	Democrat	1992	44,908,254
Ronald Reagan	Republican	1980	43,904,153

Who Is on Our Paper Money?

$1
George Washington

$2
Thomas Jefferson

$5
Abraham Lincoln

$10
Alexander Hamilton

$20
Andrew Jackson

$50
Ulysses S. Grant

$100
Benjamin Franklin

$500*
William McKinley

$1,000*
Grover Cleveland

$5,000*
James Madison

$10,000*
Salmon P. Chase

$100,000*
Woodrow Wilson

*Bills above $100 are no longer made.

Who Is on Our Coins?

Dime
Franklin D. Roosevelt

Half-dollar
John F. Kennedy

Cent
Abraham Lincoln

Nickel
Thomas Jefferson

Quarter
George Washington

Dollar
Sacagawea

Presidents of the United States

1. George Washington

Born: Feb. 22, 1732, Wakefield, Virginia
Died: Dec. 14, 1799, Mount Vernon, Virginia
Term of office: April 30, 1789—March 3, 1797
Age at inauguration: 57
Party: Federalist
Vice President: John Adams
First Lady: Martha Dandridge Custis Washington

2. John Adams

Born: Oct. 30, 1735, Braintree (now Quincy), Massachusetts
Died: July 4, 1826, Braintree, Massachusetts
Term of office: March 4, 1797—March 3, 1801
Age at inauguration: 61
Party: Federalist
Vice President: Thomas Jefferson
First Lady: Abigail Smith Adams

3. Thomas Jefferson

Born: April 13, 1743, Shadwell, Virginia
Died: July 4, 1826, Monticello, Virginia
Term of office: March 4, 1801—March 3, 1809
Age at inauguration: 57
Party: Democratic Republican
Vice President: Aaron Burr, George Clinton
First Lady: Martha Skelton Jefferson

4. James Madison

Born: March 16, 1751, Port Conway, Virginia
Died: June 28, 1836, Orange, Virginia
Term of office: March 4, 1809—March 3, 1817
Age at inauguration: 57
Party: Democratic Republican
Vice President: George Clinton, Elbridge Gerry
First Lady: Dolley Todd Madison

CHECK IT OUT!

George Washington is the only president who was unanimously elected. He received every single vote!

5. James Monroe

Born: April 28, 1758, Westmoreland County, Virginia
Died: July 4, 1831, New York City, New York
Term of office: March 4, 1817—March 3, 1825
Age at inauguration: 58
Party: Democratic Republican
Vice President: Daniel D. Tompkins
First Lady: Elizabeth Kortright Monroe

6. John Quincy Adams

Born: July 11, 1767, Braintree, Massachusetts
Died: Feb. 23, 1848, Washington, DC
Term of office: March 4, 1825—March 3, 1829
Age at inauguration: 57
Party: Democratic Republican
Vice President: John C. Calhoun
First Lady: Louisa Johnson Adams

7. Andrew Jackson

Born: March 15, 1767, Waxhaw, South Carolina
Died: June 8, 1845, Nashville, Tennessee
Term of office: March 4, 1829—March 3, 1837
Age at inauguration: 61
Party: Democrat
Vice President: John C. Calhoun, Martin Van Buren
First Lady: Rachel Robards Jackson

8. Martin Van Buren

Born: Dec. 5, 1782, Kinderhook, New York
Died: July 24, 1862, Kinderhook, New York
Term of office: March 4, 1837—March 3, 1841
Age at inauguration: 54
Party: Democrat
Vice President: Richard M. Johnson
First Lady: Hannah Hoes Van Buren

9. William Henry Harrison

Born: Feb. 9, 1773, Berkeley, Virginia
Died: April 4, 1841, Washington, DC*
Term of office: March 4, 1841—April 4, 1841
Age at inauguration: 68
Party: Whig
Vice President: John Tyler
First Lady: Anna Symmes Harrison

10. John Tyler

Born: March 29, 1790, Greenway, Virginia
Died: Jan. 18, 1862, Richmond, Virginia
Term of office: April 6, 1841—March 3, 1845
Age at inauguration: 51
Party: Whig
Vice President: (none)**
First Lady: Letitia Christian Tyler, Julia Gardiner Tyler†

11. James Knox Polk

Born: Nov. 2, 1795, Mecklenburg, North Carolina
Died: June 15, 1849, Nashville, Tennessee
Term of office: March 4, 1845—March 3, 1849
Age at inauguration: 49
Party: Democrat
Vice President: George M. Dallas
First Lady: Sarah Childress Polk

12. Zachary Taylor

Born: Nov. 24, 1784, Orange County, Virginia
Died: July 9, 1850, Washington, DC*
Term of office: March 5, 1849—July 9, 1850
Age at inauguration: 64
Party: Whig
Vice President: Millard Fillmore
First Lady: Margaret (Peggy) Smith Taylor

William Henry Harrison had the longest inauguration speech and the shortest term of any president. After giving a speech lasting 105 minutes in the cold rain, he developed pneumonia and died 32 days later.

ed in office, natural causes
ce president John Tyler took over the duties of the president when William Henry Harrison died in office, leaving the vice presidency vacant.
esident Tyler's first wife died in 1842. He remarried in 1844.

13. Millard Fillmore

Born: Jan. 7, 1800, Cayuga County, New York
Died: March 8, 1874, Buffalo, New York
Term of office: July 10, 1850—March 3, 1853
Age at inauguration: 50
Party: Whig
Vice President: (none)*
First Lady: Abigail Powers Fillmore

14. Franklin Pierce

Born: Nov. 23, 1804, Hillsboro, New Hampshire
Died: Oct. 8, 1869, Concord, New Hampshire
Term of office: March 4, 1853—March 3, 1857
Age at inauguration: 48
Party: Democrat
Vice President: William R. King
First Lady: Jane Appleton Pierce

15. James Buchanan

Born: April 23, 1791, Mercersburg, Pennsylvania
Died: June 1, 1868, Lancaster, Pennsylvania
Term of office: March 4, 1857—March 3, 1861
Age at inauguration: 65
Party: Democrat
Vice President: John C. Breckenridge
First Lady: (none)**

16. Abraham Lincoln

Born: Feb. 12, 1809, Hardin, Kentucky
Died: April 15, 1865, Washington, DC[†]
Term of office: March 4, 1861—April 15, 1865
Age at inauguration: 52
Party: Republican
Vice President: Hannibal Hamlin, Andrew Johnson
First Lady: Mary Todd Lincoln

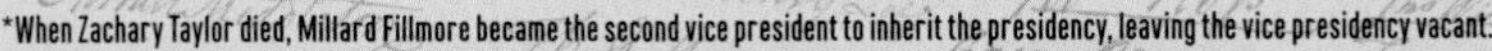

*When Zachary Taylor died, Millard Fillmore became the second vice president to inherit the presidency, leaving the vice presidency vacant.
**Buchanan was the only president who never married. A favorite niece, Harriet Lane, acted as White House hostess during his administration.
†Assassinated

17. Andrew Johnson

Born: Dec. 29, 1808, Raleigh, North Carolina
Died: July 31, 1875, Carter Station, Tennessee
Term of office: April 15, 1865—March 3, 1869
Age at inauguration: 56
Party: Democrat (nominated by Republican Party)
Vice President: (none)*
First Lady: Eliza McCardle Johnson

18. Ulysses Simpson Grant

Born: April 27, 1822, Point Pleasant, Ohio
Died: July 23, 1885, Mt. McGregor, New York
Term of office: March 4, 1869—March 3, 1877
Age at inauguration: 46
Party: Republican
Vice President: Schuyler Colfax, Henry Wilson
First Lady: Julia Dent Grant

19. Rutherford Birchard Hayes

Born: Oct. 4, 1822, Delaware, Ohio
Died: Jan. 17, 1893, Fremont, Ohio
Term of office: March 4, 1877—March 3, 1881
Age at inauguration: 54
Party: Republican
Vice President: William A. Wheeler
First Lady: Lucy Webb Hayes

20. James Abram Garfield

Born: Nov. 19, 1831, Orange, Ohio
Died: Sept. 19, 1881, Elberon, New Jersey**
Term of office: March 4, 1881—Sept. 19, 1881
Age at inauguration: 49
Party: Republican
Vice President: Chester A. Arthur
First Lady: Lucretia Rudolph Garfield

On March 1, 1872, Ulysses S. Grant established Yellowstone as the country's first national park.

*Andrew Johnson became president when Abraham Lincoln was assassinated, leaving the vice presidency vacant.
**Assassinated

21. Chester Alan Arthur

Born: Oct. 5, 1829, Fairfield, Vermont
Died: Nov. 18, 1886, New York City, New York
Term of office: Sept. 20, 1881—March 3, 1885
Age at inauguration: 51
Party: Republican
Vice President: (none)*
First Lady: Ellen Herndon Arthur

22. Grover Cleveland

Born: March 18, 1837, Caldwell, New Jersey
Died: June 24, 1908, Princeton, New Jersey
Term of office: March 4, 1885—March 3, 1889
Age at inauguration: 47
Party: Democrat
Vice President: Thomas A. Hendricks
First Lady: Frances Folsom Cleveland

23. Benjamin Harrison

Born: Aug. 20, 1833, North Bend, Ohio
Died: March 13, 1901, Indianapolis, Indiana
Term of office: March 4, 1889—March 3, 1893
Age at inauguration: 55
Party: Republican
Vice President: Levi P. Morton
First Lady: Caroline Scott Harrison (died in 1892)

24. Grover Cleveland

Born: March 18, 1837, Caldwell, New Jersey
Died: June 24, 1908, Princeton, New Jersey
Term of office: March 4, 1893—March 3, 1897
Age at inauguration: 55
Party: Democrat
Vice President: Adlai E. Stevenson
First Lady: Frances Folsom Cleveland

Grover Cleveland is the only president elected to two nonconsecutive terms.

*Chester Alan Arthur became president when James Garfield was assassinated, leaving the vice presidency vacant.

25. William McKinley

Born: Jan. 29, 1843, Niles, Ohio
Died: Sept. 14, 1901, Buffalo, New York*
Term of office: March 4, 1897—Sept. 14, 1901
Age at inauguration: 54
Party: Republican
Vice President: Garret A. Hobart, Theodore Roosevelt
First Lady: Ida Saxton McKinley

26. Theodore Roosevelt

Born: Oct. 27, 1858, New York City, New York
Died: Jan. 6, 1919, Oyster Bay, New York
Term of office: Sept. 14, 1901—March 3, 1909
Age at inauguration: 42
Party: Republican
Vice President: Charles W. Fairbanks
First Lady: Edith Carow Roosevelt

27. William Howard Taft

Born: Sept. 15, 1857, Cincinnati, Ohio
Died: March 8, 1930, Washington, DC
Term of office: March 4, 1909—March 3, 1913
Age at inauguration: 51
Party: Republican
Vice President: James S. Sherman
First Lady: Helen Herron Taft

28. (Thomas) Woodrow Wilson

Born: Dec. 28, 1856, Staunton, Virginia
Died: Feb. 3, 1924, Washington, DC
Term of office: March 4, 1913—March 3, 1921
Age at inauguration: 56
Party: Democrat
Vice President: Thomas R. Marshall
First Lady: Ellen Axon Wilson, Edith Galt Wilson**

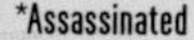

*Assassinated
**Wilson's first wife died early in his administration and he remarried before leaving the White House.

29. Warren Gamaliel Harding

Born: Nov. 2, 1865, Corsica (now Blooming Grove), Ohio
Died: Aug. 2, 1923, San Francisco, California*
Term of office: March 4, 1921—Aug. 2, 1923
Age at inauguration: 55
Party: Republican
Vice President: Calvin Coolidge
First Lady: Florence Kling De Wolfe Harding

30. (John) Calvin Coolidge

Born: July 4,1872, Plymouth Notch, Vermont
Died: Jan. 5, 1933, Northampton, Massachusetts
Term of office: Aug. 3, 1923—March 3, 1929
Age at inauguration: 51
Party: Republican
Vice President: Charles G. Dawes
First Lady: Grace Goodhue Coolidge

31. Herbert Clark Hoover

Born: Aug. 10, 1874, West Branch, Iowa
Died: Oct. 20, 1964, New York City, New York
Term of office: March 4, 1929—March 3, 1933
Age at inauguration: 54
Party: Republican
Vice President: Charles Curtis
First Lady: Lou Henry Hoover

32. Franklin Delano Roosevelt

Born: Jan. 30, 1882, Hyde Park, New York
Died: April 12, 1945, Warm Springs, Georgia*
Term of office: March 4, 1933—April 12, 1945
Age at inauguration: 51
Party: Democrat
Vice President: John N. Garner, Henry A. Wallace, Harry S Truman
First Lady: Anna Eleanor Roosevelt

CHECK IT OUT!

Two presidents, John Adams and Thomas Jefferson, died on the same day—July 4, 1826. Another president, James Monroe, died on July 4, 1831. A fourth, Calvin Coolidge, was born on July 4, 1872.

*Died in office, natural causes

33. Harry S Truman

Born: May 8, 1884, Lamar, Missouri
Died: Dec. 26, 1972, Kansas City, Missouri
Term of office: April 12, 1945—Jan. 20, 1953
Age at inauguration: 60
Party: Democrat
Vice President: Alben W. Barkley
First Lady: Elizabeth (Bess) Wallace Truman

34. Dwight David Eisenhower

Born: Oct. 14, 1890, Denison, Texas
Died: March 28, 1969, Washington, DC
Term of office: Jan. 20, 1953—Jan. 20, 1961
Age at inauguration: 62
Party: Republican
Vice President: Richard M. Nixon
First Lady: Mamie Doud Eisenhower

35. John Fitzgerald Kennedy

Born: May 29, 1917, Brookline, Massachusetts
Died: Nov. 22, 1963, Dallas, Texas*
Term of office: Jan. 20, 1961—Nov. 22, 1963
Age at inauguration: 43
Party: Democrat
Vice President: Lyndon B. Johnson
First Lady: Jacqueline Bouvier Kennedy

36. Lyndon Baines Johnson

Born: Aug. 27, 1908, Stonewall, Texas
Died: Jan. 22, 1973, San Antonio, Texas
Term of office: Nov. 22, 1963—Jan. 20, 1969
Age at inauguration: 55
Party: Democrat
Vice President: Hubert H. Humphrey
First Lady: Claudia (Lady Bird) Taylor Johnson

*Assassinated

37. Richard Milhous Nixon

Born: Jan. 9, 1913, Yorba Linda, California
Died: April 22, 1994, New York City, New York
Term of office: Jan. 20, 1969–Aug. 9, 1974
Age at inauguration: 56
Party: Republican
Vice President: Spiro T. Agnew (resigned), Gerald R. Ford
First Lady: Thelma (Pat) Ryan Nixon

38. Gerald Rudolph Ford

Born: July 14, 1913, Omaha, Nebraska
Died: Dec. 26, 2006, Rancho Mirage, California
Term of office: Aug. 9, 1974–Jan. 20, 1977
Age at inauguration: 61
Party: Republican
Vice President: Nelson A. Rockefeller
First Lady: Elizabeth (Betty) Bloomer Warren Ford

39. James Earl (Jimmy) Carter

Born: Oct. 1, 1924, Plains, Georgia
Term of office: Jan. 20, 1977–Jan. 20, 1981
Age at inauguration: 52
Party: Democrat
Vice President: Walter F. Mondale
First Lady: Rosalynn Smith Carter

40. Ronald Wilson Reagan

Born: Feb. 6, 1911, Tampico, Illinois
Died: June 5, 2004, Los Angeles, California
Term of office: Jan. 20, 1981–Jan. 20, 1989
Age at inauguration: 69
Party: Republican
Vice President: George H. W. Bush
First Lady: Nancy Davis Reagan

41. George Herbert Walker Bush

Born: June 12, 1924, Milton, Massachusetts
Term of office: Jan. 20, 1989–Jan. 20, 1993
Age at inauguration: 64
Party: Republican
Vice President: James Danforth (Dan) Quayle
First Lady: Barbara Pierce Bush

CHECK IT OUT!

There have been two father-son presidential combinations: John Adams and John Quincy Adams, and George H. W. Bush and George W. Bush. In addition, President William Henry Harrison was the grandfather of President Benjamin Harrison.

42. William Jefferson (Bill) Clinton

Born: Aug. 19, 1946, Hope, Arkansas
Term of office: Jan. 20, 1993—Jan. 20, 2001
Age at inauguration: 46
Party: Democrat
Vice President: Albert (Al) Gore Jr.
First Lady: Hillary Rodham Clinton

43. George Walker Bush

Born: July 6, 1946, New Haven, Connecticut
Term of office: Jan. 20, 2001—Jan. 20, 2009
Age at inauguration: 54
Party: Republican
Vice President: Richard B. (Dick) Cheney
First Lady: Laura Welch Bush

44. Barack Hussein Obama Jr.

Born: Aug. 4, 1961, Honolulu, Hawaii
Term of office: Jan. 20, 2009—
Age at inauguration: 47
Party: Democrat
Vice President: Joseph R. (Joe) Biden Jr.
First Lady: Michelle Robinson Obama

President Barack Obama was born in Honolulu, Hawaii, to a white mother who had grown up in Kansas and a black father from Kenya, Africa. As a young child, Obama was one of only a few black students at his school. He became an outstanding student at college and at Harvard Law School. After law school he worked to help poor families in Chicago, Illinois, get better health care and more educational programs. In 1996, he became an Illinois state senator, and in 2004 was elected to the U.S. Senate. In 2008, Obama won the Democratic nomination for president and became the first African American to be elected to the highest office in the country.

U.S. History

Free to be U.S.

For hundreds of years, the promise of freedom has attracted people to America from all over the world. Settlers came seeking the right to practice their chosen religions and to speak their minds without fear of punishment or government interference. They came for the right to make personal choices, large and small, and to live their lives as they pleased.

A Brave Declaration

In 1775, American colonists went to war for freedom. They wrote down their reasons for making war against their ruler, King George III of Britain, in the Declaration of Independence. The patriots who wrote this document were very brave. They knew that to revolt against Britain was treason, and that everyone who signed the Declaration could be hanged. Today the Declaration of Independence remains a symbol of freedom and courage, and a reminder that every person deserves the right to "life, liberty, and the pursuit of happiness."

Ten Top Rights

America won its independence in 1783. In 1787, members of Congress approved the U.S. Constitution, a document containing rules by which the new country would operate. Some members weren't completely happy with the Constitution. They thought it didn't say enough about people's rights. They wanted to add amendments that would guarantee citizens freedom of speech, of religion, and of the press, the right to a trial by jury, and other rights. In 1791, the Bill of Rights, consisting of the first ten amendments to the Constitution, was ratified by Congress.

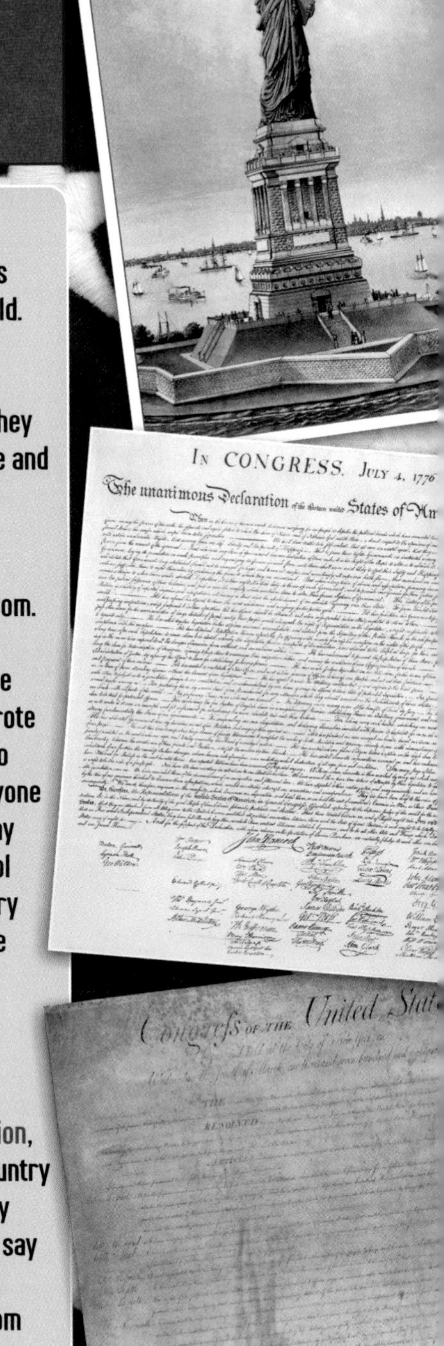

☆ Star-Spangled Country ☆

In September, 1814, the United States was at war with Britain again. A lawyer named Francis Scott Key was aboard an American ship being held by the British as the ship began to bomb Fort McHenry in Maryland. The bombardment lasted all night. At dawn, Key saw the American flag still waving across the harbor and knew the attack had failed. The poem he wrote about it was published and set to the tune of an English song. But "The Star-Spangled Banner" didn't become our national anthem until March 3, 1931.

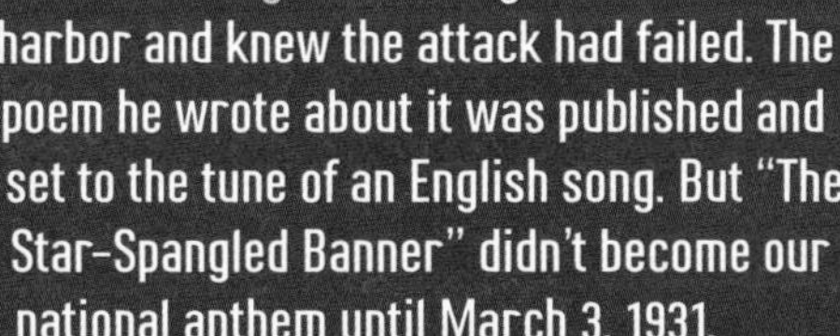

TAKE a LOOK

Read through the Bill of Rights on page 244. Key words and phrases are printed in red. Think about all the rights U.S. citizens enjoy. Are there other rights people should have? If you could add an amendment to the Constitution, what would it be?

In 1775, delegates from the colonies came together at the Second Continental Congress to prepare for war with Britain. John Hancock, the president of the Congress, was the first to sign the Declaration of Independence. Hancock signed his name in large, bold letters. Some people use the term *John Hancock* to mean a signature.

John Hancock

CHECK IT OUT!

U.S. History Highlights: 1000–1700

c. 1000	Viking explorer Leif Ericson explores North American coast and founds temporary colony called Vinland.
1492	On first voyage to America, Christopher Columbus lands at San Salvador Island in Bahamas.

1513	Juan Ponce de Leon discovers Florida. Vasco Nuñez de Balboa crosses Panama and sights Pacific Ocean.
1520	Ferdinand Magellan, whose ships were first to circumnavigate world, discovers South American straits, later named after him.
1521	Hernán Cortéz captures Mexico City and conquers Aztec Empire.
1534–1539	Jacques Cartier of France explores coast of Newfoundland and Gulf of St. Lawrence. Hernando de Soto conquers Florida and begins three-year trek across Southeast.
1540	Francisco Vásquez de Coronado explores Southwest, discovering Grand Canyon and introducing horses to North America.

1541	Hernando de Soto discovers Mississippi River.

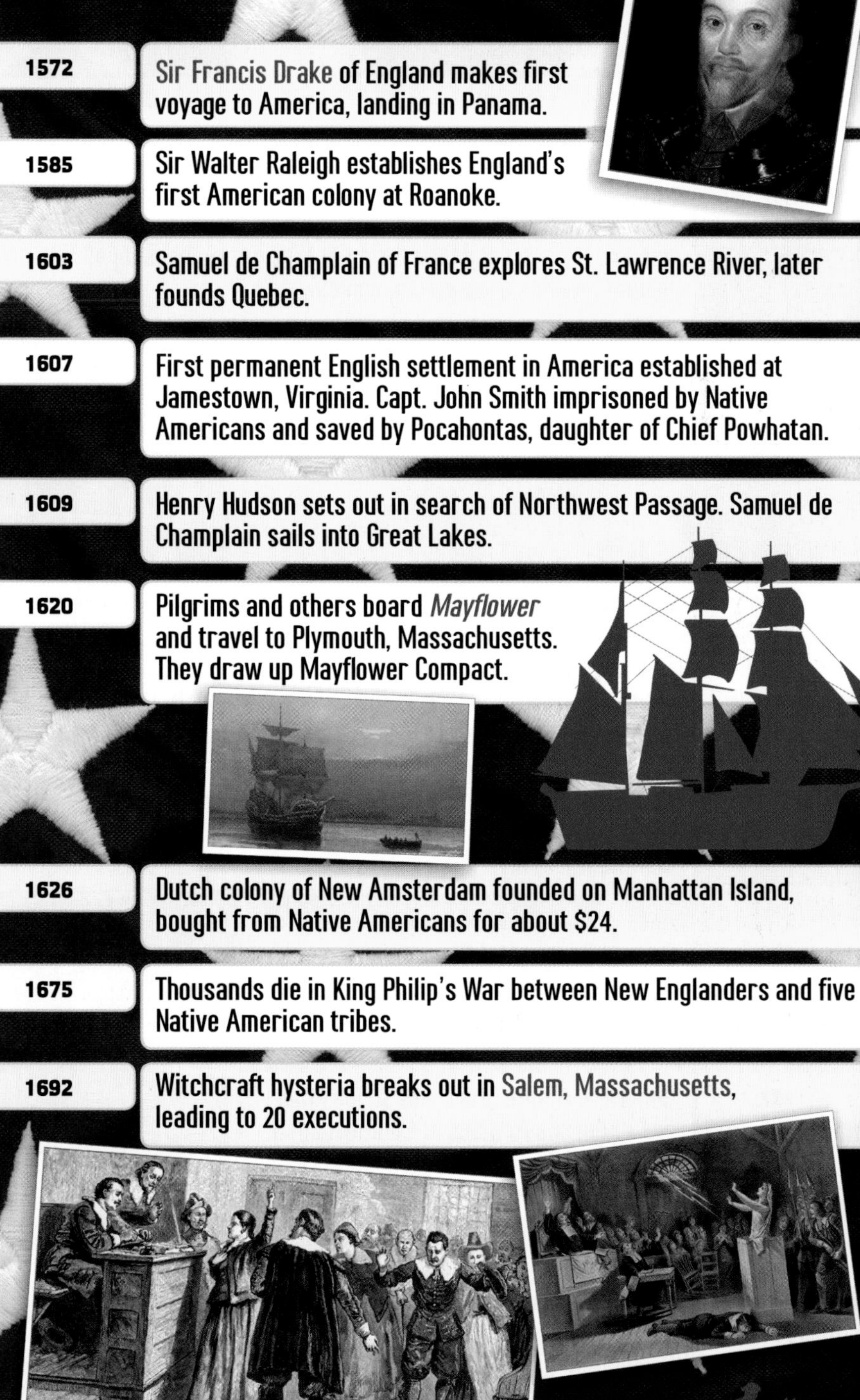

1572	Sir Francis Drake of England makes first voyage to America, landing in Panama.
1585	Sir Walter Raleigh establishes England's first American colony at Roanoke.
1603	Samuel de Champlain of France explores St. Lawrence River, later founds Quebec.
1607	First permanent English settlement in America established at Jamestown, Virginia. Capt. John Smith imprisoned by Native Americans and saved by Pocahontas, daughter of Chief Powhatan.
1609	Henry Hudson sets out in search of Northwest Passage. Samuel de Champlain sails into Great Lakes.
1620	Pilgrims and others board *Mayflower* and travel to Plymouth, Massachusetts. They draw up Mayflower Compact.
1626	Dutch colony of New Amsterdam founded on Manhattan Island, bought from Native Americans for about $24.
1675	Thousands die in King Philip's War between New Englanders and five Native American tribes.
1692	Witchcraft hysteria breaks out in Salem, Massachusetts, leading to 20 executions.

U.S. History Highlights: 1700s–1800s

1754	French and Indian War begins.
1763	Treaty of Paris ends French and Indian War.
1765	Parliament passes Stamp Act (tax on newspapers, legal documents, etc.) and Quartering Act (requiring housing of British soldiers in colonists' homes).
1770	Five Americans, including Crispus Attucks, a black man said to be the leader, perish in Boston Massacre (March 5).
1773	British Parliament passes Tea Act, leading to Boston Tea Party (Dec. 16).
1775	American Revolution begins with battles of Lexington and Concord (April 19). Second Continental Congress appoints George Washington as commander of Continental Army.
1776	Second Continental Congress approves Declaration of Independence on July 4.
1777	Congress adopts Stars and Stripes flag and endorses Articles of Confederation. Washington's army spends winter at Valley Forge, Pennsylvania.
1783	Treaty of Paris signed (Sept. 3), officially ending American Revolution.
1787	Constitution accepted by delegates to Constitutional Convention in Philadelphia on Sept. 17.
1803	Louisiana Purchase from France doubles size of U.S.

Lewis and Clark expedition sets out from St. Louis, Missouri. New Jersey begins gradual emancipation of slaves. Alexander Hamilton killed in duel with Aaron Burr.

War of 1812 with Britain begins by close vote in Congress.

War of 1812 ends.

Erie Canal opens.

Mexican War begins when U.S. troops are attacked in disputed Texas territory.

Gold Rush brings hundreds of thousands to California. Elizabeth Blackwell is first American woman to receive medical degree.

Democratic Party splits into Northern and Southern wings. South Carolina is first Southern state to secede from Union after election of Abraham Lincoln.

Civil War begins with attack on Ft. Sumter in South Carolina (April 12).

Pres. Lincoln issues Emancipation Proclamation, freeing slaves in ten states.

Gen. Lee surrenders to Gen. Grant at Appomattox Court House, Virginia (April 9). Pres. Lincoln assassinated by John Wilkes Booth in Washington, DC.

Fifteenth Amendment, guaranteeing right to vote for all U.S. citizens, is ratified (Feb. 3).

After mysterious explosion of battleship Maine in Havana harbor (Feb. 15), Spanish-American War breaks out (April 25).

U.S. History Highlights: 1900s–Present

1903 Orville and Wilbur Wright conduct first powered flight near Kitty Hawk, NC (Dec. 17).

1909 Expedition team led by Robert E. Peary and Matthew Henson plants American flag at North Pole (April 6). W.E.B. DuBois founds National Association for the Advancement of Colored People (NAACP).

1917 Congress declares war on Germany (April 6) and Austria-Hungary (Dec. 7), bringing U.S. into World War I.

1918 Armistice Day ends World War I (Nov. 11).

1920 Nineteenth Amendment establishes women's right to vote (Aug. 26).

1927 Charles Lindbergh completes nonstop solo flight from New York to Paris (May 20—21).

1929 Stock market crash on "Black Tuesday" (Oct. 29) ushers in Great Depression.

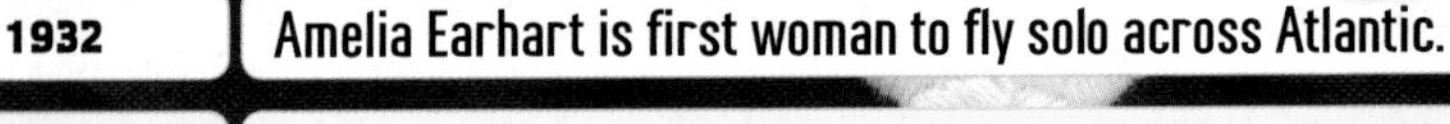

1932 Amelia Earhart is first woman to fly solo across Atlantic.

1941 Japanese planes attack Pearl Harbor, HI, killing 2,400 U.S. servicemen and civilians (Dec. 7). U.S. declares war on Japan (Dec. 8). Germany and Italy declare war on U.S. (Dec. 11). U.S. declares war on Germany and Italy (Dec. 11).

1945 Germany surrenders, ending war in Europe (May 7). Atomic bombs dropped on Hiroshima (Aug. 6) and Nagasaki (Aug. 9); Japan surrenders (Aug. 14), ending World War II.

1950 North Korea invades South Korea, beginning Korean War (June 25).

1954 Supreme Court orders school desegregation in *Brown v. Board of Education* decision (May 17).

1958 In response to Soviet launch of *Sputnik*, U.S. launches *Explorer I*, first American satellite.

1962 Lt. Col. John H. Glenn Jr. is first American to orbit Earth.

1963 Dr. Martin Luther King Jr. delivers his "I Have a Dream" speech in Washington, DC (Aug. 28). Pres. Kennedy assassinated in Dallas, TX (Nov. 22).

1965	Black nationalist Malcolm X assassinated in New York City (Feb. 21). Pres. Johnson orders U.S. Marines into South Vietnam (March 8).
1968	Dr. Martin Luther King Jr. is assassinated by James Earl Ray in Memphis, TN (April 4). After winning California presidential primary, Sen. Robert F. Kennedy of New York is assassinated by Sirhan Sirhan in Los Angeles, CA (June 5).
1969	Neil Armstrong and Edwin "Buzz" Aldrin of *Apollo 11* are first men to walk on Moon (July 20).
1972	Congress debates Equal Rights Amendment.
1973	Supreme Court disallows state restrictions on abortions (*Roe v. Wade*). U.S. signs Paris peace accords ending Vietnam War (Jan. 27). Vice Pres. Spiro Agnew resigns after threat of indictment for tax evasion (Oct. 10).
1974	Pres. Nixon resigns, elevating Vice Pres. Ford to presidency (Aug. 9).
1981	*Columbia* completes first successful space shuttle mission (April 12—13). Sandra Day O'Connor becomes first female Justice of Supreme Court.
1983	Sally Ride, aboard space shuttle *Challenger*, is first American female astronaut.
1986	Space shuttle *Challenger* explodes in midair over Florida.
1991	U.S. sends aircraft, warships, and 400,000 troops to Persian Gulf to drive Iraq's armed forces from Kuwait in Operation Desert Storm (Jan. 17). Ground war begins six weeks later and lasts only 100 hours (Feb. 24—28).
2001	On Sept. 11, hijackers overtake four U.S. planes, crashing two of them into World Trade Center in New York City. In all, 2,800 lives are lost.
2003	Suspecting weapons of mass destruction, U.S. declares war on Iraq (March 20). Official combat ends May 1.
2007	After hitting all-time high, stock market starts decline.
2008	U.S. is formally declared to be in recession. Sen. Barack Obama, first African American major presidential candidate, is elected president.

Declaration of Independence

(Phrases in red are key ideas.)

In Congress, July 4, 1776

The unanimous Declaration of the thirteen united States of America

When in the Course of human events, it becomes necessary for one people to dissolve the political bands which have connected them with another, and to assume among the powers of the earth, the separate and equal station to which the Laws of Nature and of Nature's God entitle them, a decent respect to the opinions of mankind requires that they should declare the causes which impel them to the separation.

We hold these truths to be self-evident, that all men are created equal, that they are endowed by their Creator with certain unalienable Rights, that among these are Life, Liberty and the pursuit of Happiness. —That to secure these rights, Governments are instituted among Men, deriving their just powers from the consent of the governed, —That whenever any Form of Government becomes destructive of these ends, it is the Right of the People to alter or to abolish it, and to institute new Government, laying its foundation on such principles and organizing its powers in such form, as to them shall seem most likely to effect their Safety and Happiness. Prudence, indeed, will dictate that Governments long established should not be changed for light and transient causes; and accordingly all experience hath shown, that mankind are more disposed to suffer, while evils are sufferable, than to right themselves by abolishing the forms to which they are accustomed. But when a long train of abuses and usurpations, pursuing invariably the same Object evinces a design to reduce them under absolute Despotism, it is their right, it is their duty, to throw off such Government, and to provide new Guards for their future security. —Such has been the patient sufferance of these Colonies; and such is now the necessity which constrains them to alter their former Systems of Government. The history of the present King of Great Britain is a history of repeated injuries and usurpations, all having in direct object the establishment of an absolute Tyranny over these States. To prove this, let Facts be submitted to a candid world.

He has refused his Assent to Laws, the most wholesome and necessary for the public good.

He has forbidden his Governors to pass Laws of immediate and pressing importance, unless suspended in their operation till his Assent should be obtained; and when so suspended, he has utterly neglected to attend to them.

He has refused to pass other Laws for the accommodation of large districts of people, unless those people would relinquish the right of Representation in the Legislature, a right inestimable to them and formidable to tyrants only.

He has called together legislative bodies at places unusual, uncomfortable, and distant from the depository of their public Records, for the sole purpose of fatiguing them into compliance with his measures.

He has dissolved Representative Houses repeatedly, for opposing with manly firmness his invasions on the rights of the people.

He has refused for a long time, after such dissolutions, to cause others to be elected; whereby the Legislative powers, incapable of Annihilation, have returned to the People at large for their exercise; the State remaining in the mean time exposed to all the dangers of invasion from without, and convulsions within.

He has endeavoured to prevent the population of these States; for that purpose obstructing the Laws for Naturalization of Foreigners; refusing to pass others to encourage their migrations hither, and raising the conditions of new Appropriations of Lands.

He has obstructed the Administration of Justice, by refusing his Assent to Laws for establishing Judiciary powers.

He has made Judges dependent on his Will alone, for the tenure of their offices, and the amount and payment of their salaries.

He has erected a multitude of New Offices, and sent hither swarms of Officers to harrass our people, and eat out their substance.

He has kept among us, in times of peace, Standing Armies without the Consent of our legislatures.

He has affected to render the Military independent of and superior to the Civil power.

He has combined with others to subject us to a jurisdiction foreign to our constitution, and unacknowledged by our laws; giving his Assent to their Acts of pretended Legislation:

For Quartering large bodies of armed troops among us:

For protecting them, by a mock Trial, from punishment for any Murders which they should commit on the Inhabitants of these States:

For cutting off our Trade with all parts of the world:

For imposing Taxes on us without our Consent:

For depriving us in many cases, of the benefits of Trial by Jury:

For transporting us beyond Seas to be tried for pretended offences:

For abolishing the free System of English Laws in a neighbouring Province, establishing therein an Arbitrary government, and enlarging its Boundaries so as to render it at once an example and fit instrument for introducing the same absolute rule into these Colonies:

For taking away our Charters, abolishing our most valuable Laws, and altering fundamentally the Forms of our Governments:

For suspending our own Legislatures, and declaring themselves invested with power to legislate for us in all cases whatsoever.

He has abdicated Government here, by declaring us out of his Protection and waging War against us.

He has plundered our seas, ravaged our Coasts, burnt our towns, and destroyed the lives of our people.

He is at this time transporting large Armies of foreign Mercenaries to compleat the works of death, desolation and tyranny, already begun with circumstances of Cruelty & perfidy scarcely paralleled in the most barbarous ages, and totally unworthy the Head of a civilized nation.

He has constrained our fellow Citizens taken Captive on the high Seas to bear Arms against their Country, to become the executioners of their friends and Brethren, or to fall themselves by their Hands.

He has excited domestic insurrections amongst us, and has endeavoured to bring on the inhabitants of our frontiers, the merciless Indian Savages, whose known rule of warfare, in an undistinguished destruction of all ages, sexes and conditions.

In every stage of these Oppressions We have Petitioned for Redress in the most humble terms: Our repeated Petitions have been answered only by repeated injury. A Prince whose character is thus marked by every act which may define a Tyrant, is unfit to be the ruler of a free people.

Nor have We been wanting in attentions to our Brittish brethren. We have warned them from time to time of attempts by their legislature to extend an unwarrantable jurisdiction over us. We have reminded them of the circumstances of our emigration and settlement here. We have appealed to their native justice and magnanimity, and we have conjured them by the ties of our common kindred to disavow these usurpations, which, would inevitably interrupt our connections and correspondence. They too have been deaf to the voice of justice and of consanguinity. We must, therefore, acquiesce in the necessity, which denounces our Separation, and hold them, as we hold the rest of mankind, Enemies in War, in Peace Friends.

We, therefore, the Representatives of the united States of America, in General Congress, Assembled, appealing to the Supreme Judge of the world for the rectitude of our intentions, do, in the Name, and by Authority of the good People of these Colonies, solemnly publish and declare, That these United Colonies are, and of Right ought to be Free and Independent States; that they are Absolved from all Allegiance to the British Crown, and that all political connection between them and the State of Great Britain, is and ought to be totally dissolved; and that as Free and Independent States, they have full Power to levy War, conclude Peace, contract Alliances, establish Commerce, and to do all other Acts and Things which Independent States may of right do. And for the support of this Declaration, with a firm reliance on the protection of divine Providence, we mutually pledge to each other our Lives, our Fortunes and our sacred Honor.

The Bill of Rights

The First 10 Amendments to the Constitution

(The first 10 amendments, known collectively as the Bill of Rights, were adopted in 1791.)

Amendment I

Congress shall make no law respecting an establishment of religion, or prohibiting the free exercise thereof; or abridging the freedom of speech, or of the press; or the right of the people peaceably to assemble, and to petition the Government for a redress of grievances.

Amendment II

A well regulated Militia, being necessary to the security of a free State, the right of the people to keep and bearArms, shall not be infringed.

Amendment III

No Soldier shall, in time of peace be quartered in any house, without the consent of the Owner, nor in time of war, but in a manner to be prescribed by law.

Amendment IV

The right of the people to be secure in their persons, houses, papers, and effects, against unreasonable searches and seizures, shall not be violated, and no Warrants shall issue, but upon probable cause, supported by Oath or affirmatior and particularly describing the place to be searched, and the persons or things to be seized.

Amendment V

No person shall be held to answer for a capital, or otherwise infamous crime, unless on a presentment or indictment of a Grand Jury, except in cases arising in the land or naval forces, or in the Militia, when in actual service in time of War or public danger; nor shall any person be subject for the same offence to be twice put in jeopardy of life or limb; nor shall be compelled in any criminal case to be a witness against himself, nor be deprived of life, liberty, or property, without due process of law; nor shall private property be taken for public use, without just compensation.

Amendment VI

In all criminal prosecutions, the accused shall enjoy the right to a speedy and public trial, by an impartial jury of the State and district wherein the crime shall have been committed, which district shall have been previously ascertained by law, and to be informed of the nature and cause of the accusation; to be confronted with the witnesses against him; to have compulsory process for obtaining witnesses in his favor, and to have the Assistance of Counsel for his defence

Amendment VII

In Suits at common law, where the value in controversy shall exceed twenty dollars, the right of trial by jury shall be preserved, and no fact tried by jury, shall be otherwise re-examined in any Court of the United States, than accordin to the rules of the common law.

Amendment VIII

Excessive bail shall not be required, nor excessive fines imposed, nor cruel and unusual punishments inflicted.

Amendment IX

The enumeration in the Constitution, of certain rights, shall not be construed to deny or disparage others retained by the people.

Amendment X

The powers not delegated to the United States by the Constitution, nor prohibited by it to the States, are reserved t the States respectively, or to the people.

(Phrases in red are key id

Important Supreme Court Decisions

Marbury v. Madison **(1803)**

The Court struck down a law "repugnant to the constitution" for the first time and set the precedent for judicial review of acts of Congress.

Dred Scott v. Sanford **(1857)**

Dred Scott, a Missouri slave, sued for his liberty after his owner took him into free territory. The Court ruled that Congress could not bar slavery in the territories. This decision sharpened sectional conflict about slavery.

Plessy v. Ferguson **(1896)**

This case was about the practice of segregating railroad cars in Louisiana. The Court ruled that as long as equal accommodations were provided, segregation was not discrimination and did not deprive black Americans of equal protection under the Fourteenth Amendment. This decision was overturned by *Brown v. Board of Education* (1954).

Brown v. Board of Education **(1954)**

Chief Justice Earl Warren led the Court to decide unanimously that segregated schools violated the equal protection clause of the Fourteenth Amendment. Efforts to desegregate Southern schools after the Brown decision met with massive resistance for many years.

Miranda v. Arizona **(1966)**

The Court ruled that Ernesto Miranda's confession to certain crimes was not admissible as evidence because he had been denied his right to silence and to legal counsel. Now police must advise suspects of their "Miranda rights" when they're taken into custody.

Roe v. Wade **(1973)**

In a controversial decision, the Court held that state laws restricting abortion were an unconstitutional invasion of a woman's right to privacy.

Chief Justices of the U.S. Supreme Court

Chief Justice	Tenure	Appointed by
John Jay	1789—1795	George Washington
John Rutledge	1795	George Washington
Oliver Ellsworth	1796—1800	George Washington
John Marshall	1801—1835	John Adams
Roger B. Taney	1836—1864	Andrew Jackson
Salmon P. Chase	1864—1873	Abraham Lincoln
Morrison R. Waite	1874—1888	Ulysses S. Grant
Melville W. Fuller	1888—1910	Grover Cleveland
Edward D. White	1910—1921	William H. Taft
William H. Taft	1921—1930	Warren G. Harding
Charles E. Hughes	1930—1941	Herbert Hoover
Harlan F. Stone	1941—1946	Franklin D. Roosevelt
Fred M. Vinson	1946—1953	Harry S Truman
Earl Warren	1953—1969	Dwight D. Eisenhower
Warren E. Burger	1969—1986	Richard M. Nixon
William H. Rehnquist	1986—2005	Ronald Reagan
John G. Roberts Jr.	2005—	George W. Bush

Weather

What Causes Weather?

Weather has a huge effect on our lives. It determines what kind of clothing we choose to wear, what we eat, and how we spend our day. Weather changes constantly, but all weather is a result of three key factors—pressure, temperature, and humidity (the amount of water in the air).

Warning: Contents Under Pressure

We walk around under an ocean—an ocean of air called the atmosphere, which is always pushing down on us. This atmospheric pressure keeps changing, and when it does, so does the weather. High air pressure produces clear, sunny weather. Low pressure brings cloudy, stormy weather. Meteorologists use an instrument called a barometer to measure the pressure.

Taking Some Heat

Every day the Sun heats up Earth and the air above it. The warm air rises and cooler air rushes in, which creates wind. If the air warms gradually and rises gently, we get a nice breeze. If it warms quickly, heavy-duty winds and storms can result.

It's Raining, It's Pouring

When the Sun strikes water—whether a puddle or an ocean—the heat turns water molecules into vapor. The vapor rises, cools, and condenses to form clouds. When the clouds become too heavy, water falls from them as rain or snow. This cycle of evaporation, condensation, and precipitation never stops. There is the same amount of water on Earth today as there was at the beginning. So the water you drink today could have been sipped by a dinosaur millions of years ago!

TAKE a LOOK

The water cycle never stops, but some places get more rain than others. Check page 248 to find the wettest and driest places in the United States.

CHECK IT OUT!

The line where cold and warm air masses collide is called a front. A cold front occurs when cold air pushes warm air out of its way. Cold fronts can bring stormy and even severe weather. A warm front occurs when warm air pushes away cold air, and it can bring gray, drizzly weather. (On a weather map, a cold front is indicated by a blue line with triangles below. Warm fronts are shown as red lines with half-circles above.)

U.S. Weather Extremes

The numbers below are based on 30-year averages of temperature, wind, snowfall, rainfall, and humidity at weather stations in the 48 continental states (not Alaska and Hawaii).

5 Driest Places

Location	Annual Precipitation
Yuma, AZ	3.01 in. (7.65 cm)
Las Vegas, NV	4.49 in. (11.40 cm)
Bishop, CA	5.02 in. (12.75 cm)
Bakersfield, CA	6.49 in. (16.48 cm)
Alamosa, CO	7.25 in. (18.41 cm)

5 Wettest Places

Location	Annual Precipitation
Mount Washington, NH	101.91 in. (258.85 cm)
Quillayute, WA	101.72 in. (258.37 cm)
Astoria, OR	67.13 in. (170.51 cm)
Mobile, AL	66.29 in. (168.38 cm)
Pensacola, FL	64.29 in. (163.27 cm)

5 Coldest Places

Location	Average Temperature
Mount Washington, NH	27.2°F (2.66°C)
International Falls, MN	37.4°F (3.00°C)
Marquette, MI	38.7°F (3.72°C)
Duluth, MN	39.1°F (3.94°C)
Caribou, ME	39.2°F (4.00°C)

5 Hottest Places

Location	Average Temperature
Key West, FL	78.1°F (25.61°C)
Miami, FL	76.7°F (24.83°C)
Yuma, AZ	75.3°F (24.05°C)
West Palm Beach, FL	75.3°F (24.05°C)
Fort Wayne, FL	74.9°F (23.83°C)

El Azizia, Libya, holds the world record for heat. The temperature there reached 136°F (57.78°C) on September 13, 1922. The lowest temperature on record is –128.6°F (–89.22°C), at Vostok Station, Antarctica, on July 21, 1983.

Worst U.S. Natural Disasters

Drought
When: Peak periods in 1930, 1934, 1936, 1939, and 1940
Where: Many states
This was the longest drought of the twentieth century. During 1934, dry regions stretched from New York and Pennsylvania across the Great Plains to the California coast. A great "Dust Bowl" covered some 50 million acres in the south central plains during the winter of 1935—1936.

Earthquake
When: April 18, 1906
Where: San Francisco, CA
An earthquake accompanied by fire destroyed more than 4 square miles (10 sq km) and left at least 700 dead or missing.

Flood
When: May 31, 1889
Where: Johnstown, PA
More than 2,200 died in a flood that caused fires and explosions.

Hurricane
When: August 27—September 15, 1900
Where: Galveston, TX
More than 6,000 died from the devastating combination of high winds and tidal waves.

Tornado
When: March 18, 1925
Where: Missouri, Illinois, and Indiana
Called the Great Tri-State Tornado, this twister caused 695 deaths and ripped along an unbroken path of 219 miles (352 km) after touching down near Ellington, MO.

Blizzard
When: March 11—14, 1888
Where: East Coast
Four hundred people died, and 40—50 inches (101.6—127 cm) of snow fell in the Blizzard of '88. Damage was estimated at $20 million.

CHECK IT OUT!

Hurricane Katrina, which hit the Gulf Coast in 2005, was the costliest natural disaster in U.S. history and the third-deadliest hurricane. The massive storm was responsible for 1,833 deaths and $81 billion in damages.

Weights & Measures

Weight and See

What if you never knew how many glasses of milk you could pour from a quart or liter container?

What if you bought a pair of sneakers in your size and they were big enough for Bozo the Clown?

What if a pound of peaches weighed a ton? A ton of bricks holding up a building weighed only a few pounds?

In other words, what if there were no standardized weights and measurements?

Standard Procedure

Every day we depend on measurement standards for precise information that will keep us safe and healthy and allow us to plan our lives. Weight and measurement standards are regulated by countries, and inspectors enforce the standards. Scales to weigh meat and fruit at the grocery store are regularly checked. The contents of boxed and canned food are measured and weighed to make sure they match what the label says.

Mainly Metric

The standard system of measurement for most developed nations is the metric system. In America, scientists and engineers use metric measurements, but people use the "inch-pound" system for everyday life. English colonists brought this system with them when they began to arrive in the 1600s.

A Perfect Ten

The metric system is based on the decimal system, whose foundation is the number 10. It lets us weigh and measure things more precisely than the American system. But every American measurement can be converted into metric, and vice versa. In 1959, the United States and other English-speaking nations agreed to make a foot equal exactly 0.3048 meters and a pound equal exactly 453.59237 grams.

1 FOOT = 0.3048 METERS

1 POUND = 453.59237 GRAMS

TAKE a LOOK

This chapter shows you how to convert most American measurements to metric, and vice versa. Use the information to go metric for a day, starting from when you wake up. Ask a family member to measure your height. Then measure everything else you use, eat, or drink all day. Measure your height again at night and convert all the measurements to metric. You may find something surprising in your results. (Learn more on page 271.)

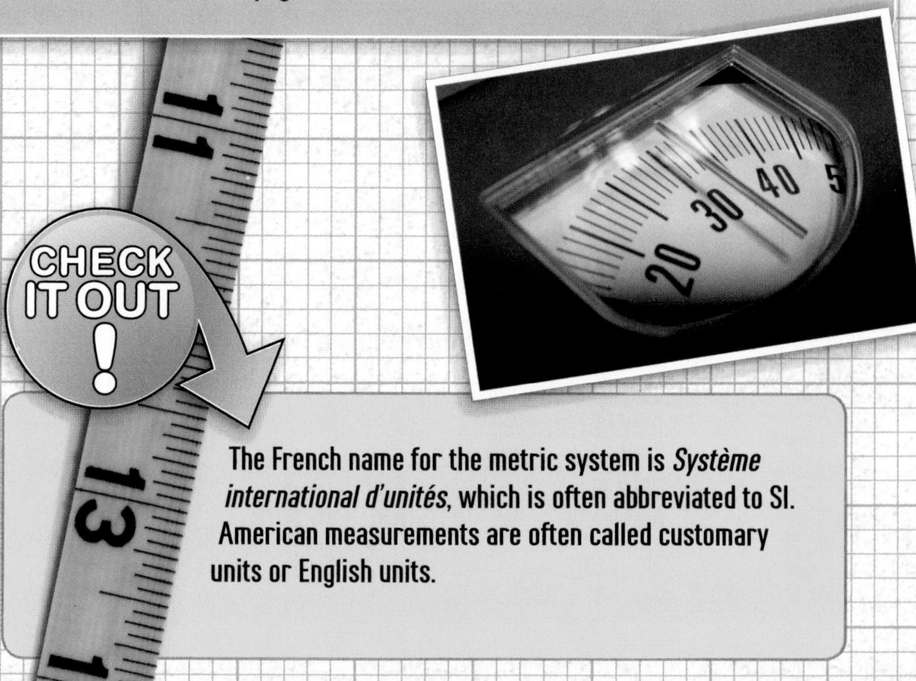

CHECK IT OUT!

The French name for the metric system is *Système international d'unités*, which is often abbreviated to SI. American measurements are often called customary units or English units.

Simple Metric Conversion Table

To convert	To	Multiply by
centimeters	feet	0.0328
centimeters	inches	0.3937
cubic centimeters	cubic inches	0.0610
degrees	radians	0.0175
feet	centimeters	30.48
feet	meters	0.3048
gallons	liters	3.785
grams	ounces	0.0353
inches	centimeters	2.54
kilograms	pounds	2.205
kilometers	miles	0.6214
knots	miles/hour	1.151
liters	gallons	0.2642
liters	pints	2.113
meters	feet	3.281
miles	kilometers	1.609
ounces	grams	28.3495
pounds	kilograms	0.4536

Converting Household Measures

To convert	To	Multiply by
dozens	units	12
baker's dozens	units	13
teaspoons	milliliters	4.93
teaspoons	tablespoons	0.33
tablespoons	milliliters	14.79
tablespoons	teaspoons	3
cups	liters	0.24
cups	pints	0.50
cups	quarts	0.25
pints	cups	2
pints	liters	0.47
pints	quarts	0.50
quarts	cups	4
quarts	gallons	0.25
quarts	liters	0.95
quarts	pints	2
gallons	liters	3.79
gallons	quarts	4

Temperature Conversions

Fahrenheit	Celsius
475	246.1
450	232.2
425	218.3
400	204.4
375	190.6
350	176.7
325	162.8
300	148.9
275	135.0
250	121.1
225	107.2
212	100.0
110	43.3
105	40.6
100	37.8
95	35.0
90	32.2
85	29.4
80	26.7
75	23.9
70	21.1
65	18.3
60	15.6
55	12.8
50	10.0
45	7.2
40	4.4
35	1.7
32	0.0
30	–1.1
25	–3.9
20	–6.7
15	–9.4
10	–12.2
5	–15.0
0	–17.8
–5	–20.6
–10	–23.3
–15	–26.1
–20	–28.9
–25	–31.7
–30	–34.4
–35	–37.2
–40	–40.0
–45	–42.8

Fractions and Their Decimal Equivalents

Fraction	Decimal	Fraction	Decimal	Fraction	Decimal
1/2	0.5000	2/7	0.2857	5/9	0.5556
1/3	0.3333	2/9	0.2222	5/11	0.4545
1/4	0.2500	2/11	0.1818	5/12	0.4167
1/5	0.2000	3/4	0.7500	6/7	0.8571
1/6	0.1667	3/5	0.6000	6/11	0.5455
1/7	0.1429	3/7	0.4286	7/8	0.8750
1/8	0.1250	3/8	0.3750	7/9	0.7778
1/9	0.1111	3/10	0.3000	7/10	0.7000
1/10	0.1000	3/11	0.2727	7/11	0.6364
1/11	0.0909	4/5	0.8000	7/12	0.5833
1/12	0.0833	4/7	0.5714	8/9	0.8889
1/16	0.0625	4/9	0.4444	8/11	0.7273
1/32	0.0313	4/11	0.3636	9/10	0.9000
1/64	0.0156	5/6	0.8333	9/11	0.8182
2/3	0.6667	5/7	0.7143	10/11	0.9091
2/5	0.4000	5/8	0.6250	11/12	0.9167

Length or Distance
U.S. Customary System

1 foot (ft.)	=	12 inches (in.)				
1 yard (yd.)	=	3 feet	=	36 inches		
1 rod (rd.)	=	5 ½ yards	=	16 ½ feet		
1 furlong (fur.)	=	40 rods	=	220 yards	=	660 feet
1 mile (mi.)	=	8 furlongs	=	1,760 yards	=	5,280 feet

An international nautical mile has been defined as 6,076.1155 feet.

Six Quick Ways to Measure if You Don't Have a Ruler

1. Most credit cards are 3 3/8 inches by 2 1/8 inches.
2. Standard business cards are printed 3 ½ inches wide by 2 inches long.
3. Floor tiles are usually manufactured in 12-inch squares.
4. U.S. paper money is 6 1/8 inches wide by 2 5/8 inches tall.
5. The diameter of a quarter is approximately 1 inch, and the diameter of a penny is approximately ¾ of an inch.
6. A standard sheet of paper is 8 ½ inches wide and 11 inches long.

World History

Ask Your Mummy

This chapter is about the history of the world since ancient times, before people wrote down accounts of events as a regular practice. Without recorded eyewitness accounts, how do we know what happened? Scientists and historians have learned a lot from their mummies!

A Cold Case

Take the case of Otzi, a 5,300-year-old mummy found in 1991, frozen in the Alps between Austria and Italy. Archaeologists could tell what Otzi had for his last meal, where he lived, and much more. They could also tell he knew something about natural medicine. They found a deep wound in his hand and several kinds of mosses in his stomach, including a kind known to have healing powers.

A Lot of Garbage?

Mummies have been found on every continent in the world. We can learn about the past not just from human remains but from what humans threw out when they were alive. Bone slivers and plant parts tell what families ate for supper and what they grew in their gardens. A broken fork or a splinter of pottery can reveal how civilized mealtimes were. What will our trash say about us in the future?

WORDS AND PICTURES

Today we have our pick of ways to study history. We can read journals, diaries, letters, ship's logs, and other primary-source documents to learn firsthand what people were experiencing. We can look at photographs or videos that capture a precise moment. We can even watch history as it's happening on the Internet or on TV. On January 20, 2009, millions of viewers around the world watched as Barack Obama was sworn in as the first African American president of the United States.

TAKE a LOOK

Behind every date and event in history are people—famous people and ordinary people. The more we know about the people, the more meaning history has. Pick a date or event in this chapter and do some research to learn more about the people involved. Or choose one of the famous people featured here and find some interesting details about him or her that aren't generally known.

There are various terms used for dating eras and periods in history. BC stands for "before Christ," or the years before Jesus Christ lived. The same period of time, which includes prehistoric times and ancient history, can also be called BCE ("before the common era"). CE means "common era." It refers to the same period of time as AD, which stands for "*anno Domini.*" That means "in the year of our Lord," or after the birth of Christ.

Ancient History Highlights

Date	Event
4.5 billion BC	Planet Earth formed.
3 billion BC	First signs of life (bacteria and green algae) appear in oceans.
3.2 million BC	*Australopithecus afarensis* roams Earth (remains, nicknamed Lucy, found in Ethiopia in 1974).
1.8 million BC	*Homo erectus* ("Upright Man"). Brain size twice that of *australopithecine* species.
100,000 BC	First modern *Homo sapiens* live in East Africa.
4500–3000 BC	Sumerians in Tigris and Euphrates valleys develop city-state civilization. First phonetic writing.
3000–2000 BC	Pharaonic rule begins in Egypt with King Menes. Great Sphinx of Giza constructed. Earliest Egyptian mummies created.
2000–1500 BC	Israelites enslaved in Egypt.
1500–1000 BC	Ikhnaton develops monotheistic religion in Egypt (circa 1375 BC). His successor, Tutankhamun, returns to earlier gods. Moses leads Israelites out of Egypt into Canaan. Ten Commandments. End of Greek civilization in Mycenae with invasion of Dorians.
800–700 BC	First recorded Olympic Games (776 BC). Legendary founding of Rome by Romulus (753 BC).
700–600 BC	Founding of Byzantium by Greeks (circa 660 BC). Building of Acropolis in Athens by Solon, Greek lawmaker (630—560 BC).
600–500 BC	Confucius (551—479 BC). develops philosophy of Confucianism in China. Siddhartha Gautama (Buddha) (563—483 BC) founds Buddhism in India.
300–241 BC	First Punic War (264—241 BC). Rome defeats Carthaginians and begins domination of Mediterranean. Invention of Mayan calendar in Yucatán (more exact than older calendars). First Roman gladiatorial games (264 BC). Archimedes, Greek mathematician (287—212 BC).
250–201 BC	Construction of Great Wall of China begins.
149–146 BC	Third Punic War. Rome destroys Carthage.
100–51 BC	Julius Caesar (100—44 BC) invades Britain and conquers Gaul (France). Spartacus leads slave revolt against Rome (73 BC). Birth of Jesus (variously given 7 BC to 4 BC).

People of Ancient History

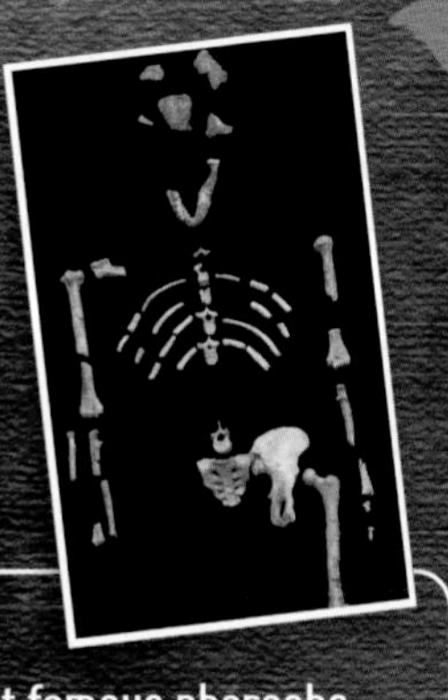

Lucy

In 1974, in Hadar, Ethopia, scientists discovered a nearly complete skeleton of an *Australopithecus afarensis*, or early human being, which they named Lucy. The skeleton provided scientists with critical insight into the history of humans.

Tutankhamun

Tutankhamun, or King Tut, was one of the most famous pharaohs, or rulers, of ancient Egypt. He began ruling at age ten and died before he was twenty. There are no written records about his life. Most of the information known comes from what Howard Carter discovered in King Tut's tomb in 1922.

Confucius

Confucius was a thinker and educator in ancient China. His beliefs and teachings about the way a person should live and treat others greatly influenced the Chinese culture and inspired the Ru school of Chinese thought. Later his beliefs spread to other parts of the world, and his type of belief system came to be known as Confucianism.

Buddha

Siddhartha Gautama was born the son of a wealthy ruler in what is modern-day Nepal. One day he was confronted with the suffering of people outside his kingdom, and he left his life of privilege. Siddhartha searched for enlightenment through meditation and eventually found his own path of balance in the world. He earned the title Buddha, or "Enlightened One," and spent the rest of his life helping others to reach enlightenment.

Julius Caesar

As a great politician, military leader, and dictator, Julius Caesar expanded the Roman Empire. He led Rome in conquering Gaul (France), ended the civil war, and instituted many social reforms. His rule ended with his assassination by many of his fellow statesmen on March 15, the Ides of March.

World History Highlights: AD 1–1499

Date	Event
AD 1–49	Crucifixion of Jesus Christ (probably AD 30).
312–337	Under Constantine the Great, eastern and western Roman empires reunited and new capital, Constantinople, established.
350–399	Huns (Mongols) invade Europe (circa 360).
622–637	Muhammad flees from Mecca to Medina. Muslim empire grows (634). Arabs conquer Jerusalem (637).
c. 900	Vikings discover Greenland.
c. 1000	Viking raider Leif Erickson discovers North America, calls it Vinland. Chinese invent gunpowder.
1211–1227	Genghis Khan invades China, Persia, and Russia.
1215	King John of England forced by barons to sign Magna Carta, limiting royal power.
1231–1252	Inquisition begins as Pope Gregory IX creates special court to locate and punish heretics. Torture used (1252).
1251	Kublai Khan comes to prominence in China.
1271–1295	Marco Polo of Venice travels to China.
circa 1325	Renaissance begins in Italy.
1337–1453	English and French fight for control of France in Hundred Years' War.
1347–1351	About 25 million Europeans die from "Black Death" (bubonic plague).
1368	Ming dynasty begins in China.
1429	Joan of Arc leads French against English.
1452	Leonardo da Vinci, painter of *Mona Lisa* and other masterpieces, born near Florence, Italy.
1492–1498	Columbus discovers Caribbean Islands and Americas, returns to Spain (1493). Second voyage to Dominica, Jamaica, Puerto Rico (1493—1496). Third voyage to Orinoce (1498).
1497	Vasco da Gama sails around Africa and discovers sea route to India (1498). John Cabot, employed by England, explores Canadian coast.

People of AD 1–1499

Constantine

Known as Constantine the Great, he served as the emperor of Rome from 312 to 337. He created a "new" Rome by bringing religious tolerance to the empire and laying a foundation for western culture. He moved the center of the empire from Rome to the Greek colony of Byzantium, which he renamed Constantinople.

Muhammad

As a prophet from Mecca, Muhammad worked to restore the faith of Abraham. He spread the religion of Islam and the belief in one true God, Allah. His teachings were recorded in the Koran. As his teachings spread, many aristocrats in Mecca began to oppose him. Muhammad fled to Medina, an event that marks the beginning of the Muslim calendar. In 629, he won over his opposition in Mecca. By the time he died in 632, most of the Arabian Peninsula followed his political and religious ideas.

Genghis Khan

Born around 1162 in Mongolia, Genghis Khan was a warrior and ruler who united the tribes of Mongolia and founded the Mongol Empire. He spent his life establishing and increasing his empire by conquering China, Russia, and parts of Persia.

Joan of Arc

At the age of thirteen, Joan of Arc heard the voices of saints telling her to help the French king defeat the English. She presented herself to the king and led the French army to victory at Orléans, forcing the English out of the region. She was later captured by the English, accused of heresy, and burned at the stake. Joan of Arc was hailed as a hero in France for her bravery and made a saint.

Leonardo da Vinci

Italian-born Leonardo da Vinci was one of the most farsighted, multitalented, and relentless thinkers of the time. He was a great artist, inventor, engineer, mathematician, architect, scientist, and musician whose works and insights (created new discoveries) and influenced generations.

World History Highlights: 1500–1899

Date	Event
1509	Henry VIII becomes king of England.
1513	Juan Ponce de León explores Florida and Yucatán Peninsula for Spain.
1517	Martin Luther pins his 95 theses on door of Wittenberg Castle Church in Wittenberg, Germany, starting Protestant Reformation.
1520	Ferdinand Magellan discovers Straits of Magellan and Tierra del Fuego for Spain.
1547	Ivan IV, known as Ivan the Terrible, crowned czar of Russia.
1558	Elizabeth I, Henry VIII's daughter, becomes queen of England.
1585–1587	Sir Walter Raleigh's men reach Roanoke Island, Virginia.
1588	Spanish Armada attempts to invade England and is defeated.
1609	Henry Hudson explores Hudson River and Hudson Bay for England.
1632	Italian astronomer Galileo Galilei is first person to view space through a telescope and confirms belief that Earth revolves around Sun.
1687	Sir Isaac Newton publishes his theories on gravity and his laws of motion.
1721	Peter I, known as Peter the Great, crowned czar of Russia.
1756	Seven Years' War breaks out, involving most European countries.
1778	James Cook discovers Hawaii.
1789	Parisians storm Bastille prison, starting French Revolution.
1804	Scottish explorer John Ross begins expedition to find Northwest Passage in Arctic.
1821	Mexico gains its independence from Spain.
1845	Irish potato crops are ruined by blight, or fungus, creating famine that leads millions to starve to death or emigrate to America.
1859	Charles Darwin publishes *The Origin of Species*.
1898	Spanish-American war begins.

People of 1500–1899

Ferdinand Magellan

As a Portuguese explorer, Magellan sailed under both the Portuguese and Spanish flags. To find a route to India by sailing west, he sailed around South America to the Pacific Ocean, discovering the Strait of Magellan along the way. Although he was killed in the Philippines and did not complete the journey, his ships made it back to Spain to become the first to circumnavigate the globe.

Elizabeth I

Queen Elizabeth I ruled England, leading her country through war with wisdom and courage. She was a beloved queen who brought prosperity and a rebirth of learning to England, making the country a major European power. For this reason, the era in which she ruled became known as the Elizabethan Age.

Galileo

Galileo Galilei was a great Italian thinker whose contributions in philosophy, astronomy, and mathematics shaped the way we view the world. He helped develop the scientific method and establish the mathematical laws of falling motion. He advanced the development of the telescope to the point where he could use it to view objects in space and prove that Earth revolved around the Sun. His findings and beliefs were radical at the time and led to his excommunication from the Catholic Church.

Sir Isaac Newton

The contributions of this English physicist and mathematician laid the foundation of many modern sciences. Newton's discovery of white light and its composition of colors paved the way for studies in modern optics. His laws of motion gave a basis to modern physics and his law of universal gravity created a framework for classic mechanics.

Peter the Great

Crowned czar of Russia at the age of ten, Peter ruled jointly with his half brother until his brother's death. As sole ruler, Peter expanded the Russian empire to reclaim access to the Baltic Sea and establish trade with Europe. He reorganized government, founding the city of St. Petersburg as the new capital of Russia and creating the Russian army and navy.

World History Highlights: 1900–Present

Date	Event
1905	Albert Einstein formulates his theory of relativity.
1911	Marie Curie wins Nobel Prize for chemistry.
1914	Archduke Franz Ferdinand, heir to Austrian-Hungarian throne, assassinated in Sarajevo, setting off events that lead to World War I.
1918	Massive worldwide flu epidemic kills more than 20 million people.
1919	Treaty of Versailles signed, ending World War I.
1927	American Charles Lindbergh is first to fly solo across Atlantic Ocean.
1939	Germany invades Poland, sparking World War II. Britain and France declare war on Germany. U.S. remains neutral.
1941	Japan attacks U.S. by bombing American ships at Pearl Harbor, Hawaii. U.S. declares war on Japan and enters World War II.
1945	Germany surrenders. U.S. drops atomic bombs on two Japanese cities, Hiroshima and Nagasaki. World War II ends. United Nations, international peacekeeping organization, formed.
1948	Israel proclaims its independence. Gandhi, nonviolent leader of Indian Nationalist movement against British rule, assassinated.
1950	North Korea invades South Korea, starting Korean War.
1964	U.S. begins sending troops to Vietnam to assist South Vietnam during Vietnamese civil war.
1973	Paris Peace Accords signed, ending Vietnam War.
1989	Chinese army shoots and kills protestors in China's Tiananmen Square. Berlin Wall separating East and West Germany torn down.
1991	President Frederik Willem de Klerk negotiates to end apartheid in South Africa. Union of Soviet Socialist Republics (USSR) dissolved into independent states.
1994	Nelson Mandela elected president of South Africa in first free elections.
1997	Mother Teresa, champion of poor in Calcutta, India, dies.
2003	U.S. invades Iraq, aided by Britain and other allies.
2006	Iraqi dictator Saddam Hussein captured and killed for crimes against humanity.
2009	World leaders meet in London at G-20 summit to discuss methods of boosting world's troubled economy.

People of 1900–Present

Albert Einstein

Called the greatest scientist of the 20th century, physicist Alfred Einstein developed revolutionary theories about how the world works, especially the connection between matter and energy. Einstein's knowledge was applied to the development of the atomic bomb, which he said made him very sad. Today calling somebody an "Einstein" means that he or she is a genius, but young Albert Einstein was known more for playing tricks in school than for getting good grades.

Marie Curie

Polish-French chemist Marie Curie is best known for discovering the radioactive element radium, for which she won a Nobel Prize. She also discovered an element called polonium, named for her birthplace, Poland. Although radium is used to treat and diagnose diseases, repeated or excessive exposure can cause serious illness and even death. After years of working with radium, Marie Curie died in 1934 from radiation poisoning.

Mohandas Gandhi

To the people of India, Mohandas Gandhi was the Mahatma, or Great Soul. Gandhi believed in tolerance for all religious beliefs. He led peaceful protests to bring about social change and freedom from British rule. India was granted freedom in 1947, but fighting between Hindus and Muslims continued. Gandhi spoke out against the fighting, angering many and resulting in his assassination. In America, Dr. Martin Luther King Jr. modeled his nonviolent strategy of fighting racism on Gandhi's methods.

Nelson Mandela

In 1994, Nelson Mandela was elected the first black president of South Africa. That was the first year in which South Africans of all races could vote, because of the end of the government's previous policy of racial segregation, called apartheid. Mandela served many years in prison for leading protests against apartheid and became a world-famous symbol of racial injustice. After his release from prison, he led discussions with white leaders that led to the end of apartheid and to a nonracial form of government.

Mother Teresa

Born Agnes Gonxha Bojaxhiu, Mother Teresa was a Roman Catholic nun who became known as the "Saint of the Gutters" for her work with poor people. She founded a religious order in India to provide food, schools, health care, and shelters for the poor, sick, and dying. Mother Teresa received numerous awards for her work, including the Nobel Peace Prize. In 2003, Pope John Paul II approved the first step toward declaring Mother Teresa a saint in the Roman Catholic Church.

Index

Answers

Animals, p. 7: In cats, camels, and giraffes, the front and back legs on each side of the body move together as a pair. In other animals, the two front legs move together, followed by the two back legs.

Flags & Facts, Countries of the World, p. 47: The four country flags that show the Southern Cross are Australia, New Zealand, Papua New Guinea, and Samoa.

Flags & Facts, States of the United States, p. 83: The 21 flags with a star or stars are Alaska, Arizona, Arkansas, California, Georgia, Illinois, Indiana, Kansas, Maine, Massachusetts, Mississippi, Nevada, New Hampshire, Missouri, North Carolina, North Dakota, Ohio, Rhode Island, Tennessee, Texas, and Utah. The 26 flags on a solid blue background are Alaska, Connecticut, Delaware, Idaho, Indiana, Kansas, Kentucky, Louisiana, Maine, Michigan, Minnesota, Montana, Nebraska, Nevada, New Hampshire, New York, North Dakota, Oklahoma, Oregon, Pennsylvania, South Carolina, South Dakota, Utah, Vermont, Virginia, and Wisconsin. The 8 flags with birds are Illinois, Iowa, Louisiana, Michigan, New York, North Dakota, Oregon, and Utah. The flags of California and Missouri feature bears. The flag of Maine is the only one with a moose.

Languages, p. 132: They that thrive well take counsel of their friends = It's good to get advice from your friends; Stand and unfold thyself = Tell me who you are; Mere prattle, without practice = It's all just talk; Headstrong liberty is lash'd with woe = Too much freedom can be trouble

Weights & Measures, p. 251: You may find you're taller in the morning than at night. At night, when you're lying down, your spine relaxes and spreads out. During the day, gravity pulls your body down, pressing your vertebrae together and making you shorter.

Photo Credits

Front cover: car, © Ethan Miller/Gettyimages; Demi Lovato and Selena Gomez, © WireImage/Gettyimages; iPhone, © Rick Friedman/Corbis; LeBron James, © Anthony J. Causi/Icon SMI/Corbis; dinosaur, © Louie Psihoyos/Corbis; globe, © Janrysavy/iStockphoto; penguin, © Jan Martin Will/Shutterstock

Animals p. 6: zebra, stock.xchng, © Barbara Schneider; polar bears, wikipedia, © Alan D. Wilson; p. 7: wolf, stock.xchng, © GMDee; small dog, wikipedia, © Danielle deLeon; cat, stock.xchng, © mettus.com; p. 10: giant tortoise, wikipedia © Childzy; p. 12: cows, stock.xchng, © Watje 11; oysters, stock.xchng, © Samuel Rosa; kangaroos, stock.xchng, © Charlie Lawrence; p. 13: firefly, wikipedia, © Ken Ishikawa; p. 14: Arabian camel, wikipedia, © John O'Neill; humpback whale, wikipedia, © Whit Welles; p. 15: pipistrelle bat, wikipedia, © Maolf; p. 17: poodle, stock.xchng, © Bethan Hazell; Labrador retriever, stock.xchng, © Marcelo Britofilho; Persian cat, stock.xchng, © bonvivant

Buildings & Landmarks p. 22: Channel Tunnel, wikipedia, © Extrememachine UK; p. 23: Mausoleum of Halicarnassus, wikipedia, © Nevit Dilmen; Tehri Dam, wikipedia, © Wind's child; p. 24: Tacoma Narrows bridge, wikipedia, © WSDOT/Travisl; p. 25: Dubai, wikipedia, © EVO; Singapore, wikipedia, © JeCCo

Calendars & Holidays p. 27: Julius Caesar, wikipedia, © Andrew Bossi; Moon, wikipedia, © Luc Viatour

Environment p. 40: windmills, wikipedia, © Wagner Christian; p. 42: landfill, wikipedia, © P. Cezary; p. 42: paper and paperboard, stock.xchng, © Tim Meijer

Flags & Facts, Countries of the World p. 46: Giza Pyramids, wikipedia, © Ricardo L. Berato; pp. 48–49: world map © stockmaps.com/GeoNova Publishing, Inc.; p. 50: birds, stock.xchng, © Rainer Schmied; p. 52: Bengal tiger, stock.xchng, © Thad Zajdowicz; p. 56: emerald bracelet, stock.xchng, © Lavinia Marin; p. 57: Lego blocks, stock.xchng, © Craig Rodway; p. 58, Great Pyramid of Khufu, stock.xchng, © James Farmer; p. 60: Cologne Cathedral, stock.xchng, © Dirk Ziegener; p. 61: cashews, stock.xchng, © Sonny Leon; guinea pig, stock.xchng, © Kim André Silkebaekken; p. 62: geyser, stock.xchng, © Dr. Zsolt Zátrok; Taj Mahal, stock.xchng, © Dr. Zsolt Zátrok; p. 64: Koran, stock.xchng, © Ramzi Hashisho; p. 67: fishing on the Niger River, stock.xchng, © Dennis Hunink; p. 68: sugarcane, stock.xchng, © clix; p. 74: fruit pie, stock.xchng, © Enrica Bressan; p. 75: sailing ship, stock.xchng, © Stella Levi; p. 78: porcelain statue, stock.xchng, © clix

Flags & Facts, States of the United States p. 82: Golden Gate Bridge, wikipedia, © Rich Nieworoski Jr.; Grand Canyon, wikipedia, © Luca Galuzzi; p. 88: woolly mammoth, stock.xchng, © Lavinia Marin; p. 91: surfer, stock.xchng, © Michelle Dennis; p. 96: deer, stock.xchng, © BCreavis; p. 98: Carlsbad Caverns, wikipedia, © Dave Bunnell; Babe Ruth, © Library of Congress; p. 99: bullfrog, wikipedia, © Carl D. Howe; p. 100: beaver, wikipedia, © Stevehdc; p. 101: Mount Rushmore, wikipedia, © Jim Bowen; p. 102: Texas bluebonnets, wikipedia, © stickywikit

Geography p. 114: map of North America, © stockmaps.com/GeoNova Publishing, Inc.; p. 116: Mount McKinley, wikipedia, © 2006 Derek Ramsey

Health & Wellness p. 127: fishing, stock.xchng, © Esa Oksman

Inventors & Inventions p. 128: telephone, stock.xchng, © Dawn Allyn; Wright Brothers flyer, John T. Daniels, © Library of Congress

Plants p. 146: speckled flower, stock.xchng, © Patricia Oliveira

Pop Culture p. 150: *American Idol*, © Getty Images for Fox; Jonas Brothers, © Associated Press; Taylor Swift, © Ethan Miller/Gettyimages; p. 151: Miley Cyrus, © Ethan Miller/Gettyimages; p. 152: Heath Ledger, © Gettyimages; p. 153: Ashley Tisdale, © Jason Merritt/Gettyimages; Will Smith © WireImage/Gettyimages; p. 154: David Cook, © AP Images for Fox; Dylan and Cole Sprouse, © Bryan Bedder/Gettyimages; p. 155: Blake Lively, © WireImage/Gettyimages; p. 156: Carrie Underwood, © Associated Press; Beyoncé Knowles, © Associated Press; p. 157: Jennifer Hudson, © Gettyimages; p. 158: Stephenie Meyer, © WireImage/Gettyimages

Population p. 160: middle, stock.xchng, © Dr. Zsolt Zátrok; bottom, stock.xchng, © Wynand Delport; p. 161: top, stock.xchng, © Mark Forman; p. 162; penguin on ice floe, stock.xchng, © Jan Will; St. Peter's Square, wikipedia, © David Iliff; p. 165: Los Angeles skyscrapers, wikipedia, © BDS2006; Dallas, wikipedia, © fcn80

Religion p. 168: girl praying, stock.xchng, © Eper Agi; children around menorah, stock.xchng, © Sarah Alevsky; Pope Benedict XVI, wikipedia, © Fabio Pozzebom/ABr; p. 169: Ganges River, wikipedia, © Babasteve

Science p. 176: Mt. Mayon, wikipedia, © Tomas Tam; igneous rock, wikipedia, © Stan Zurek

Sports p. 194: all photos, © Associated Press; p. 195: LeBron James, © Associated Press; Peyton Manning, © Gettyimages; p. 196: Santonio Holmes, © Gettyimages; p. 197: Heisman Trophy, wikipedia, © Robert J. La Verghetta; p. 199: Cole Hamels, © Sports Illustrated/Gettyimages; p. 201, Ty Lawson, © Sports Illustrated/Gettyimages; p. 202: Venus and Serena Williams, © Associated Press; Henrik Zetterberg, © Gettyimages; p. 203: Tiger Woods, © Associated Press

U.S. Government p. 214: Supreme Court west facade, wikipedia, © wadester16; p. 217: gavel, wikipedia, © Jonathunder

Weather p. 246: weathervane, wikipedia, © Prof DEH; ocean beach, wikipedia, © Mila Zinkova; p. 247: storm, wikipedia, © Emergent Property, 2002; p. 248: Mt. Washington, wikipedia, © WWoods

Weights & Measures p. 250: kitchen scale, stock.xchng, © Miles Pfefferle; p. 251: bathroom scale, stock.xchng, © Peter_W

World History p. 254: Otzi the Iceman, © Vienna Report Agency/Sygma/Corbis; Great Wall of China, stock.xchng, © Joan Ho